AMERICAN PHILANTHROPY

American

THE CHICAGO HISTORY OF AMERICAN CIVILIZATION

Daniel J. Boorstin, EDITOR

Philanthropy

Robert H. Bremner

Second Edition

THE UNIVERSITY OF CHICAGO PRESS

CHICAGO AND LONDON

ROBERT H. BREMNER, Professor Emeritus at Ohio State University, is the author of *From the Depths: The Discovery of Poverty in the United States* and *The Public Good: Philanthropy and Welfare in the Civil War Era*.

The University of Chicago Press, Chicago 60637
The University of Chicago Press, Ltd., London

Library of Congress Cataloging in Publication Data

Bremner, Robert Hamlett, 1917–
   American philanthropy / by Robert H. Bremner. — 2nd ed.
     p.   cm. — (The Chicago history of American civilization)
   Bibliography: p.
   Includes index.
   1. Charities—United States—History.   2. Voluntarism—United
States—History.   3. Philanthropists—United States—History.
I. Title. II. Series.
HV91.B67   1988   87-23739
361.7′0973—dc19   CIP

ISBN 0-226-07324-6 (cloth); 0-226-07325-4 (paper)

Editor's Preface

We have long thought of ourselves immodestly as a nation of philanthropists. But in our generation American private philanthropy has dwarfed all our earlier good works, and the United States government has become a philanthropist on an unprecedented scale. Having cast ourselves in the role of a philanthropic nation—only to be blamed all over the world for the shortsightedness and selfishness of our good works—we should now try to discover precisely what our tradition has been.

Americans today need to understand the meaning of philanthropy and to see what is distinctive about our ways of doing good. Faithful Christians have often remarked that one of God's purposes in creating poverty was to make charity possible. In the United States, as Mr. Bremner shows in this volume, the emphasis has generally been quite different. One of God's purposes in creating American wealth, it is said, must have been to make philanthropy possible. Without great wealth, how could there by great philanthropy?

In this pioneering volume, Mr. Bremner gives us some

much-needed help in defining our philanthropic tradition. He is neither a sentimentalist, a cynic, nor a muckraker. He is a ruthless and sympathetic historian. He does not suggest that Americans are by nature any more selfless or alturistic than other peoples. He does show how the peculiarly American situation has given a special character to our efforts to do good by private means. He shows both the opportunities offered by our great wealth, and the temptations to disingenuousness (accentuated recently, for example, by our tax laws). He shows how the dogmas of individualism and of equal opportunity, and the chance to rise in the world, have made the spirit of philanthropy sometimes seem at odds with the spirit of democracy.

Mr. Bremner does not deny that Americans, like other men, have often wanted simply to help their fellow men. But he shows how the facts of our history—our colonial origins, the American Revolution, the institution of slavery and the efforts to abolish it, the rise of an American Standard of Living, and the accumulation of industrial wealth—have provided temptations to misuse philanthropic slogans for personal, political, or economic ends, just as they have provided opportunities for the unalloyed philanthropic spirit.

By putting a familiar, but largely unexamined, American institution into the mainstream of our civilization, Mr. Bremner admirably serves the purposes of the "Chicago History of American Civilization," which aims to make each aspect of our culture a window to all our history. The series contains two kinds of books: a *chronological* group, which provides a coherent narrative of American history from its beginning to the present day, and a *topical* group, which deals with the history of varied and significant aspects of American life. This book is one of the topical group.

Mr. Bremner's work has stood the test of time, and since

its publication in 1960 has become the standard brief survey of American philanthropy. In the intervening years there has been a renewed interest in the role of private philanthropy and voluntarism in American life, with new efforts to redefine the role of public philanthropy. In this edition Mr. Bremner brings his interpretations up to date in three new chapters, and discusses some aspects of philanthropy that have acquired a new prominence. He has expanded the list of Important Dates and thoroughly revised his bibliographic essay to guide the reader into the growing literature on a subject of perennial interest.

DANIEL J. BOORSTIN

Contents

ix

Illustrations

Introduction

It's a serious, stern, responsible deed,
To help an unfortunate soul in his need.
And your one reward, when you quiet his plaint,
Is to feel like an opulent, careworn saint.

CLARENCE DAY

Ever since the seventeenth century, when Cotton Mather announced that Boston's helpfulness and readiness to every good work were well and favorably known in Heaven, Americans have regarded themselves as an unusually philanthropic people. In the twentieth century, celebration of American philanthropy has reached such heights that one can scarcely read a newspaper or magazine without being reminded, in editorials or advertisements, that the United States is the country with a heart, that giving is the great American game, and that philanthropy ranks as one of the leading industries of the age. Americans seem never to tire of saying, or of hearing, that they are generous to a fault— the most compassionate, open-handed people the world has ever known. The philanthropic streak in the national character is taken so much for granted that it is sometimes deemed more a genial failing than an asset or virtue.

1

As this tendency suggests, the word philanthropy and the ideas it carries with it arouse mixed emotions in American breasts. Many Americans have been concerned lest their countrymen's generosity be abused. But on a deeper level there is something about philanthropy that seems to go against the democratic grain. We may be willing to help others, but we are not humble enough to appreciate the efforts of those who would bend down to help us. "Don't try to uplift me," we say. "I can lift myself." We expect rich men to be generous with their wealth, and criticize them when they are not; but when they make benefactions, we question their motives, deplore the methods by which they obtained their abundance, and wonder whether their gifts will not do more harm than good.

Criticism of philanthropy and distrust of philanthropists are of course not peculiar to the United States, but there has been no lack of either in this country. Our literature abounds in portaits of foolish or hypocritical philanthropists. Newspaper and magazine editors decry the activities of "do gooders" and "bleeding hearts"; conservatives denounce "sentimental humanitarianism"; and radicals sneer at the "palliatives" offered by "mere philanthropic reform." The prejudice against philanthropy is felt even by its practitioners. Many of our most active and generous benefactors resent being called philanthropists and deny that their works have a philanthropic purpose. Until quite recently theoretical writings on the subject of philanthropy seem to have consisted mainly, and sometimes exclusively, in condemnations of "unwise giving."

Whether we approve or disapprove of philanthropy, the fact remains that it has been one of the principal methods of social advance. And we do not need to exaggerate the extent of our generosity to recognize that voluntary benevolence has played a large role and performed important functions in

2

American society. Here, as elsewhere, philanthropy has covered a wider field than charity; the problems of the poor have not been philanthropy's only or even primary concern. The aim of philanthropy in its broadest sense is improvement in the quality of human life. Whatever motives animate individual philanthropists, the purpose of philanthropy itself is to promote the welfare, happiness, and culture of mankind.

We are all indebted to philanthropic reformers who have called attention to and agitated for abatement of the barbarities inflicted by society on its weaker members. We are all, in some degree, beneficiaries of philanthropy whenever we attend church, go to college, visit museums or concert halls, draw books from libraries, obtain treatment at hospitals, or spend leisure hours in parks. Most of us use, or may have occasion to use, institutions and services now tax-supported, which originated as philanthropic enterprises. We continue to rely on philanthropy for the support of scientific research, for experimentation in the field of social relations, and for diffusion of knowledge in all branches of learning.

The record of American philanthropy is so impressive that it would require several lengthy volumes to list its achievements. In a book as brief as this one, some of those achievements can only be alluded to, and many important benefactors and benefactions must be omitted. The author extends his apologies to readers who may look in vain in the following pages for mention of favorite philanthropists; many of the author's favorites have been left out too. The book is not an encyclopedia of good works but a narrative of some of the major trends in American philanthropy, broadly defined, set against the background of the main developments in American social history. The study is a survey of voluntary activity in the fields of charity, religion, education, humanitarian reform, social service, war relief, and foreign aid. It deals with representative donors, whether of money or service, with promoters of moral and social reform, and with the various institutions and associations Americans have founded to conduct their philanthropic business. The author hopes that the book will advance the growing interest in philanthropy as a subject of research and that the story told in the following pages will offer occasional insights into the character of American civilization.

NOTE ON THE 1987 EDITION

For this edition I have added three chapters dealing with trends and issues in philanthropy in the United States since 1960, updated Important Dates, and revised Suggested Reading. In some cases I have used the list of dates to call attention to significant and interesting events I have been unable to incorporate in the brief narrative. Similarly, works cited in Suggested Reading are intended to help students make fuller investigations of topics mentioned in the text.

In recent years a number of institutions and agencies have fostered the study of many aspects of philanthropy and non-profit enterprise. Despite the valuable work already accomplished there is general agreement that much remains to be done to promote wider understanding and appreciation of the roles philanthropy and voluntarism play in American life. The renewal of interest in the study and teaching of the history of philanthropy gives me great pleasure, and I am happy to have had an opportunity to prepare the present edition of *American Philanthropy* for the use of a new generation of readers.

I

Doing Good in the New World

> If any man ask, Why it is so necessary to do good?
> I must say, it sounds not like the question of a good
> man.
>
> COTTON MATHER

The earliest American philanthropists, as far as European records go, were those gentle Indians of the Bahama Islands who greeted Columbus at his first landfall in the New World. In view of the cruelty and exploitation these natives were to suffer at the hands of white men there is something ominous in Columbus's report that they were "ingenuous and free" with all they had, gave away anything that was asked of them, and bestowed each gift "with as much love as if their hearts went with it."

From other Indians pioneer white settlers obtained a wealth of practical assistance in the difficult task of adjusting to life in an alien land. The names of most of these benefactors are forgotten, but one at least is familiar to every schoolboy. Squanto, who had once been kidnapped by an Englishman and carried off to be sold into slavery, escaped from bondage and returned to New England. There, during the starving time at Plymouth in the winter of 1620–21, Squanto proved "a special instrument sent of God" for the good of the enfeebled, bewildered Pilgrims. He taught them, in the words of William Bradford, "how to set their corn, where to take fish, and to procure other commodities, and was also their pilot to bring them to unknown places for their profit, and never left them till he died." Sad to relate, Squanto used his connections with the Pilgrims to extort gifts for himself from other Indians, and so his hands, like those of some other eminent philanthropists, were not entirely clean. On his deathbed he asked the governor "to pray for him that he might go to the Englishman's God in Heaven, and bequeathed sundry of his things to sundry of his English friends as remembrances of his love. . . ."

Philanthropy is philanthropy wherever and by whomever practiced. When we speak of American philanthropy, however, we usually have in mind an imported product rather than an indigenous growth. Our systems and principles of benevolence, both public and private, originated in Europe before the colonization of America began. They were brought to this country by Europeans, and their subsequent development was influenced by European experience and theory. For many years our philanthropic institutions sought and received support from abroad; and until quite recently those institutions were copies of European models. All we can lay claim to on the score of uniqueness is that philanthropy *in* America took such a firm root and grew so prodigiously that it early assumed a stature and significance all its own.

To understand why this happened we must remember, first, that the age of colonization coincided with one of the great periods of European philanthropy. The seventeenth century saw the launching of heroic missionary enterprises, a revival of interest in charitable works, the development in England of a system of tax-supported poor relief, and the organization of a host of associations for specialized philanthropic purposes. America inspired some of these undertakings and benefited directly or indirectly from nearly all of them, for the discovery of the New World affected the conscience as well as the cupidity of the Old. Almost every effort at colonization had, or claimed to have, a philanthropic motivation: there were natives to be converted to Christianity, poor men to be provided with land and work, and a wilderness to be supplied with the institutions of civilization. It is not too much to say that many Europeans regarded the American continent mainly as a vastly expanded field for the exercise of benevolence.

The real founders of American philanthropy, however, were men and women who crossed the Atlantic to establish communities that would be *better* than, instead of like or different from, the ones they had known at home. The Puritan leader John Winthrop (1588–1649) forthrightly stated their purpose in the lay sermon, "A Model of Christian Charity," which he preached on the ship "Arbella" to "the great company of religious people" voyaging from old to New England in the year 1630. Winthrop used "Charity" as a synonym for love rather than in the modern sense of aid to the poor; and the "Model" he proposed was not a new scheme of benevolence but a code of conduct for a company of Christians who had entered into a convenant with God. The Puritans' God permitted no breach of contract but demanded strict performance of each article in the covenant. Therefore, as Winthrop said, "in this duty of love we must love brotherly without dissimulation, we must love one another with a pure heart fervently, we must bear one another's burdens, we must not look only on our own things but also on the things of our brethren.

7

Neither must we think that the Lord will bear with such failings at our hands as He doth from those among whom we have lived. . . ."

Like later philanthropists, Winthrop justified disparities in wealth and condition as divinely ordained. He had no wish to tamper with God's design, and he did not hesitate to distinguish between "the great ones," high and eminent in power and dignity," and "the poor and inferior sort" of men. Winthrop looked upon such distinctions as necessary for the good and preservation of society. He was convinced, however, that no man was made richer or more honorable than his neighbor for his own sake, but only "for the glory of his creator and the common good of the creature man." The poor must not rise up against their superiors; neither should the rich and mighty be allowed to eat up the poor. Differences in condition existed, not to separate and alienate men from one another, but to make them have more need of each other, and to bind them closer together "in the bond of brotherly affection." And those differences, important and essential though Winthrop believed them to be, seemed less significant to him than "our community as members of the same body." "We must be knit together in this work as one man," he said. "We must delight in each other, make others' conditions our own, rejoice together, mourn together, labor and suffer together. . . ." The common objective—"to improve our lives to do more service to the Lord"—must never be lost sight of and "the care of the public" must take precedence over all private interests.

Winthrop's vision of a community united and exalted by religious dedication was not to be realized even in Puritan New England. The mean and despised were not content to remain in the state to which God had assigned them; the powerful showed little disposition to forego opportunities to profit at the expense of the weak; and neither rich nor poor was willing to remain for long under the rule of divinely commissioned magistrates. Competition, individualism, and self-interest proved too strong to be suppressed, and what Roger Williams, in a letter to Winthrop's son, called "the common trinity of the world—Profit, Preferment, Pleasure"—soon made their appearance. Even so, Winthrop's ideal was never entirely forsaken. The forces of disunity, although they could not be held down, did not quite prevail; and, not only in the colonial period, but in later eras as well, Americans continued to feel under a special obligation to bring the duty of neighborly and brotherly love, everywhere professed, into "familiar and constant practice."

Half a century after Winthrop and the Puritans started to build their city upon a hill in New England, William Penn (1644–1718) began his holy experiment in Pennsylvania. Although Penn founded the colony as a refuge for Quakers and members of other persecuted sects, the idea of withdrawing from or renouncing the world had no place in his plans. "True Godliness," he said, "don't turn men out of the World, but enables them to live better in it, and excites their Endeavors to Mend it." To Penn and the Quakers there was no conflict between efforts to live better in the world and endeavors to improve it. The two were inseparably bound together, and the one was the means of achieving the other. Living better in the world meant following the rule of moderation or, more specifically, observing diligence (the middle path between drudgery and idleness) and frugality (as opposed to the extremes of miserliness and extravagance) in one's daily affairs. Mending the world was to be accomplished by employing the rewards

9

of diligence and frugality for benevolent and humanitarian purposes—not casually and incidentally, but wholeheartedly—as the major business of life.

A good deal of the hostility the Quakers encountered arose from the fact that they regarded the conduct of daily life as much, if not more, a part of religious observance than formal worship. But the Quaker outlook, radical in its belief in separation of church and state and in its insistence upon the individual's right of freedom of conscience, was conservative in its attitude toward social organization. Penn, no less than Winthrop, deemed class distinctions an essential part of the divine order. God has not placed men "on the level," he said, but has arranged them in descending orders of subordination and dependency; due respect for these God-ordained differences required "Obedience to Superiors, Love to Equals, . . . *Help* and *Countenance* to Inferiors."

Assumptions of social superiority and inferiority, however, were typical of seventeenth-century thought rather than peculiar to the Quakers. Penn himself emphasized the responsibilities rather than the privileges that went with rank. He took the doctrine of stewardship both seriously and literally, believing that men were indebted to God not only for their wealth but for their very being, and accountable to Him for the way they spent their lives as well as their fortunes. His concept of stewardship was free of the condescension with which it is so often associated because, in his case, the doctrine of stewardship was joined to an equally serious and literal belief in the brotherhood of man. Penn was, after all, one of "The People called Friends," and, like other Quakers, he rejected the Calvinistic notion of the Elect. Whatever the differences in material conditions among men, all men were children of God, carriers of His seed, and spiritually equal in His sight.

Penn anticipated Benjamin Franklin in admiration for industry, thrift, and the other economic virtues that are now attributed to the middle class. Practical man that he was, Penn certainly had an appreciation for the value of money, but he believed that God gave men wealth to use rather than to love or hoard. Of all the vices, avarice struck him as worst. The spectacle of men, already comfortably fixed, who scrambled by day and plotted by night to increase their wealth moved him to scorn. "They are running up and down," he commented, "as if it were to save the life of a condemned innocent." Their conduct, personally disgraceful, was socially ruinous; for the reason the poor had too little was that the rich, already possessing too much, were striving to pile up even more.

Next to avarice Penn abhorred waste, display, and the pursuit of pleasure. Here again Penn's puritanical attitude expressed his social conscience: if all the money wasted on luxury and extravagance were put to public use, the wants of the poor would be well satisfied. To be sure, mortal man required diversion; but (or so Penn said), "The best recreation is to do good." There will be time enough for making merry "when the pale faces are more commiserated, the pinched bellies relieved and naked backs clothed, when the famished poor, the distressed widow, and the helpless orphan . . . are provided for."

Penn's writings, personal influence, and deeds left an indelible influence on Quakerdom and, through its followers, on nearly all subsequent humanitarian movements. Penn was, however, an Englishman. He visited America only twice, at widely spread intervals, and his total stay in this country amounted to no longer than four years. It is not Penn, therefore, but a native Yankee, the grandson of two of the founders of Massachusetts, who must be considered the chief exponent of do-goodism in colonial America.

Cotton Mather (1663–1728), unfortunately better re-membered today for his part in the witchcraft trials than for his benevolent activities, is one of the commanding figures in the history of American philanthropy. The son of a president of Harvard, and himself one of the founders of Yale, Mather was the most prolific and conspicuously learned writer of the colonial period. Of the approximately four hundred and fifty works he is known to have published, one of the least pretentious, *Bonifacius*, or as it is usually known, *Essays To Do Good* (1710), enjoyed the greatest and longest popularity. In it Mather proposed that men and women, acting either as individuals or as members of voluntary associations, should engage in "a perpetual endeavor to do good in the world." Such advice, coming from a son of the Puritans, was hardly novel. It was the method Mather outlined rather than the objective that was new. And it was this individualistic, voluntary method—taken not from the Quakers, whom Mather disliked, but from the German Pietists, especially August Hermann Francke of Halle—that was destined to characterize Amer-ican philanthropy for many years to come.

In the passage quoted at the head of this chapter, Mather disposed in summary fashion of one of the persistent objections to the gospel and practice of doing good. It is interesting, however, to consider why Mather himself thought it so necessary to do good. He regarded the performance of good works as an obligation owed to God rather than as a means of salvation; yet, as a constant expounder of the doctrine of stewardship, he had no doubt that God would punish the unfaithful steward. Moreover, as he was frank enough to admit and bold enough to proclaim, doing good was a reward in itself. To help the unfortunate was an honor, a privilege, "an incomparable pleasure." Not content to let the case rest here, Mather cited an entire

catalog of worldly advantages including long life and
business success he thought would surely accrue to the
benevolent. Besides, as Mather took pains to point out,
doing good was sound policy, a mild but effective
instrument of social control. Pious example, moral leadership, voluntary effort, and private charity were the means by
which competing and conflicting interests in society might
be brought into harmony.

To Mather charity emphatically did begin at home; for he
believed that each man must start his career of doing good
by correcting whatever was amiss in his own heart and life.
Yet for all the emphasis on personal reform, Mather's was a
social gospel. Keep a list of the needy in your neighbornood,
he urged his readers; be on the lookout for persons who may
require help, and seize each opportunity to be useful with
"rapturous assiduity." Always bear in mind that "charity to
the *souls* of men" is the highest form of benevolence. Send
preachers, Bibles, and other books of piety to heathens at
home and abroad; support the church, and keep a watchful
eye on the spiritual health of the community. Very often, he
said, the poor need "admonitions of piety" quite as much as
alms. "Cannot you contrive to mingle a spiritual charity with
your temporal bounty?"

Mather's own charitable gifts were sufficient to make him
a one-man relief and aid society. But Mather's real
contribution to the practice of philanthropy lay in his
recognition of the need for enlisting the support of others in
benevolent enterprises. He was a tireless promoter of
associations for distributing tracts, supporting missions,
relieving needy clergymen, and building churches in poor
communities. At the same time, in sermons and private
conversations, he called the attention of the rich to the
needs, physical as well as spiritual, of the poor. From
personal experience he learned that the recompense of the

charitable was multiplication of occasions to be serviceable. "Those who devote themselves to good devices," he drily observed, "usually find a wonderful increase of their opportunities." In a beautiful simile he likened a good deed to "a stone falling into a pool—one circle and service will produce another, till they extend—who can tell how far?"

Despite, or as Mather would have said, because of his sincere concern for the poor, he advocated extreme care in the bestowal of alms. "Let us try to do good with as much application of mind as wicked men employ in doing evil," was his motto. Giving wisely was therefore an even greater obligation than giving generously; and withholding alms from the undeserving as needful and essentially benevolent as bestowing them on the deserving. In a famous and widely approved sermon delivered in 1698 Mather told the good people of Boston: "Instead of exhorting you to augment your charity, I will rather utter an exhortation . . . that you may not *abuse* your charity by misapplying it." He was disturbed by the increase of idleness and fearful that an excess of benevolence might nourish and confirm the idle in their evil ways. "The poor that can't work are objects for your liberality," he said. "But the poor than *can* work and *won't*, the best liberality to them is to *make* them." The thing to do was to cure them of their idleness: "Find 'em work; set 'em to work; keep 'em to work. Then, as much of your bounty to them as you please."

The most famous tribute to the *Essays To Do Good* came from an unlikely source. In youth—actually boyhood—Benjamin Franklin (1706–90) had been an enemy of the Mathers, and the pseudonym adopted in his earliest published work, Silence Dogood, was an unkind thrust at Cotton Mather. In old age, however, Franklin advised Samuel Mather, Cotton's son, that the *Essays* had influenced his conduct throughout life. "I have always set a greater value on the character of a *doer of good*, than on any other kind of reputation," he wrote, "and if I have been . . . a useful citizen, the public owes the advantage of it to that book."

Franklin did not acknowledge and possibly was not aware of the influence Quakerism exerted on his character and career. Nevertheless there was much in his approach to life that bore witness to his prolonged association with the Friends. He did not learn the virtues of discretion, moderation, and attention to his business from his first master, his brother James; in these, as in so many other arts, Franklin was self-taught. Yet he presumably derived something, if only concern for reputability, from the example of solid Quaker businessmen for whom he worked as a young man and whose patronage he solicited when he entered business for himself. At any rate it was a happy circumstance that Franklin, with his Puritan background and avowed indebtedness to Mather, should have carried out his highly successful experiments in useful living in the city founded by William Penn.

In addition to numerous similarities, there was a significant difference between Franklin's views and those of Penn and Mather. Penn demanded that money, instead of being hoarded or spent on impious luxuries, should be used for comforting the poor. Mather dreamed of a city in which each house would have an alms-box bearing the message *"Think* on the Poor." Franklin, however, conceived of a society in which there would be no poor and little need for relief or charity. He sprang from a different class and addressed himself to a different audience than Penn or Mather. Far from forgetting his humble origin, he traded on it throughout life. In the successive volumes of *Poor Richard's Almanack* Franklin spoke to "leather-aproned" folk as a man of their own sort. As he preached it, the gospel of industry, frugality, and sobriety was worldly wisdom rather than spiritual discipline. Contrary to what is sometimes assumed, Franklin did not advise his readers to seek riches or tell them how to gain wealth. If he had really wanted to do so, with his knowledge of the world, he could have offered more practical suggestions than maxims of self-help. It was the road to independence, not the "Way to Wealth," that Franklin pointed out. "Be *industrious* and *free:* be *frugal* and *free,*" he counseled—free among other things of dependency upon the uncertain charity of the world.

In conducting his own affairs Franklin observed the maxims of the *Almanack*, if not to the letter, closely enough to become financially independent at a relatively early age. At forty-two he sold his printing house and devoted most of the rest of his life to serving the public. Long before quitting business, however, he had begun to practice what he so often preached to others: "Leisure is Time for doing something useful." It goes without saying that Franklin used his leisure to advance his own knowledge and reputation; but he employed it as earnestly for social as for self-improvement. Although the fact is well known, it is worth recalling that instead of patenting and seeking profit from his inventions, Franklin willingly gave the products of his ingenuity to the world. He introduced a secular spirit into the do-good gospel and shifted the emphasis from pious works and personal charity to efforts to further the general welfare. To Franklin, God was "the Great Benefactor." His religion consisted in the belief that men should show their gratitude to God "by the only means in their power, promoting the happiness of his other children."

Franklin was above all a man of the eighteenth century and it is not wise to insist too strongly on the modernity of his approach to social problems. In much that he did or suggested, however, it is possible to recognize principles that later came to be recognized as characteristic of both enlightened public policy and of constructive philanthropy. Preventing poverty always impressed him as a more sensible course than relieving it. In calling for repeal of the poor laws on the ground that public provision for the needy had an even greater tendency than almsgiving to pauperize the poor, Franklin went beyond Mather, who had warned of the abuses of private charity, and foreshadowed the scientific philanthropists and reformers of the nineteenth century. "I am for doing good to the poor," he wrote, "but I differ in opinion about the means. I think the best way of doing good to the poor is, not making them easy *in* poverty, but leading or driving them out of it." In practice Franklin relied on leading rather than driving, on persuasion and encouragement rather than coercion. Unlike some later advocates of individualism, however, Franklin was not content merely to exhort the poor to become self-supporting. He was ever mindful of the need for widening opportunities for self-help, and throughout life he strove, as he put it, "to promote the happiness of mankind" by working for the establishment of conditions in which men would be able to take care of themselves.

Franklin's philanthropic activities, although varied, followed a consistent pattern. Starting in 1727 with the Junto, a club for the mutual improvement of its members, and the library (1731) which was the Junto's first offshoot, Franklin proceeded to organize or assist in organizing a host of civic projects. He founded a volunteer fire company, developed schemes for paving, cleaning, and lighting the streets of Philadelphia, and sponsored a plan for policing the city. His political talents were never better displayed than in his ability to unite public and private support behind municipal improvements. He played a leading part in the establishment of both the Pennsylvania Hospital (1751) and the academy which became the University of Pennsylvania. Funds provided in his will made possible the founding, more than a century after his death, of a technical institute in Boston. His interest in "improving the common Stock of Knowledge" led to the formation in 1743 of the American Philosophical Society, the first and for many years the foremost American institution for promoting research in the natural and social sciences.

Franklin demonstrated that the sovereign remedy of self-help, so often prescribed for individuals, could be applied with equally beneficial results to society. He did not invent the principle of improving social conditions through voluntary associations, but more than any American before him he showed the availability, usefulness, and appropriateness of that method to American conditions. The voluntary method, as Franklin's success with it suggested, and as later events were to prove, was precisely suited to the inclinations of his countrymen.

2

Religious and Revolutionary Humanitarianism

The Humane Mania . . . Persons afflicted with this madness, feel for every species of distress, and seem to pour forth tears upon some occasions, from every pore of their bodies . . . Gracious heaven! if ever I should be visited with this species of madness, . . . my constant prayer to the divine fountain of justice and pity—shall be, that *I may never be cured of it.*

BENJAMIN RUSH

In the third and fourth decades of the eighteenth century a series of religious revivals collectively known as the Great Awakening swept over the American colonies. The revival fervor reached its peak around 1742 and thereafter quickly subsided, perishing, as Jonathan Edwards's biographer has written, in its own noise. Brief though its sway, the Great Awakening effected what may with some slight exaggeration be called an American Reformation, for by strengthening individual religiosity it encouraged a spirit of religious independence and thus weakened the authority of the churches. George Whitefield (1714–70), Jonathan Edwards (1703–58), and other preachers of the revival made religion an intensely personal concern. Their emphasis on an inner experience of spiritual rebirth revealed possibilities of a whole religious existence outside the established forms of worship. The number of churches, sects, and church members increased as a result of the Awakening, but never again would the hold of the meeting house on individual consciences be secure, and never again would organized religion provide the only outlet for men's strivings for a better life. While religious and sectarian charities continued to flourish, a vast new interest in secular and humanitarian philanthropies developed both within and without the churches.

Among the most important results of the Great Awakening were the fostering of humane attitudes and the popularization of philanthropy at all levels of society, but especially among the poorer classes. The Awakening was a mass movement. It derived its strength from, and made its greatest impact on, humble men and women, many of whom belonged to no church and were therefore beyond the reach of religious appeals for charity. The revival gave them an opportunity to indulge in sentiments usually regarded as above their proper station in life and to partake more fully in the pleasures of piety and benevolence. Of all the conversions wrought by the Great Awakening certainly the most remarkable was the transformation of do-goodism from a predominantly upper- and middle-class activity—half responsibility, half recreation—into a broadly shared, genuinely popular avocation.

The man chiefly responsible for this achievement was George Whitefield, a young English evangelist who had not yet turned twenty-five when, in the autumn of 1739, he began the most famous preaching tour in American history. On this, the second of the seven visits Whitefield was to make to the colonies, he spent fourteen months (in his own words) "ranging and hunting the American woods after poor sinners." Whitefield found the quarry eager to be caught, for the fame of his eloquence had preceded him across the Atlantic and earlier revivals in the middle colonies and New England had prepared the way for his message of the awful need and wondrous possibilities of a new birth in Christ. The Awakening was already in progress when Whitefield arrived. He linked isolated, local revivals into an intercolonial movement, and turned the torrents of religious excitement unloosed by these revivals in the direction of practical benevolence.

It was not only the suffering of the damned but the misery of the poor that Whitefield preached. Other exhorters equaled or excelled him in ability to terrorize audiences with threats of hell-fire, but none approached him in ability to move the hearts and purses of listeners. He appealed to conscience and altruism as well as to fear, pleaded as earnestly for money as for souls, and made the collection plate hardly less important than the mourners' bench. With his superb voice, extraordinary histrionic talent, and instinctive feeling for human interests he could stir vast throngs to frenzies of pity and remorse. Responding generously, even extravagantly, to Whitefield's cry for alms became more than a demonstration of piety: it was a welcome and almost essential means of relieving emotional tension.

The principal object of the donations Whitefield collected was an orphanage, modeled after Francke's celebrated institution in Halle, which he founded in the impoverished colony of Georgia in 1740. This project, although appealing, was not well thought out and proved to be a costly undertaking. Whitefield raised money for the orphanage in England as well as in America; he purchased and operated a slave-manned plantation in South Carolina to obtain additional revenue for its support; and agitated for removal of the prohibition of slavery in the Georgia charter. For thirty years Whitefield devoted as much care to the management of the institution as the circumstances of his career permitted. In the closing years of his life he tried vainly to turn the orphanage into a college. Whitefield, however, was a better fund-raiser than administrator; and despite the energy and expense he lavished on the orphan home it never fulfilled his expectations.

The indifferent success of Whitefield's pet charity did not dampen his enthusiasm for benevolence. Throughout his mature life he made it his practice to improve his acquaintance with the rich for the benefit of the poor. Like Cotton Mather, whom Whitefield resembled in this respect, if in no other, he was ever ready to find support for good causes. He took up collections for poor debtors, raised money for victims of disaster, and secured books and financial assistance for hard-pressed colonial colleges. Harvard, Dartmouth, Princeton, and the University of Pennsylvania all benefited from his assistance. If no single institution can be regarded as his monument, the reason is partly that he helped so many.

The thirty-odd years between the Great Awakening and the Revolution brought a succession of emergencies that placed severe strains on American philanthropy. During much of the period the colonies were officially, if not always actively, at war with the French and Indians. The problem of poor relief, serious even before 1740, was made still more acute by the military struggle. Disabled soldiers, displaced Acadians, and refugees from the frontier swelled the numbers of the orphaned, widowed, aged, ill, and inprovident for whom care had to be provided. The ranks of the distressed were further increased by two serious depressions, an influx of needy immigrants, recurring epidemics of smallpox, dysentery, and other diseases, and destructive fires in Charleston, South Carolina, and Boston. Despite the humanitarian sentiments spread by the Awakening, colonial society was poorly equipped to deal with these accumulated misfortunes. Private fortunes were too few and wealth neither widely enough distributed nor sufficiently fluid to permit large-scale or sustained private giving. Public relief under the poor laws was ordinarily available only to persons having legal settlement in a given community. In Massachusetts and some other colonies provincial legislatures reimbursed towns for the care of refugees and certain other needy wanderers who could not meet residence requirements for local relief. In time of depression or disaster, however, communities were hard put to care for their own poor.

In these circumstances welfare necessarily became a joint public-private partnership. Services that could not otherwise have been provided could be, and were, established through the willingness of public bodies and private citizens each to assist and supplement the philanthropic activities of the other. This cooperative approach was an expedient, but in view of the antagonism later thought to exist between governmental and voluntary efforts in the field of welfare, it stands out as one of the noteworthy aspects of colonial philanthropy. The line between public and private responsibility was not sharply drawn. In seasons of distress overseers of the poor frequently called on the churches for special collections of alms, and throughout the colonial period giving or bequeathing property to public authorities for charitable purposes remained a favorite form of philanthropy. Friendly societies organized along national, occupational, or religious lines relieved public officials of the necessity for caring for some of the poor by supplying mutual aid to members and dispensing charity to certain categories of beneficiaries. New institutions, notably the Pennsylvania Hospital and the Philadelphia Bettering House, jointly financed by taxation and private contributions, offered unsurpassed facilities for treating and sheltering the poor. Gifts from overseas, added to funds raised by colonial churches and assemblies, made possible the founding of new colleges, better support for those already in existence, and an expansion of missionary and educational work among the Indians.

The sponsors of these undertakings appealed to common sense and self-interest as well as to compassion. Certainly this was true of the friendly societies, which, in addition to performing charitable and convivial services, gave members a sense of economic security. Dr. Thomas Bond (1712–84), the principal founder of the Pennsylvania Hospital, presented the project as "a means of increasing the Number of People, and preserving many useful Members to the Public from Ruin and Distress." The Philadelphia Bettering House and similar houses of industry in other cities asked and received support on the grounds that they not only relieved but employed the destitute, promoted industry and frugality among the poor, and thereby reduced the number of beggars and paupers. Eleazar Wheelock's (1711–79) success in obtaining money for his Indian school (later Dartmouth College) stemmed partly from his argument that the spread of Christianity and civilization among the tribesmen would provide "a far better Defense than all our expensive Fortresses."

Such rationalizations, although useful in giving humane motives a practical justification, are not sufficient to explain the vigor of colonial philanthropy. More revealing than these public pronouncements is the private observation of John Smith, a Philadelphia Quaker, who wrote in his diary in 1747 that he had not yet turned any beggar away empty handed, since "a fellow feeling of the Infirmities and wants of our Brethren—as all mankind are—is a duty, and not sufficiently practiced without Administering Relief when in our power." How seriously Americans took that duty became clear in 1760 when individuals, churches, town meetings, and legislatures throughout the colonies raised impressive sums for the relief of Boston's fire sufferers. Fourteen years later the closing of Boston's harbor in punishment for the Boston Tea Party threatened that city with economic ruin and produced the greatest relief crisis in the colonial period. Once again, but even more generously than before, other town and colonies dispatched money, clothing, food, and livestock to Boston as if to prove that Americans, although not yet united politically, were already knit together by bonds of sympathy and affection.

Anthony Benezet (1713–84) was one of the men who drafted an appeal to Pennsylvania and New Jersey Quakers asking contributions for the relief of "the necessitous of every religious denomination" in Boston and other afflicted areas of New England. It was not the first time that the French-born Benezet, always frail in health and almost as poor as those he helped, had lent his assistance to such tasks. At the start of the French and Indian War he had organized relief for frontier settlers driven from their homes by Indian raids; and for more than a decade after 1756 he had been the self-appointed guardian of the Acadians in Philadelphia, obtaining grants for these French-Catholic war victims from a grudging legislature and begging gifts for them from his fellow Quakers. Benezet had come to Pennsylvania in 1731 and was by profession a schoolmaster. By 1775 he had instructed a fair portion of the youth of Philadelphia—rich and poor, boys and girls, black and white. Meanwhile, through unflagging efforts as almoner and pamphleteer, he had extended his pedagogy to the entire community. Justice, and charity in the old sense of love, were the lessons Benezet taught. Because his conscience was alert to wrong as well as misfortune, and because he not only labored to ameliorate suffering, but courageously exposed and fought injustice, he deserves to rank as one of America's first humanitarian reformers.

The most famous picture of Benezet is Benjamin Rush's recollection of him as he appeared in old age: "His face was grave, placid, and full of benignity. In one hand he carried a subscription paper and a petition; in the other he carried a small pamphlet on the unlawfulness of the African Slave-trade, and a letter directed to the King of Prussia, upon the unlawfulness of war." "He is small, old and ugly," said a French officer during the American Revolution, "but his countenance wears the stamp of a peaceful soul and the repose of a good conscience." That benign countenance masked a ready wit and sharp tongue. Benezet laughed tolerantly when he heard that an aged Acadian, long a beneficiary of his charity, had concluded that such kindness as Benezet had shown over so many years could not possibly be disinterested, and that the author of it must have some design to profit at the expense of the Acadians. For the ungenerous, however, especially those of his own sect, Benezet had nothing but scorn. He told his friend John Smith that he was weary of begging vainly of men who could afford to give a thousand pounds "without having one tear the less dropt on that account by their Heirs." It was no excuse for these men to say that they were insufficiently acquainted with the misery of the poor: they did not wait for full details before acting when they heard rumors that some extraordinary bargain might easily be attained. "The appellation of *Steward* is what we often take upon ourselves," he observed, "but indeed, in the mouth of many it is but a cant, unmeaning expression."

Benezet accompanied his services to war sufferers with an attack on war itself. Men of letters have exposed the follies of prejudice and intolerance, he observed in 1780; "Will they not endeavor too, to disgust men with the horrors of war, and to make them live together like friends and brethren?" Benezet, at least, was willing to make the endeavor and he pressed the campaign most strenuously when it was least politic to do so, that is, in the midst of war. He wrote the letter to Frederick the Great, to which Rush alluded, in 1776. Inclosed with the letter was his pamphlet, "Thoughts on the Nature of War," first printed in 1766 and reissued in the year of Independence. Benezet also sent the pamphlet to Henry Laurens, president of the Continental Congress. Two years later he prepared another antiwar tract and presented copies to members of Congress, governors of states, and influential persons on both sides of the Atlantic. "If people had never seen War kindled in countries and between neighboring Nations, they could hardly believe that man would be so inattentive to the dictates of Reason, the tender feelings of humanity, and the Gospel . . . as deliberately to engage in battles for the destruction of each other," he told his readers. We should pray, he said, "not for the destruction of our enemies, who are still our Brethren, . . . ; but for an agreement with them."

Benezet devoted much of his voluminous correspondence and some of his most trenchant pamphlets to improving relations between Indians and whites. He was not alone in this work, but unlike some of his contemporaries, who were interested mainly in baptizing the Indians and making them allies in war and trade, Benezet's concern was to obtain consideration for Indians as fellow beings, and to secure recognition for them of rights to which they—in his opinion—were as much entitled as any other people. He publicized every instance that came to his attention of the friendly disposition of Indian chiefs or tribesmen. "Is it not notorious that they are generally kinder to us than we are to them?" he asked in the last of his many pamphlets. The difference between us and them, he said, "is chiefly owing to our different ways of life, and different ideas of what is necessary and desirable." The advantage we have over them is one of education "which puts it in our power to gloss over our own conduct, however evil; and to see theirs, however defensible, in the most odious point of light."

Of all the crusades in which Benezet engaged, the most fruitful was his long struggle in behalf of the Negro. Benezet, in common with his friend John Woolman (1720–72), was troubled by the effect of slaveholding on the religion and morals of slaveowners; and, like Woolman, he was particularly distressed at the countenancing of slavery by his own sect. In 1776, after more than twenty years of effort, he succeeded in bringing Philadelphia Friends to agree to censure and disown members of the Society who refused to give up their slaves. But Benezet was animated more by love for the Negro as a brother creature than by hatred for slaveholders. In his first important defense of Negro rights, written in 1754, he argued that if we sincerely desire to live by the golden rule, "we shall never think of bereaving our fellow-creatures of that valuable blessing liberty, nor endure to grow rich by their bondage." "Let us make their case our own," he continued, "and consider what we should think, and how we should feel, were we in their circumstances."

Through experience gained as a teacher of both Negro and white children Benezet had come to believe that there was as great a variety of talent in the one race as in the other and that the notion of Negro inferiority in intellectual capacity was "a vulgar prejudice." Combatting racial prejudice and showing that white superiority was based on illegal force and unjust laws became his major mission in life. In pamphlet after pamphlet he returned to the theme of Negro equality. Thus, on the eve of the Revolution—"at a time," as Benezet said, "when the general rights and liberties of mankind" were ardently proclaimed—he raised the question that still haunts Americans: How can "those who distinguish themselves as the advocates of liberty" deny equality and justice to others on the grounds of race?

Benezet showered his letters and pamphlets on those he thought would benefit from them as liberally as a rich man might have scattered alms. Two thousand copies of *A Caution and Warning to Great Britain and Her Colonies* (1767) went to the Society of Friends in London for distribution to members of Parliament and officers of the crown. An expanded version of this attack on the slave trade appeared in 1771 under the title *Some Historical Account of Guinea*. This book, also widely distributed, made a strong impression on John Wesley, who borrowed from it in his own *Thoughts on Slavery* (1774). Thomas Clarkson, the chief English foe of the slave trade, called Benezet's work "influential, beyond any other book ever before published, in disseminating a proper knowledge and detestation of this trade."

During the 1770s Benezet enlisted the support of the young physician Benjamin Rush in the fight against the slave trade, and he encouraged the anitslavery views of his old friend and neighbor, Benjamin Franklin. Benezet lived long enough to lobby for the passage of Pennsylvania's gradual emancipation act of 1780, the first abolition law passed by any American state. After Benezet's death in 1784 Rush and Franklin reconstituted an association Benezet had founded to assist free Negroes into the Pennsylvania Society for Promoting the Abolition of Slavery. Franklin's last public act was to forward a petition of the Abolition Society to the First Congress urging that body to go to the very limit of its powers to discourage the traffic in human beings; and his last publication, as witty as anything he ever wrote, was a parody of the proslavery arguments advanced against the petition.

Benjamin Rush (1746–1813) was a generation younger than Benezet and Franklin—which means that he belonged to that remarkable group of Americans, born around the time of the Great Awakening, who came to maturity, and in a sense were reborn, during the American Revolution. Rush was a physician, teacher, soldier, statesman, writer, and, in all his callings, a reformer. The breadth of his interests was matched only by the intensity of his feelings. He approached every issue not only as though his own life were at stake but as if the fate of the world hung in balance. As a boy of fifteen he found and stated his life-mission: "to spend and be spent for the Good of Mankind is what I chiefly aim at."

Rush's ancestors included Quakers, Episcopalians, and Baptists but he grew up in an atmosphere of revivalistic Presbyterianism. His pastor, whom he eulogized in his earliest known publication, was the great revivalist Gilbert Tennent. He studied under an uncle, Samuel Finley, who was a leader of the "New Light" wing of Presbyterianism, and he received his B.A. at the Presbyterian stronghold of Princeton. Rush met Whitefield as a boy and renewed his acquaintance with him while studying medicine in London during the late 1760s. For the rest of his life Rush treasured "the original, pious and eloquent sayings" of Whitefield and felt that he had been particularly fortunate to have known him.

In later years Rush rejected the Calvinistic doctrines in which he had been trained, but he never shed his youthful religiosity. He had a puritanical attitude toward idleness, deplored the use of tobacco and distilled liquors on grounds of morals as well as health, advocated adoption of the Bible as a schoolbook, and was acutely disturbed by the sin of Sabbath-breaking. "The clergy and their faithful followers of every denomination are *too good to do good*" he complained on one occasion. "It is possible we may not live to witness the approaching regeneration of our world," he wrote a friend, "but the more active we are in bringing it about, the more fitted we shall be for that world where justice and benevolence eternally prevail." Rush was given to visions, which he called dreams, and in one of them he envisaged Philadelphia spared from justly deserved destruction on several occasions by the intervention of the Angel of Mercy who, in each emergency, was able to point out some philanthropy sufficient to appease God's wrath.

In choosing a career Rush wavered between the ministry and medicine. Although he chose medicine, we may wonder whether religion did not really win out in the end. At almost any time in his life he might have said what he actually did say in a letter written while a medical apprentice: "Though now I pursue the study of physic, I am far from giving it any pre-eminence to Divinity." The Bible passage which he took most to heart and quoted most often— "The son of Man is not come to *destroy* men's lives but to *save* them"—gave religious justification to the practice of medicine. Rush was a great physician and quite naturally believed that the principles of what he called "the healing art" could be applied to society. But his medical opinions, far from affecting his religious views, were themselves influenced by religion. There was something theological in Rush's belief in the unity of disease, something evangelical in his teaching and preaching of the one sure cure for all ailments, and a family resemblance between the drastic remedies he em-

ployed in effecting cures and the violent methods used by
the revival preachers to obtain conversions.

For Rush, as for others of his generation, the American
Revolution was the central experience of life. "This great
event has everywhere shaken the human mind to its
centre," he wrote in 1788. A quarter of a century after
Independence he said "I still believe the American
Revolution to be big with important consequences to the
world, and that the labor of no individual, however feeble
his contributions to it were, could have been spared." Rush,
not yet thirty when the war began, had already gained some
notoriety as a reformer through his tracts on temperance and
the slave trade. In 1775 he encouraged another pamphleteer, Thomas Paine, to write an appeal for American independence. Rush read drafts of the work as Paine composed it
and suggested *Common Sense* as the title. He was a member
of the Continental Congress, a signer of the Declaration of
Independence, and, for about a year, surgeon-general and
physician-general of Washington's army. In the latter posts
Rush's zeal for improving medical services embroiled him in
disputes with brother officers, and his criticism of superiors,
including Washington, forced his resignation early in 1778.

The Revolution intensified the sense of mission that
already possessed Rush. Termination of his military career,
instead of disgusting him with the struggle, strengthened
his ardor for the cause of liberty. Possibly because his
participation in the war was so brief and unsatisfying, he
continued to wage the Revolution on other fronts long after
Independence had been won. The war is over, he was fond
of saying, but the Revolution has just begun. The more
important and the more difficult task of bringing "the
principles, morals, and manners of our citizens" into
harmony with republican institutions remained to be
accomplished.

In the decade after 1783 Rush addressed himself to this task with energy and conviction seldom matched by any American reformer. "The world seems to be on the eve of a great change for the better," he exulted in 1787, and he rejoiced in the privilege of speeding the better day. In the midst of a growing medical practice he continued his political activities, took on new teaching duties, founded the Philadelphia Dispensary, the first free medical clinic in the United States, and began the study of mental disease and the experiments in humane treatment of the insane that were to be among his greatest services to the medical profession. Meanwhile he renewed his attack on slavery and strong drink; he wrote against tobacco and in favor of the sugar maple tree, cultivation of which he believed would free the world from dependence upon slave-produced West Indian cane sugar. He agitated for moderation of the criminal laws, opposed capital punishment and all public punishments, and sought to convert prisons into agencies of repentance and reform. A teacher himself, Rush tried to excite public interest in education in every form, at all levels, and for both sexes. He advocated establishment of free public schools, gave enthusiastic support to movements for broadening opportunities for higher education, and proposed reforms in school curriculum, teaching methods, and discipline. In one of his letters he referred to "a new pamphlet written by that turbulent spirit Dr. Rush, who I hope will never be quiet while there is ignorance, slavery, or misery in Pennsylvania." A correspondent, half-admiring, half-despairing of Rush's efforts, likened him to Mr. Great Heart in *Pilgrim's Progress*.

Rush professed little respect for "the cold blood of common sense" but he frequently appealed to this sentiment in his pleas for reform. Noting the moderate expense involved in treating large numbers of needy

33

patients at the Philadelphia Dispensary, he declared that the principles of mechanics had been applied to morals, "for in what other way would so great a weight of evil have been removed by so small a force?" He defined capital punishment as the punishment of murder by murder and called it an act of legal revenge which did no practical good and much demonstrable harm. In arguing for milder discipline in the classroom Rush pointed out that schoolmasters were the only despots still tolerated in free countries. He defended public expenditure for education as true economy, since, in his opinion, diffusion of education could result only in promoting order, prosperity, and morality and thus in lessening of taxes. We can never suppress vice and immorality by enacting laws against them, he asserted, but we can prevent them from becoming serious problems by making adequate provision for the instruction of the manners and morals of young people.

Varied though Rush's crusades were, and whimsical as some of his arguments seem, they were parts of a consistent and nobly conceived design. In the years of hope and promise that followed the Revolution, Rush directed his anger not at individuals but at the relics of barbarism in human institutions. The doctrines of universal salvation which he embraced in the 1780s bound him, as he said, to the whole human race. "I was animated constantly by a belief that I was acting for the benefit of the whole world, and for future ages," he recalled years later. He thought that Independence offered Americans a God-given opportunity, if not obligation, to root out old errors and vices and to erect a society whose humanity, civilization, and Christianity would be a beacon to the world. Rush was sanguine of the outcome for, as he wrote John Howard the English Prison reformer in 1789, "we are at present in a *forming* state. We have as yet but few habits of any kind, and *good* ones may be

34

acquired and fixed by a good example and proper instruction as easily as *bad* ones. . . ."

Ironically enough, it was a local emergency and the needs of Rush's own time which called forth his greatest efforts, brought him most fame, and involved him in the bitterest and longest controversies of his career. The emergency was an epidemic of yellow fever—the worst calamity of its kind in American history—which almost decimated the population of Philadelphia between August and November of 1793. In the epidemic Rush lost his sister, three of his apprentices, many of his friends, and more of his patients than he liked to admit. He himself suffered three attacks of the fever, but as long as his strength permitted he treated all who asked for his help. During one week in September he estimated that he called on and prescribed for between 100 and 120 patients a day, while his apprentices visited from 20 to 55 more. For many weeks he carried on consultations even while taking his meals; and after his own illness confined him to his home, he reported, "In my parlor, on my couch, and even in my bed I prescribe for 50 to 100 people, chiefly the poor, every day."

It was characteristic of Rush that, in the very depth of disaster, he could say, "Never was the healing art so truly delightful to me." It was also characteristic of him to deal with the epidemic in the manner of a reformer. He maintained, in the first place, that the fever was generated locally by filth and that it could be prevented by improved sanitary practices. This view involved him in protracted disputes with those who deemed his opinion a slur on the good name of Philadelphia and who insisted that yellow fever was an imported pestilence to be stopped by stricter quarantine. Even sharper controversies arose, however, over Rush's remedy for the disease. He did not claim to have discovered, but he practiced and publicized what he called "the successful mode of treating" yellow fever. The treatment consisted of extremely strong purges followed by copious bloodletting. In private letters and public pronouncements Rush boasted of "the triumphs of mercury, jalap, and blood letting." He stoutly maintained that if administered early enough the remedy was a sure cure for yellow fever. Rush's remedy, which we now know was ineffective, was widely condemned as well as devoutly praised in his own day. There can be no doubt, however, that Rush's faith in his cure and the confidence he inspired in others were factors in quieting the panic that accompanied the early stages of the epidemic.

While the doctors were disagreeing and the sick dying, with or without benefit of "the successful mode" of treatment, many residents of Philadelphia fled the city. Among those who stayed behind were the mayor, Matthew Clarkson, and a small group of public spirited citizens. These men organized themselves into a voluntary committee to carry on the normal business of the city and to provide the extraordinary services made necessary by the epidemic. To the best of their abilities and resources, and in a heroically matter-of-fact spirit, they combatted the panic, tended the sick, buried the dead, and cared for the poor, the unemployed, the abandoned, and orphaned.

Perhaps the least likely candidate for heroism in this valiant band of volunteers was the squint-eyed, close-mouthed businessman, Stephen Girard. At the time of the epidemic Girard was forty-three years old, a self-made man whose gospel was work, laissez faire, and *caveat emptor*. Born in France in 1750 (d. 1831), Girard had left home as a boy, and, after a dozen years of seafaring, had settled in Philadelphia at the start of the Revolution. For a decade or more before 1793 he had been engaged in trading ventures with the French West Indies. It was a lucrative business,

The Pennsylvania Hospital in 1800. Engraving by William Birch. (From R. M. Palmer, *Reproduction of Birch's Celebrated Views of Philadelphia*, Philadelphia, 1908.)

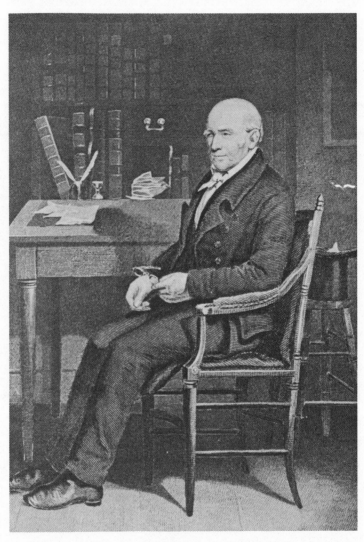

Stephen Girard. (From E. A. Duyckinck, *National Portrait Gallery of Eminent Americans.* New York: Johnson, Fry & Co., 1862.)

but sometimes dubious and always risky. In the summer of 1793 Girard's affairs were more unsettled than usual owing to the slave uprising in Santo Domingo, and for a while he was more disturbed by disorders in the West Indies than by yellow fever in Philadelphia. "It seems as if the misfortunes at Cap Francais will be fatal to me," he wrote a business associate early in September, adding that the so-called plague in Philadelphia was "only a malignant fever which, by the pernicious treatment of our doctors, has sent many of our citizens to another world." He had easily thrown off a slight case of the fever, and he resented the interruption of business caused by the panic. "It is to be hoped," he wrote, "that the month of September will bring all the inhabitants back to their homes, and that business will resume its usual trend."

Before the month was half-gone, however, Girard notified his correspondent that fear, fright, and disease had reduced the city to a deplorable condition. "I shall accordingly be very busy for a few days," he advised, "and if I have the misfortune to be overcome by the fatigues of my labor I shall have the satisfaction of having performed a duty which we owe to one another." The few days stretched into two months. The duty, voluntarily assumed, was the arduous and unpleasant one of administering the pesthouse established in an old mansion on Bush Hill. With the help of another volunteer, Peter Helm, and a French doctor, Jean Devèze (emphatically not a follower of Rush), Girard made the makeshift hospital into a model institution. The managers of Bush Hill could claim no miraculous cures. Most of their patients came to them in advanced stages of the disease, and about half of them died. But Girard's business-like management, combined with the tender care he and his staff rendered to the sick and dying, turned Bush Hill from a place of horror into a haven of mercy.

Neither before nor after the epidemic were Rush and Girard on friendly terms. To Rush, Girard's character seemed as singular as his prosperity was extraordinary. He believed and repeated rumors of Girard's niggardliness toward impecunious relatives and of his despotic treatment of employees. *"Men will be Gods!"* he exclaimed in his commonplace book after recording instances of Girard's arrogance. For his part, Girard never tired of denouncing American doctors as charlatans, "ignorant jackasses," and "executioners of the human race." From Girard's point of view almost the worst crime committed by the doctors was the harm they did to commerce by frightening the population out of town when yellow fever returned in 1794, 1797, and 1798. He railed at preventive measures such as quarantine which interfered with trade, and declared that the only way of dealing with the fever was to take care of the sick, especially the sick poor. In his opinion it was fear that made people ill and the doctors rather than the disease that killed. After the epidemic of 1798 he wrote Jean Devèze that, of all the patients he had tended, "I do not suppose I cured one; nevertheless, you will agree with me that in my capacity as Physician of Philadelphia I have been very moderate and, that no one of my confreres has killed less than I."

Girard would be remembered as one of America's greatest philanthropists even if his work at Bush Hill were entirely forgotten. He provided financial assistance to the United States government during and after the War of 1812, when his generous subscriptions made possible the floating of a war loan and the establishment of the Second Bank of the United States. Girard's chief fame, however, came after his death in 1831 and as a result of the provisions of his will. Never before had an American bequeathed such a large estate to charitable and public purposes. A childless widower, at odds with his relatives, Girard made bequests to the city of Philadelphia for improvement of certain streets, to the state of Pennsylvania for development of canals, to the Masonic order to create a loan fund (and to cancel a debt owed to Girard), to the Pennsylvania Hospital, and to a number of philanthropic institutions and organizations in Philadelphia. The bulk of his estate he set aside (shades of Whitefield!) for founding a boarding school for poor, white, male orphan children. Girard's munificence set a high standard for later millionaires, some of whom, impressed by his example, persisted in establishing or endowing orphan homes many years after the need for such institutions was less pressing than it had been in Girard's day.

It is probable that Girard's interest in orphans dated back at least to the yellow-fever days. Certainly his palliative approach to philanthropy was as clearly revealed in the emergency of 1793 as was Rush's reformistic bent. Then, no less than in his later, more celebrated philanthropic bequests, Girard responded to specific needs rather than to general causes. Unlike Rush and other humanitarian reformers who came before and after him, Girard felt under no obligation to cure or prevent social disorders or to try to remold society by any means other than economic self-interest. Yet within the limits of a somewhat misanthropic philosophy, Girard, in times of emergency, was capable of acts of public usefulness and private kindness.

Rush and Girard are fair representatives of the two types of philanthropists the United States has produced. Their disparate interests and objectives point the directions American philanthropy was to follow through most of the nineteenth century.

3

Benevolence in the Young Republic

In the United States hardly anybody talks of the
beauty of virtue, but they maintain that virtue is
useful and prove it every day.
ALEXIS DE TOCQUEVILLE

Alexis de Tocqueville was twenty-five years old in the spring
of 1831 when he began a nine-months' journey through the
United States. The supposed purpose of the trip was to
gather material for a report on American prison systems.
From the outset, however, Tocqueville had a broader and
bolder work in mind. He was interested not only in prisons
but, as he said, in "all the mechanism of that vast American
society which everyone talks of and nobody knows." In
Democracy in America (1835) Tocqueville had a good deal to
say about the ways in which Americans performed and
justified acts of helpfulness to one another, and on the effect
of substantial equality of condition in producing mild and
humane customs. The young aristocrat was particularly
impressed by the uncertain status of the rich in a democratic
society. The rich seemed to spring up daily from the

multitude and almost as often to relapse into it again. Hence, Tocqueville said, there was no "race" of rich men in America. The rich did not form a distinct class but were connected to the rest of the people by a thousand secret ties.

The strongest of those ties, or so it seems today, was the widespread acceptance of a common set of moral values and economic principles. These values and principles were better suited to the interests of the middle and lower classes than to the development of an aristocracy, for they justified the acquisition of wealth but condemned the display, enjoyment, waste, or hoarding of it. Few Americans seriously questioned the right of any man to get rich by personal effort, but a great many voiced endless concern about the uses to which wealth was put once it had been won. Democracy imposed or sought to impose, the same rules of conduct on the rich as on other members of society. In practice the rich often flouted convention, but the pervasive influence of custom and belief tended to hold them to middle-class standards of thrift, sobriety, and responsibility.

In view of the popular prejudice against ostentatious enjoyment of riches, the luxury of doing good was almost the only extravagance the American rich of the first half of the nineteenth century could indulge in with good consciences. Even the bequeathing of large estates to one's children was frowned on. A fortune left to children is a misfortune, declared Horace Mann, since it takes away the stimulus to effort, the restraints from indulgence, "the muscles out of the limbs, the brain out of the head, and virtue out of the heart." Mann, it must be admitted, had no fortune to bequeath; but his views were shared (although not rigidly adhered to) by the rich merchant and industrialist Amos Lawrence (1786–1852). Lawrence hailed his brother Abbott's gift of $50,000 to Harvard in 1847 in these words:

"It enriches your descendents in a way that mere money never can do, and is a better investment than any you have ever made."

In an age of criticism and conscience, when vast fortunes were still a novelty, the methods by which wealth was acquired were scrutinized almost as carefully as the ways in which it was used. "They cheats one another and they calls that business," John Jacob Astor was reported to have said of the commercial classes of New York City. Emerson, who hoped and expected that the amelioration of society would come from the concessions of the rich rather than from the grasping of the poor, was discomfited by the discovery that the ways of trade were "selfish to the borders of theft, and supple to the borders, if not beyond the borders, of fraud." A Lowell physician, Dr. Joseph Curtis, advised the American Medical Association in 1849 that there was not a prison or reformatory in New England in which the hours of labor were as long, the time for meals as short, or ventilation as neglected as in the textile mills owned by Boston philanthropists. Thoreau, who remarked that philanthropy was the only virtue sufficiently appreciated by mankind, was not alone in thinking that "he who bestows the largest amount of time and money on the needy may be doing the most by his mode of life to produce the misery he strives in vain to relieve." Thus early Americans began to voice the suspicion that philanthropy was a device used by the rich to atone for their way of acquiring wealth.

Reasonable though the atonement theory of philanthropic motivation seems in the abstract, the diaries and private correspondence of pre–Civil War philanthropists betray no hints of feelings of guilt. On the contrary, these men seem to have been blandly confident that their prosperity came from God. Before retiring from business Amos Lawrence sometimes berated himself for "over-engagedness" in secular affairs; and Peter Chardon Brooks, an insurance broker and money lender who had amassed a million dollars by 1817, admitted that a self-made man was apt to value his money too highly and hug it too close. The major concern of such men, however, seems to have been to discharge the obligations of stewardship faithfully, so that, at the appointed hour, they might hear the joyful sound of "Well Done!" from the lips of their Divine Master. They gave out a feeling of religious duty, because they frankly enjoyed giving, because some appeal touched their hearts, and because, as they frequently said, they thought giving for certain purposes was a good investment.

If proof of the complex motives of philanthropy were needed, it would be supplied by the variety of objects donors chose to support. Boston boasted—alas, in the literal sense—"such a number and combination of charities as has never before been found in any city of its size," and in almost every American community well-to-do citizens contributed to the founding and support of churches, hospitals, and orphanages. A breadline in New York, a cemetery in Morristown, New Jersey, a home for fallen but repentant women in Philadelphia, and a fund to assist young brides to set up housekeeping in the vicinity of Northampton, Massachusetts, all impressed their donors as proper objects of benevolence. Some of the most important gifts went to states or cities for public purposes: Girard left money for internal improvements in Philadelphia and Pennsylvania; Theodore Lyman won some sort of immortality by supplementing legislative appropriations for the Massachusetts state reformatory; and Thomas H. Perkins and Cyrus Butler, great men in their day, would be forgotten today save for their contributions toward the establishment of asylums for the blind and insane.

It is easy to laugh at the highly specialized and seemingly

trivial purposes of many philanthropic activities. Yet who can deny, for example, that old people often suffer from failing eyesight? And who but Elias Boudinot, first president of the American Bible Society, was thoughtful enough to leave money in his will for purchasing spectacles for the aged poor? Amos Lawrence, having disengaged himself from business, rode out on fine days to distribute the tracts of the American Temperance Society and the Sunday School Union; on bad days he busied himself in selecting clothes, books, and other useful articles from storerooms in his house, bundled them into packages, and sent them off to needy students, professors, and clergymen. John Jacob Astor, not renowned for charitable giving, made an exception in favor of the Association for the Relief of Respectable Aged and Indigent Females. On the other hand, George Cheyne Shattuck, Boston's leading physician and a generous patron of education, passed up an opportunity to contribute to an old ladies' home; he preferred to give his money for such ends as the building of an observatory at his alma mater, Dartmouth. It was a halcyon day for philanthropists when a man could say, as the very rich and very generous William Appleton did in 1853, "I part with money in various ways of charity but much like to do it in my own way and not to be dictated to or even asked but in a general way, to give with others."

But giving with others was already a well-established feature of American philanthropy. The principle of voluntary association accorded so well with American political and economic theories that as early as 1820 the larger cities had an embarrassment of benevolent organizations. For the rest of the century, and even to our own day, one of the major problems of charity reformers would be to discover ways to coordinate the activities and fund drives of these competing agencies. In 1829 the

economist and publisher Matthew Carey, attempted—
without much success—to interest Philadelphians in a
single subscription campaign for the thirty-three
benevolent societies then operating in the city. During the
first half of the nineteenth century, societies for moral
reform of individual sinners, and for the redemption and
regeneration of a sinful world, multiplied even more rapidly
than relief and aid organizations. As improvements in
transportation and communication made it easier for people
to join together, local societies merged into regional and
then into national associations. William Ellery Channing,
who disliked the substitution of the group for the individual
conscience, remarked in 1829 that there was scarcely an
object, good or bad, for whose advancement an association
had not been formed.

The 1830s, an era of religious, political, and economic
ferment, was the age of the "Benevolent Empire," a
coalition of separate but closely related interdenominational
religious societies. These various organizations collected
and dispersed funds for distributing Bibles and religious
tracts, for promoting foreign and home missions, for
advancing the cause of temperance, Sabbath observance,
and the Sunday-school movement; they supplied financial
assistance to poor youths who wished to become clergymen
and labored mightily to uplift the morals of seamen. Their
combined membership ran into the hundreds of thousands
and contributions to them amounted to several million
dollars a year. Each of the societies held rousing national
conventions and had offices, life-members, and, of course,
rich angels. Elias Boudinot, Stephen Van Rensselaer, David
Olyphant, Arthur and Lewis Tappan, and other philanthropists—usually although not always Federalist-Whig in
their political leanings—took one or more of the societies to
their bosoms, made generous contributions to their trea-

suries, and exerted a dominant influence on their policies and programs. In the hard times following the panic of 1837 many contributors had to curtail their gifts to the moral reform societies. The assocations were further harassed by sectarian jealousies, by mounting sectional tensions, and by demands that they either denounce or defend the institution of slavery. The mission and tract societies adopted a policy of silence on the slavery issue, partly because it was politic to do so, and partly because (or so they maintained) their concern was with personal, not social reform.

The American Colonization Society was founded (in 1817) about the same time as the moral reform societies and derived its support from approximately the same classes. Its work, which was the transporting of free Negroes to Africa, received the blessings of statesmen, the indorsement of state legislatures, and indirect assistance from the federal government. During the 1820s the society raised enough money in the North and South to purchase land and found a struggling colony in Liberia. The society managed to send a few hundred emigrants to the colony each year—a total of 11,000 by 1860—but its operations proved a disappointment both to southerners, who seem to have expected it to rid the slave states of free Negroes, and to northerners who had hoped that the society would promote the manumission of slaves. After 1832, when William Lloyd Garrison denounced colonization as a scheme to strengthen slavery, the society lost the support of the Tappans and other militant antislavery men. Its endeavors yielded such slight returns that critics labeled it "an American humane farce." Yet simply because it was *not* an antislavery organization it continued to receive contributions from conservative philanthropists such as James Beekman of New York and Robert Winthrop and Nathan Appleton of Boston. Appleton, a founder of the Massachusetts textile industry, and sensitively aware of the property rights of slaveowners, said in 1847 that he did not regard colonization as either an attack on or a solution to slavery. He supported the Colonization Society because he thought it was engaged in an experiment to ascertain whether the African race was fit for self-government and civilization.

At least some slaveowners were, or had been, prepared to go considerably farther than Appleton. The large number of free Negroes in Maryland and Virginia testified that hundreds of slaves had obtained freedom with the consent of their masters. After the 1830s legal restrictions made manumission more difficult to practice, but even so John McDonogh, a Louisiana planter and land speculator who conceived many ambitious philanthropies, allowed his slaves to use the proceeds of their labor over a fifteen-year period to buy their liberty. McDonogh sent his freed Negroes to Liberia, but John Randolph, in one of his several wills, conferred freedom on his four hundred slaves, valued at about a half-million dollars, and provided for their colonization in other parts of the United States. After a long legal battle the court carried out the terms of the will.

Few of the very rich were identified with the abolition movement before the mid-fifties. Among the exceptions were Arthur Tappan (1786–1865) and his brother Lewis (1788–1873). The Tappans, who attributed the success of their New York silk-importing business to moral supervision of their clerks and a strictly cash, one-price system of merchandising, came close to being caricatures of blue-nosed reformers. They worried about the "unchurched poor," the desecration of the Sabbath, and the use of wine in communion services. They founded a society to establish asylums for reformed prostitutes and, when that failed, organized a Society for Promoting the Observance of the Seventh Commandment. That the Tappans were pious busybodies cannot be denied, but they were also dedicated to the gospel of stewardship. They spent their wealth generously on religious and educational philanthropies, and when the championship of unpopular causes exposed them to the wrath of street mobs and the pressure of the business community, they faced their foes with uncommon courage. It was Arthur Tappan who secured William Lloyd Garrison's release from a Baltimore jail in 1830 by paying the fine and court costs imposed on him for libeling the owner of a vessel engaged in the domestic slave trade. As an alternative to colonization they proposed schemes for educating free Negroes for citizenship in the United States. They were among the organizers of the American Anti-Slavery Society in 1833, and active workers in the society until it split in 1840. Thereafter, although somewhat reduced in influence because of Arthur's bankruptcy, they gave their support to the anti-Garrisonian political wing of the abolition movement.

Education, which loomed so large in the thought of the Tappans, also occupied a major share of the attention of other philanthropists. At the start of the century the provision of free schools for poor children was a favorite form of charity; but with the expansion and reform of the public school system philanthropists became active in endowing private academies for the children of the rich. The field of higher education, neglected by the federal government and very poorly supported by the states, gave philanthropists their greatest opportunity for service. A nation growing rapidly in population and wealth possibly needed more colleges than the twenty-odd in existence at the start of the century. As events proved, however, the nation did not require and could not support nearly all of the five hundred or more colleges that were founded between 1800 and 1860.

It would be logical to assume that supposedly practical Americans would have given first priority to the establishment of schools for engineers and technicians. In practice, however, they seem to have believed that the crying need was for institutions to train more clergymen and devout laymen. By 1830 twenty theological seminaries had been founded, with Andover, the seat of "sound, orthodox, Calvinistic principles of divinity" receiving particularly generous benefactions. Meanwhile, churches of all denominations organized a host of small colleges, many of which called themselves universities. Of all the new institutions, Amherst, founded by Congregationalists in 1821, seems to have been the pet of the philanthropists, largely because of its reputation as a feeder of ministerial students to the seminaries.

Promoters of colleges in the western states appealed to the East for financial assistance in much the same way that the colonial colleges had sought help from England. In their campaigns for funds they often claimed that the indoctrination of young westerners in sound moral principles was the best defense against the twin evils of religious indifference and political radicalism. The Tappans, who contributed to the founding of both Oberlin and Kenyon, thought that the solution to the financial problems of poor colleges and college students lay in attaching farms and workshops to classrooms. To this end they organized in 1831 a Society for Promoting Manual Training in Literary Institutions. The manual labor idea, although it furthered the founding of small schools, did not solve the needs of the larger and better-established western colleges. After the depression of 1837 a number of these institutions, finding that frequent and competing solicitations increased the resistance of eastern philanthropists, formed the Society for Promotion of Collegiate and Theological Education in the West and, for a number of years, conducted a united fund drive.

The great increase in the number of colleges made it difficult for older institutions to attract and retain philanthropic support. Even Harvard, Unitarian since 1805, suffered from the competition of younger but more religiously orthodox colleges. Bostonians had contributed slightly more than a quarter of a million dollars to Harvard between 1800 and 1830; in the next fifteen years, while raising $330,000 for Amherst, they gave but $84,000 to Harvard. Beginning in the late 1840s, however, and increasingly in the 1850s, Harvard began to receive the gifts of Abbott Lawrence, Samuel Appleton, and other industrialists. Numerous institutions were favored by the families or individuals whose names they bore or adopted, but in at least one instance, Rutgers, college authorities made the mistake of renaming the institution in honor of a prospective benefactor who failed to make the expected princely donation. On the other hand, a public lecture by Mark Hopkins, the president of Williams College, made such a favorable impression on Amos Lawrence that the philanthropist made a large unsolicited gift to the college and followed his initial donation with several more.

The federal government was the recipient of another unsolicited and quite unprecedented gift in the form of James Smithson's bequest of approximately $500,000. Smithson, a British chemist who died in 1829, left his fortune to a nephew with the proviso that if the latter died without issue (as he obligingly did) the entire estate should pass "to the United States of America to found at Washington, under the name of the Smithsonian Institution, an establishment for the increase and diffusion of knowledge among men." Upon the death of the nephew in 1835 Congress debated the constitutionality and propriety of accepting the gift, John C. Calhoun opposing and John Quincy Adams favoring acceptance. As President, Adams had been unsuccessful in his efforts to expand the activities of the federal government in education and research; now, however, he was not to be denied, and in 1836 Congress voted to accept the bequest. Not until ten years later, after further controversy and debate, and after the loss of the original gift through unwise investment (Congress appropriated $500,000 to cover the loss) did "the establishment" at last come into being. Adams again played an important role in securing approval of the act that set up the institution, but it remained for Joseph Henry, the brilliant physicist who served as director of the Smithsonian from its founding in 1846 until his death more than thirty years later, to establish research and publication as the means by which the institution was to carry out its mission of increasing and diffusing knowledge among men.

While Congress was still debating what to do with the Smithson gift, another institute for disseminating knowledge opened in Boston. The donor, John Lowell, retired from business after the death of his wife and two young daughters and spent the rest of his brief life in restless travel through Europe and the Middle East. Shortly before his death in 1836 he put his will into final shape, directing that a sum of $250,000 be used to found the Lowell Institute. Lowell stipulated that the endowment, instead of being spent on buildings, should be used to sponsor public lectures to instruct the people of Boston in science, literature, history, and religion. Although imparting more knowledge to serious-minded Bostonians might seem like carrying coals to Newcastle, the Institute opened in 1840 with a series of lectures on geology by Benjamin Silliman. Through a policy of generous remuneration the institute was able to bring to its platforms some of the foremost men of letters and science of both the old and new worlds.

Beginning in the 1840s, as the founding of Lowell Institute and the Smithsonian Institution suggest, scientific research and intellectual inquiry—as opposed to moral instruction and reform—began to figure more prominently as objects of American philanthropy. Louis Agassiz, who came to the United States to lecture at Lowell Institute, remained to become professor of zoology and geology at Harvard. There his work was supported by the gifts of Abbott Lawrence, Francis Gray, and other Boston capitalists as well as by grants from the Massachusetts legislature. Agassiz's insatiable requirements for funds for his museum of comparative zoology gave philanthropists an object lesson in the cost of scientific research. At about the same time, by founding Cooper Union in New York City, Peter Cooper (1791–1883) continued the Franklin tradition of advancing science and art "in their application to the varied and useful purposes of life." George Peabody (1795–1869), the American-born banker who lived in London after 1837, made it possible for his countrymen to display their industries and inventions at the Crystal Palace Exhibition of 1851 and through his gift of the Peabody Institute enriched Baltimore's cultural life with an art gallery, lecture hall, and conservatory of music. Peabody's and Henry Grinnell's underwriting of the expenses of polar expeditions during the 1850s popularized geographical exploration as an object of philanthropic support. Similarly, the bequest of John Jacob Astor, which established the Astor Library in New York, and the gifts of Joshua Bates for the founding of the Boston Public Library in 1852, presaged what was to become one of the standard forms of philanthropy in the second half of the nineteenth century.

Promoters of two patriotic undertakings met difficulty in raising money for objects that would, offhand, seem to have had popular appeal. The Bunker Hill Monument Association of Boston ran out of money and into debt three years after laying the cornerstone of the monument in 1825. Construction had to be suspended for almost a decade. The obelisk was not completed until the 1840s, after Amos Lawrence and Judah Touro of New Orleans had each contributed $10,000 and a "Ladies Fair" had raised $30,000 for the project. Meanwhile, the Washington National Monument Society, founded in 1833, sought subscriptions for a memorial to George Washington in the national capital. More than fifty years passed before the beautiful shaft was finished, for although the society had collected enough money to begin construction in 1848, funds were exhausted by 1855, and for many years thereafter efforts to obtain additional support from private citizens or the federal government yielded disappointing returns. Partisan feelings and, in the case of the Washington Monument, religious considerations were partly responsible for the indifference and even hostility to these undertakings. But more important was the fact that the sense of national patriotism was still comparatively weak in pre–Civil War America, despite Fourth of July orations and the vogue of eulogistic biographies and histories.

In contrast to the lagging support accorded patriotic monuments, Americans gave enthusiastically and liberally for foreign relief. In the 1820s volunteer committees arranged balls, fairs, auctions, debating contests, and theatrical benefits to raise money for the cause of Greek independence. The committees employed nearly all the devices of modern charity drives to levy contributions for Greek relief from merchants, shippers, laborers, and school children, and brought a number of Greek war orphans to this country for adoption. In the autumn of 1832, when the starving people of Cape Verde Islands rowed out to a ship hoping to buy food, they were astonished to learn that the vessel had been sent from the United States for the express purpose of relieving their necessities. Individuals and churches in New England, Philadelphia, and New York had heard of their need and had raised thousands of dollars for their assistance. Boston gentlemen sent a relief ship to the Madeira Islands in 1843 and were rewarded when appreciative islanders sent the ship back laden with casks of choice old Madeira. The Irish famine of 1846–47, the worst calamity of the entire period, called forth the largest and most widely shared response from the American people. New York's merchant prince A. T. Stewart and other Irish-Americans showed sympathy in abundance, but generosity cut across national and religious lines. To carry the contributions of Massachusetts alone required two sloops of war, four merchant ships, and two steamers. It was both fitting and ironic that the Boston bluebloods, Josiah Quincy and Robert Winthrop, the latter an Episcopalian descendant of Puritan John Winthrop, should have taken leading parts in organizing relief efforts for the distressed people of Catholic Ireland.

American readiness to assist the unfortunate in foreign lands seemed to bear out Tocqueville's view that democracy, by destroying barriers of class and privilege, fostered a general feeling of compassion for all members of the human race. But in the 1830s and 1840s thoughtful Americans were less concerned about the consequences of democracy than about the work that remained to be done for its realization. There was need, said William Ellery Channing in 1841, for "vigorous efforts, springing from love, sustained by faith" for diffusing knowledge, self-respect, self-control, morality and religion through all classes of the population. At the time these were the areas in which philanthropy was most interested and best fitted to serve.

4

Saints and Scolds

What is it we heartily wish of each other? Is it to be pleased and flattered? No, but to be convicted and exposed, to be shamed out of our nonsense of all kinds. . . .

RALPH WALDO EMERSON

With some exceptions, like the Tappans, contributions to moral reform and gifts to the unfortunate involved few sacrifices by donors. Not even the Tappans insisted that the rich should give away all they possessed, and Amos Lawrence once reflected that the more he gave the more he seemed to have. Some men, like Girard, gave up their money only after death; others, like Lawrence, gave liberally of their income during life but made no significant charitable bequests. "I have given in my lifetime what I felt it was my duty to give," Edward Delavan, the angel of the temperance movement, said in his will. "I think my family is entitled to what is left of my estate." Generally speaking, philanthropists made their contributions out of surplus wealth and stopped giving whenever they thought it prudent to do so.

To some guardians of conscience neither the ends nor the means of conventional giving warranted the name of philanthropy. Emerson, in "Self-Reliance" (1841), warned the "foolish philanthropist" not to come to his door begging for "your miscellaneous popular charities; the education at colleges of fools; the building of meeting-houses to the vain end to which many now stand; alms to sots, and the thousandfold Relief Societies." Thoreau scorned "a charity which dispenses the crumbs that fall from its overload tables, which are left after its feasts!" He wondered at the boasts of men who gave one-tenth of their income to charity while keeping nine-tenths for themselves; and he asked whether such a distribution was to be explained by the generosity of the givers or by "the remissness of the officers of justice."

There were a number of philanthropists in the pre–Civil War period, however, who were as little impressed by the common run of charities as Emerson, who were as alert as Thoreau to inhumane social practices, and who offered more than passive resistance to injustice. These reformer-philanthropists conducted a general inquest into the abuses of their time and were more than willing to point out better ways of doing things. Not all the causes they championed were unpopular, but they did have to contend with complacency, and, at times, sentimentality. Mainly it was inertia—passive goodwill combined with prejudice against change and reform—rather than active opposition that they encountered. The vehemence of their agitation shocked persons of milder temperaments and easier consciences. Their peculiarities, prejudices, and blind spots are all too apparent, as are the inadequacies of some of the remedies they proposed. They were neither revolutionaries nor visionaries, and perhaps were not much more sensitive to wrong than ordinary men and women; but they had a much stronger than ordinary sense of personal responsibility for ending or mitigating wrongs. They became excited about issues in which their own interests were not involved, and they had the energy and daring to carry their feelings into action.

The miscellaneous popular charities whose numbers increased during the hard times of 1816–21, and in each succeeding depression, were among the principal targets of the reformers. The trouble with such agencies, in the opinion of Joseph Tuckerman (1778–1840) of Boston and John Griscom (1774–1840) of New York, two of the most influential of the charity reformers, was that while relieving the sentiments of the comfortable classes, they did more harm than good to the poor. The American charity reformers, like their British and Continental counterparts with whom they were in frequent communication, were obsessed by a fear of pauperism. They wanted to help the poor but were so fearful of pauperizing them that the only commodity they dared offer was advice. That they gave liberally: hints on household management, admonitions on waste, intemperance, and idleness, and sermons on the virtues of self-help.

Individualistic and moralistic in outlook though the charity reformers were, they were not as naïve as they sometimes seem. Tuckerman, Griscom, and their associates put in motion schemes for the spread of savings banks, life insurance, and benefit societies among the poor; and in the course of their attack on pauperism they lent support to a host of reform movements. The material as well as the moral state of the poor engaged the attention of Robert M. Hartley (1796–1881), who founded the New York Association for Improving the Condition of the Poor in 1843 and managed it for the next three decades. Under Hartley's leadership the A.I.C.P. devoted part of its energies to "incidental labors" for social betterment, particularly in the fields of housing, sanitation, and child welfare.

Although suspicious of unwise private charity, the reformers were even more critical of public poor relief. Tuckerman urged repeal of existing poor laws and abolition of all public assistance except that furnished in closely supervised institutions. England attempted a revision of her poor laws along these lines in 1834, but public opinion in the United States (where the votes of the poor counted more at the polls) would not accept such a drastic step. Nevertheless during the 1820s legislatures in several states ordered investigations of prevailing methods of poor relief. The reports of the investigating committees confirmed the reformers' charges that some of the poor were maintained in their own homes at the taxpayers' expense; others, however, were either farmed out to contractors at a stipulated price or "sold" to the person who bid the lowest sum for keeping them. Since the bidders themselves were often desperately poor, the money paid them for keeping paupers constituted a kind of relief—"a species of economy" (said the New York report) "much boasted of by some of our town officers." With rare unanimity the reports indorsed the almshouse or poor farm—utilized by the more populous communities for a century or more—as the most humane and economical method of caring for paupers. A well-regulated institution, such as the one at Poughkeepsie, New York, employed its inmates at picking oakum, washing, spinning, cooking, and farm work, and fed and clothed each at an annual cost of twenty-five dollars. "Our house of industry," reported the gratified managers, "affords an opportunity to economize, and to support our paupers at least 50 percent less than formerly."

Amos Lawrence. (From Freeman Hunt, *Lives of American Merchants.*
New York: Derby & Jackson, 1858.)

BOYS
having HOMES
are
NOT RECEIV
HERE

"Please Sir, May I Have a Bed." Newsboys' Lodging House of Children's Aid Society of New York, 1854. (From Charles Loring Brace, *The Dangerous Classes of New York*. New York: Wynkoop & Hallenbeck, 1872.)

The reformers were more successful in inducing communities to build almshouses than in policing them once they had been established. The poorhouses founded in the 1820s and 1830s soon become catchalls for victims of every variety of misery, misfortune, and misconduct. The old and the young, the vagrant and the abandoned, the feeble-minded, insane, and disabled, were all herded together in buildings that were poorly constructed, foully maintained, and wretchedly furnished. "Common domestic animals are usually more humanely provided for than the paupers in some of these institutions" was the verdict of one investigatory commission at midcentury. In New York in the 1850s a committee of the state senate found evidence of such "filth, nakedness, licentiousness, . . . and . . . gross neglect of the most ordinary comforts and decencies of life" that it forbore to publish its findings in detail lest the report disgrace the state.

The children in prison rather than those in pauper asylums first aroused the sympathy of nineteenth-century reformers. John Griscom, representing the New York Society for the Prevention of Pauperism, and Thomas Eddy, who had been active in prison reform movements since the 1790s, worked for five years after 1819 to get youthful offenders out of jails and into reformatories. Through their efforts the New York House of Refuge, the first reformatory for juvenile delinquents in the United States, was founded in 1825. Shortly afterward, Philadelphia, traditionally the center of American prison reform activities, built a similar House of Refuge; and Boston, under the prodding of Mayor Josiah Quincy, soon established a House of Reformation which, in the opinion of informed students, might have served as a model for all correctional institutions. The success of the Boston House of Reformation led Theodore Lyman in the 1840s to make gifts totaling almost $75,000 for the establishment of the first state juvenile reformatory at Westborough, Massachusetts.

While other humanitarians were demanding special institutions for wayward youth, Charles Loring Brace (1826–90), a twenty-seven-year-old city missionary in the Five Points district of New York, developed a comprehensive program for combatting delinquency at its source. The New York Children's Aid Society, organized by Brace in 1853, provided religious meetings, workshops, industrial schools, and lodging houses for the poorest and most neglected children of the metropolis. Brace, who regarded these undisciplined and often homeless youngsters as menaces to society, described the Children's Aid Society as "a moral and physical disinfectant." He was particularly interested in the possibility of "draining" New York of destitute children. Beginning in 1854 the Children's Aid Society annually sent hundreds of boys and girls to foster homes in the West. The success of the emigration scheme rested in part on the demand for unpaid farm labor. To Brace this circumstance did not lessen the charity of those who gave poor children homes in return for work. Brace, like Cotton Mather, believed the best charity that could be offered the idle was an opportunity to work, and he was convinced that boys and girls were better off in Christian homes, especially farm homes, than in any institution.

Brace's informal placement methods set off a long controversy. Roman Catholics complained that Catholic children were being sent to Protestant homes; westerners protested that the Children's Aid Society was filling western jails and reformatories with petty criminals; and welfare workers objected that the society did not carefully scrutinize the homes in which it placed children. Brace investigated the charges, modified his methods, and persisted in his labors for almost forty years. His work did much to popularize foster-home care for dependent children as opposed to institutionalization, and his preventive "child-saving" approach, adopted at a time when so much emphasis was placed on correctional or reformatory methods, exercised a wholesome influence on later development in child welfare.

The founding of juvenile reformatories was part of the larger movement for prison reform. In the United States this movement went back at least to 1776 when a Society for Alleviating the Miseries of Public Prisons had been organized in Philadelphia. By the 1820s, after half a century of experience in substitution of confinement for corporal punishment, two rival systems of prison discipline had emerged: the Pennsylvania or "separate" plan used at the great and costly Eastern State Penitentiary of Cherry Hill, and the Auburn or "congregate" system developed in New York State. In the former, inmates lived, worked, ate, and slept in solitary cells; under the Auburn plan prisoners were locked up alone at night, but worked and ate together during the day, theoretically in absolute silence and subject to harsh punishment for breaking rules against communicating with one another.

Each of the methods had staunch advocates. The Pennsylvania system appealed to humanitarians because of the supposed penitential benefits of solitary confinement, while the Auburn plan found support among persons impressed by its demonstrated economy. Auburn won the indorsement of the influential Boston Prison Discipline Society, which, under the leadership of Louis Dwight, a former agent of the Tract and Bible Societies, issued propaganda for adoption of the congregate system throughout the nation. On the other hand Samuel Gridley Howe, Horace Mann, Charles Sumner, and many other reformers remained partisans of the Pennsylvania system.

The dispute produced a spate of pamphlets, the most valuable of which was Dorothea Dix's *Remarks on Prisons and Prison Discipline* (1845), and Nathaniel Hawthorne made a visionary prison reformer the villain of *The Blithedale Romance* (1852). In the heat of the controversy legislatures and prison administrators initiated reforms in the construction and management of penitentiaries that for a brief period made American prisons rank among the most progressive in the world.

In the long run it proved impossible to maintain interest in prison reform at the high level necessary to effect lasting improvement. Other issues intervened, and reformers soon found prison discipline a less interesting subject of debate and speculation than projects for preventing crime. Before interest had cooled, however, a New York Quaker, Isaac Hopper (1771–1852), had begun his work of helping discharged prisoners find homes and jobs. Meanwhile in Boston a shoemaker named John Augustus (1785–1859) voluntarily assumed and performed the duties of probation officer. Over a period of almost twenty years Augustus devoted the earnings of his shop and applied the contributions of well-wishers to bailing and rehabilitating drunkards and persons convicted of petty crimes. Necessarily selective in the bestowal of assistance, since his resources were limited, he nevertheless helped many unfortunates who were "undeserving" by conventional standards. Augustus was "extraordinarily given to help the helpless and love the unlovely," said the radical preacher Theodore Parker. "Ministers preach benevolence and beneficence—he *went* and *did* it."

Three more famous philanthropists, among the most justly celebrated America has produced, also *went* and *did* acts of extraordinary usefulness to classes previously neglected and often deemed beyond help. The Reverend

Thomas Hopkins Gallaudet (1787–1851), Dr. Samuel Gridley Howe (1801–76), and Dorothea Dix (1802–87) were not specially qualified by training for the service that won their fame. They abandoned their intended careers in order to help deaf mutes and the blind, and to rescue the insane from cages in jails and almshouses. Gallaudet, a graduate of Andover Theological Seminary, demonstrated to the nation that deaf mutes could be educated. He founded the first American school for the deaf, gained support for this work from private donors, state legislatures, and even Congress, and lived to see state schools for the deaf widely established. Howe's special field was instruction of the blind, and his most celebrated feat was teaching Laura Bridgman—blind, deaf, and mute—the use of language and a variety of manual skills. But before Howe became a teacher of the blind in the 1830s, he had fought in the Greek War of Independence and administered relief to Greek civilians; and long after he won renown as head of Perkins Institution, he plunged into other causes, and embarked on new crusades to educate the feeble-minded and teach the mute to speak. Howe was a latter-day Benjamin Rush in the multiplicity of his interests, in his love of liberty, aptitude for controversy, and unquenchable optimism. Even oysters, he said, were capable of improvement!

As for Dorothea Dix, her career offers one of the best examples the nineteenth century affords of sustained and constructive agitation for humanitarian reform. She was not a pioneer in the field of better treatment of the insane. Much had already been accomplished when she began her work. Several reputable hospitals for the mentally ill had been founded by incorporated bodies; John McLean and other donors had given money for improving and expanding facilities for the insane, and a number of states had opened publicly supported asylums. Nearly all of these institutions made at least nominal provision for caring for the dependent insane at low cost. So much progress seemed to have been made in the years just before Miss Dix's investigations that there was danger, not that her proposals would seem outlandish, but that further action and expenditure for the insane might seem superfluous. Dorothea Dix's task was the difficult one of puncturing complacency, indicating omissions, specifying mistakes and abuses, and stirring the public conscience to greater exertions.

Like another great agitator, Anthony Benezet, Miss Dix was a teacher by profession. Largely self-taught, she had conducted a successful school for daughters of Boston's leading families and had tutored the children of her friend and pastor, William Ellery Channing. In the winter of 1841, somewhat at loose ends following a long illness, she agreed to teach a Sunday-school class for women prisoners in the East Cambridge jail. Here she found insane women locked in unheated cells. Anyone might have done what she then did. She petitioned the court for warmer quarters for these women. But Dorothea Dix was not content to stop there. She made it her business to find out how the insane were cared for in the rest of Massachusetts. After two years she was ready to report her findings in a *Memorial to the Legislature of Massachusetts* (1843), a document which proved that Victorian decorum was not inconsistent with the presentation of sordid social truths.

"I proceed, gentlemen," Miss Dix began, "briefly to call your attention to the *present* state of insane persons confined within the Commonwealth, in *cages, cellars, stalls, pens; chained, naked, beaten with rods,* and *lashed* into obedience." Armed with facts, figures, names, places, and dates, she cited instance after instance of the mistreatment or neglect of the mentally ill. Poor-law officials, as she pointed out, found it cheaper to "lodge" the pauper insane in jails and almshouses than to send them to asylums. In any case, the number of dependent insane and idiotic persons was at least twice as large as the total capacity of the three asylums in the state. Fortunately she had friends as well as facts at her disposal. Horace Mann lent his assistance, and Samuel Gridley Howe was chairman of the legislative committee to which the *Memorial* was referred. Howe's committee indorsed both the findings and conclusions of her investigation and secured passage of a bill enlarging the Worcester Asylum to provide more space for poor patients.

Massachusetts was the first phase of a forty-year campaign that took Miss Dix throughout the United States, into Canada, Scotland, England, Italy, and Turkey, and spread her influence as far as Japan. It would be incorrect to imply that she single-handedly worked a revolution in the care of the insane. Yet it is true that her "sad, patient, deliberate" investigations resulted in the founding of many new state hospitals and at least a temporary improvement in the treatment of the mentally ill. Wherever she went her methods were essentially the same: inquiry and research to determine the facts about the number and condition of the insane; efforts to arouse public opinion through articles in the press and memorials to the legislature; and cultivation of powerful figures in and out of public office. She professed a ladylike repugnance of politics, but she had a real talent for political maneuver. She knew when to sprinkle her humanitarian pleas with the salt of economy and often concluded her appeals by observing that "it is cheaper to take charge of the insane in a curative institution than to support them elsewhere for life." She was adept at discovering the most influential men in legislatures and in bringing them into her camp. The men she feared most were not those who openly opposed her but those who said they sympathized with her aims, wept over her reports, and then found compelling, noble reasons for steeling their hearts against compassion.

Such a man was President Franklin Pierce, at whose hands Miss Dix suffered one of her few major defeats. In 1848 she sent a *Memorial* to Congress in which she estimated that not more than one-twelfth of the insane population of the country could be accommodated in existing hospitals and asylums. As a means of dealing with the problem she proposed federal assistance in financing care of the insane through land grants to the states. Grants of this sort had frequently been made for education and internal improvements, and, on two occasions, for schools for the deaf. In 1854, after six years of lobbying by Miss Dix, both houses of Congress passed her bill. It apportioned 12,225,000 acres of public land among the states for the support of insane asylums and institutions for the deaf.

President Pierce, professing regret for having to do so, vetoed the bill. He acknowledged that the duty of providing for those who suffered from want and disease of body or mind was "among the highest and holiest" of human obligations, but he said he feared the effect of Miss Dix's bill would be "prejudicial rather than beneficial to the noble offices of charity," since it would dry up the normal springs of benevolence. "If Congress have the power to make provision for the indigent insane . . . ," he warned, "it has the same power to provide for the indigent who are not insane; and thus to transfer to the Federal Government the charge of all poor in all the states." For his part, continued Pierce, "I cannot find any authority in the Constitution for making the Federal Government the great almoner of public charity throughout the United States."

Of course Miss Dix and her supporters were not asking the federal government to play such a role, or to assume exclusive responsibility for all the poor in all the states. They wanted only to have a portion of the public lands granted to the states to enable them to fulfill their obligations better than they were then able. But to Pierce principle was more important than policy, and his principle, as a critic has remarked, was that no power that might be abused should be used. Yet Pierce sensed the implications of the Dix bill accurately. Had it become law, not only the care of the insane but all public welfare programs might have developed quite differently. As it was the United States had to wait another eighty years before the federal government began to assist and strengthen state programs for certain categories of needy persons.

To Horace Mann (1796–1859) and some other friends of Miss Dix, Howe, and Gallaudet, the improvement of common schools for normal children seemed an even more urgent matter than the establishment of institutions for the afflicted. No nineteenth-century reform movement had a broader base than the crusade for good schools, and none was expected to yield greater benefits. The educational reformers maintained that raising the general level of culture through more and better schools was the only sure way of accomplishing a thoroughgoing reform of society. A nation that made education freely available to all would not neglect its unfortunate members; it would not have to bear the burdens of pauperism, crime, immorality, and intemperance; and it would be prepared to meet social crises with wisdom and humanity.

The task of the reformers, however, was not to praise education, which nearly everybody did, but to obtain adequate financial support for it. They did not ask free schools for the poor, since both private philanthropists and public authorities were ready to provide that. They wanted free, public, entirely tax-supported education for all children—rich, poor, and middling—without any stigma of charity attached to it. The story of their struggle to win this objective lies outside the realm of the history of philanthropy, and yet it involves the difficult problem of the relationship of philanthropy to reform. Theoretically, philanthropy pioneers, proves the value of a service, then allows the community or the state to assume responsibility for the task, and moves on to some new field. In practice, as in the public school controversy when societies operating charity schools presented one of the numerous obstacles to the establishment of tax-supported educational systems, philanthropy may become a vested interest and display no eagerness to surrender its prerogatives. Fortunately there are philanthropists and philanthropists, and no one would deny that title to Horace Mann, the lawyer, politician, bureaucrat, college president, and reformer.

Mann had been a poor boy who studiously observed the maxims of self-help in his own career, and he preached those maxims with less humor and even more zeal than Benjamin Franklin. It was characteristic of him to find Richard Henry Dana's *Two Years before the Mast* deficient in statistics, wanting in moral lessons, and too full of descriptions. But Mann's earnestness and seriousness were well suited to his time and purpose, and he revealed in all his works a dedication to great ends. He was a figure of some prominence in Massachusetts politics when, in 1837, he accepted the relatively minor post of secretary of the state board of education. His long tenure in this office gave him an opportunity to canvass every shortcoming in the existing school system and to promote improvements in instruction, discipline, curriculum, textbooks, and the training of teachers. His *Annual Reports*, each as carefully prepared as a legal brief and as hortatory as a sermon, aroused interest and controversy not only in Massachusetts but in nearly every other state.

Like Howe and other humanitarian reformers of his day Mann found in phrenology an apparent scientific justification for his belief in the improvability and infinite educability of the human race. He had unbounded faith in the practical uses of education, particularly in overcoming poverty. But it was the common welfare rather than individual success that excited him, and it was the religious doctrine of stewardship much more than scientific rationalism that guided his thought. He believed that property owners were indebted to the social intelligence of preceding generations for their wealth and that they were therefore obligated to use it to transmit the common body of knowledge to future generations through schools. He was disappointed that rich men contributed little beyond their taxes to public education. When Abbott Lawrence, in making a gift of $50,000 to Harvard, said, "Elementary education appears to be well provided for in Massachusetts," Mann replied that salaries for women teachers in the public schools averaged $68.40 for the entire school term and that the average number of books in school libraries was twenty-five. In his last *Annual Report* he took a hard look at Massachusetts' latest wonder, the reform school at Westborough. "One tenth part of its cost," said Mann, "would have done more in the way of prevention than its whole amount can accomplish in the way of reclaiming."

In 1848, convinced that a man or child must be free before he could be educated, Mann gave up his official post and reentered politics on an antislavery platform. During the 1850s, in response to the Fugitive Slave Law, the Kansas-Nebraska Act, and the struggle for Kansas, other reformers also put the cause of the Negro above their earlier interests. Miss Dix was an exception to the general rule because she, in order not to jeopardize her usefulness to the insane, refused to become involved in the sectional controversy. But Howe, as impetuous in full-bearded middle age as in his Byronic youth, flung himself wholeheartedly into the abolition movement. Charles Sumner, the foremost peace orator of the 1840s, was anything but pacifistic in his utterances about slavery and slaveholders in the 1850s, and Gerrit Smith, a generous contributor to the peace movement, had concluded by the late 1850s that there was no possibility of ending slavery by peaceful means. Smith gave financial assistance to John Brown and was so deeply implicated in Brown's plans for direct action against slavery that he became temporarily insane after the debacle at Harpers Ferry. Theodore Parker and a few other clergymen, not content to denounce slavery from the pulpit, enrolled in vigilance committees that raised funds to speed fugitives to Canada or pay for the legal defense of Negroes held under the Fugitive Slave law. Prominent lawyers offered their services free of charge or at nominal costs as counsel to fugitives, and philanthropists who had once given money to colonize Negroes in Africa now contributed funds to send white settlers to Kansas. Amos Lawrence's son discharged his obligation of stewardship by paying for rifles shipped to the free-soil settlers.

If philanthropy means spending time and effort and risking personal safety to aid the downtrodden, the ranks of pre–Civil War philanthropists must be broadened to include the men and women who violated federal laws to shelter fugitives, as well as those who raided the South to rescue or abduct slaves. Levi Coffin, reputed head of the Underground Railway, is said to have assisted about one hundred fugitives a year over a period of more than thirty years. The intrepid Harriet Tubman, herself a fugitive, repeatedly returned to the South to lead her fellows to freedom. Some who engaged in this dangerous work paid a heavy price. John Brown sacrificed not only his own life but those of two of his sons. Reverend Charles Torrey, who resigned from a Providence pulpit to work for abolition, died in a southern jail for his efforts. Calvin Fairbanks spent more than seventeen years in prison in Kentucky as punishment for abducting slaves and, according to his own account, received something like 35,000 lashes at the hands of his jailer. One Rush R. Sloane of Sandusky, Ohio, paid a fine of $3,000 for assisting fugitives to Canada, while Thomas Garrett of Wilmington, Delaware, convicted of numerous breaches of the Fugitive Slave law, surrendered all his property in payment of fines totaling $8,000. This doughty old Quaker, undeterred by his punishment, continued to give aid and comfort to refugees until 1861. "The war came a little too soon for my business," he said. "I wanted to help off three thousand slaves. I had only got up to 2,700."

The Civil War came too soon for all the philanthropists. None of their work was finished and parts of it were hardly begun when the fighting started, bringing new opportunities for service.

5

Civil War Philanthropies

Long, too long America,
Traveling roads all even and peaceful you learn'd
    from joys and prosperity only,
But now, ah now, to learn from crises of
    anguish . . .
And now to conceive and show to the world what
    your children en-masse really are, . . .

WALT WHITMAN

The first need of the Civil War was for men to fight it; the next was for civilians to support and succor the armies; and the third was for marshaling material and spiritual resources into an overpowering will to victory. In April 1861 neither the North nor the South anticipated a struggle of the magnitude and duration that in fact took place. Both parties looked, as Lincoln said in his Second Inaugural Address, "for an easier triumph, and a result less fundamental and astounding." Throughout the war, patriots on each side, from Lincoln and Davis down, complained of laxity, indifference, self-seeking, and internal opposition that weakened war efforts. Yet from the very beginning the war roused the charitable energies and impulses of the American people, and of American women in particular, as they had never been aroused before. Charitable enterprises were of great importance, not only in providing needed supplies and services to the troops, but in building up civilian morale and the will to win.

"The uprising of the women of the land" (as the Reverend Henry W. Bellows, chairman of the United States Sanitary Commission, called the phenomenon) began on the day Lincoln summoned 75,000 militia to meet the challenge of Fort Sumter. Women in several New England cities, soon followed by others from New York to Iowa and California, organized to aid soldiers and their families. Before the war ended something like 15,000 soldiers' aid societies had been founded and almost every northern home had been canvassed for funds and supplies. One of the first women to volunteer for more onerous duties, and almost the last to leave the field, was Dorothea Dix. Although nearing sixty, she presented herself at the War Department in the first week of the war and shortly thereafter accepted the post of Superintendent of Female Nurses. Miss Dix's specifications for female nurses—and she was not one to relax her standards—were mature years, good health, and plainness in person and dress. "No bows, no curls, no jewelry, and no hoop-skirts," she decreed.

With or without Miss Dix's approval, for her authority was challenged by the Medical Bureau of the Army, an estimated thirty-two hundred women served as nurses with Union forces. Among them were six hundred Roman Catholic nuns, frowned upon by Miss Dix, but highly esteemed by the troops and hospital surgeons. More to the superintendent's liking were the three Woolsey sisters, daughters of the president of Yale, and Katherine Prescott

Wormeley, whose father was a British admiral. Illness cut short Louisa May Alcott's career as a nurse, but she served long enough to gather material for *Hospital Sketches* (1863), her first successful book. Most of the regular female nurses served in hospitals behind the lines, but "Mother" Mary Ann Bickerdyke, once a student at Oberlin and an herb-doctor at the start of the war, worked with such devotion and efficiency in battle zones that she became one of the authentic heroes of the war. Harriet Tubman, following Massachusetts troops to the South, mingled hospital chores with scouting and spying behind enemy lines. After every important battle free-lance "reliefers" and nurses hastened to the field. The most celebrated and ubiquitous of these independent operators was Clara Barton (1821–1912). A former teacher and Patent Office clerk, Miss Barton displayed her genius for obtaining relief supplies and getting them promptly to places of need long before she succeeded in organizing the American Red Cross. The prestige she gained through her war work helped in the later undertaking.

In zeal for war relief the women of the Confederacy equaled their sisters in the North. They organized hundreds of aid associations and during the first year of the war assumed almost complete responsibility for clothing southern troops. Soldiers on their way to or from the front found hospitality, entertainment, and medical service in Wayside Inns maintained by volunteers. Nursing appealed as strongly to southern as to northern women. They took battle casualties into their homes, and after Gettysburg some of them were permitted to go to the battlefield to tend their wounded. In 1862 the "petticoat gunboat" fever struck the Confederacy; in state after state women took collections at prayer meetings and Sunday schools, and held fairs, bazaars, raffles, and concerts to raise money to build gunboats. In the South, as in the North, there were drives for gifts to widows and orphans of war heroes. Southern sympathies and pocketbooks seem to have been particularly susceptible to appeals for the relief of families of men killed either in defense of the flag of the Confederacy or in pulling down the emblem of the Union.

Measured by money expended, the largest charitable efforts, North and South, were devoted to relieving families of servicemen. Oft-repeated warnings of the dangers of unwise giving were forgotten for the moment as community and state-wide relief organizations solicited contributions from farmers, merchants, railroad companies, factory owners, and workers, and showered gifts on the needy. Local, county, and state aid in the form of enlistment bounties and direct relief to dependent families seems to have been even more bountiful. Wartime generosity brought increased public debt and higher taxes, factors which had considerable bearing on the revival of hostility to public poor relief in the postwar years.

Religious charities flourished on both sides of the battle lines. "Both read the same Bible, and pray to the same God; and each invokes His aid against the other," mused Lincoln in 1864. The Bible Society of the Confederacy, with some assistance from the American Bible Society, labored to collect Bibles and testaments for distribution to southern soldiers; and the Evangelical Tract Society of Petersburg, Virginia, published a religious paper and kept rebel troops well supplied with tracts against swearing, drinking, and gambling. In the North, the work of the Christian Commission was generously supported by the evangelical churches, the Young Men's Christian Associations, the American Tract Society, and business firms such as the Baldwin Locomotive Company, which gave 10 percent of annual earnings during the war years. The Christian

Commission waged an aggressive campaign to furnish Union soldiers with material and spiritual comforts. It sent boxes of food, clothing, and religious literature to troops and employed a large staff of delegates, mainly clergymen on leave from their congregations, to distribute supplies, preach sermons, and conduct prayer meetings in army camps and to perform such helpful services as they could for the sick and wounded.

It remained for another organization, broader in scope and more scientific in intent than any of those so far mentioned, to demonstrate the real usefulness of philanthropy in wartime. The United States Sanitary Commission, which despite its official-sounding name was privately financed and directed, was organized in June 1861 by a group of humanitarians and reformers led by Henry W. Bellows, a Unitarian clergyman of New York City, and Dr. Elisha Harris, a well-known sanitary reformer. These men, and others like them throughout the nation, were impressed by the achievements of the British Sanitary Commission in the Crimean War and were determined to make use of the medical and sanitary knowledge acquired at such tragic cost in that conflict. Their aim, in large part realized, was to unite local relief societies into a national organization that would do much more than supplement the work of official agencies: it would use its money, influence, and knowledge to improve conditions in military camps and hospitals so as to prevent needless suffering and loss of life through disease.

In short, the tasks of the Sanitary Commission were to organize and direct the activities of thousands of women's societies and to bring the force of informed opinion to bear on the administration and military leaders. To accomplish these difficult and delicate assignments the Commission, a purely voluntary association, had to rely on persuasion and moral pressure. It would have been strange indeed if such an audacious undertaking had won universal acceptance. As it was Lincoln viewed the inception of the commission without enthusiasm and wondered whether it might not become "a fifth wheel to the coach." The Medical Bureau, indifferent to the commission at the start, was later often hostile. Secretary of War Stanton impeded rather than advanced its operations. And religious groups affiliated with the Christian Commission condemned the Sanitary Commission as godless. On the other hand Sanitary agents won the respect of field commanders and received enthusiastic backing from Catholics, Jews, and Protestants of liberal or advanced views. Working in or for the Sanitary Commission were veterans of prewar humanitarian crusades: Samuel Gridley Howe, for example, and able women such as Louisa Lee Schuyler, whose administrative talents later advanced many postwar reform movements. The commission was unusually fortunate in having as its first secretary-general the energetic Frederick Law Olmsted. Already famous in 1861 (and still remembered) for his books on the Old South, Olmsted brought to the Sanitary Commission the vision and foresight that he afterward applied to the planning and construction of some of America's greatest public parks.

From first to last the Sanitary Commission carried on inspections of camps and hospitals to uncover and help correct defects in sanitary arrangements, drainage, water supply, ventilation, and diet. It helped secure a needed reorganization of the Medical Bureau, promoted improvements in hospital design, and developed better and more humane methods of transporting the wounded. Through its local branches it collected food, clothing, bandages, and other supplies; stored them in supply depots; and distributed them through its agents in hospitals, on battlefields, and in emergency shelters. The commission provided lodges and feeding stations for soldiers in the major cities, established hospitals for convalescents, and maintained offices to assist distressed soldiers in obtaining back pay and bounties or pensions due them. It maintained a hospital directory—later adopted by the Army—that enabled relatives and other interested persons to locate the wounded and missing, collected and tabulated vital statistics on military personnel, and prepared and distributed thousands of medical monographs to surgeons in the armed forces. The greatest service rendered by the Sanitary Commission was to save lives; without it the number of deaths from disease in the Union forces—high as it was— would have been much larger. It influenced later developments in hospital administration, nursing service, and medical and surgical practice. That the commission was a precedent for the American Red Cross goes without saying; of more immediate importance was the fact that it gave to thousands of civilians a sense of purpose and participation in the struggle for the Union.

Contributing to or raising funds for the Sanitary Commission was one practical means of obtaining that sense of participation. Numerous charitable campaigns and the Greek and Irish relief drives had already demonstrated the formidable talent of American women for fund-raising. All earlier efforts were dwarfed, however, by the giant Sanitary Fairs that the women of northern cities staged in 1863 and 1864. Through admission fees, sales or auctions of gifts, and encouragement to conspicuous giving, these carnivals of benevolence netted about half the total cash contributions to the Sanitary Commission. Fair managers received and profitably disposed of such diverse items as pianos, threshing machines, watches, jewelry, a famous trotting horse, an album containing the autographs of all the presidents of the United States, and a cardboard representation of the

American eagle "feathered" with hair cut from the heads of the president and members of the cabinet. In addition to his autograph and hair Lincoln donated a copy of his Gettysburg address and the original draft of the Emancipation Proclamation. Cornelius Vanderbilt and A. T. Stewart, determined not to be outdone by the other, each gave the New York Fair $100,000. Everywhere the fairs yielded quantities of goods of all kinds—a mixed blessing as far as the commission was concerned, since the sudden increase in supplies created storage and transportation problems. In spite of large sums collected at the fairs, financial questions gave the commissioners many anxious hours. Generally speaking, the branches and local societies, quick and generous in contributions of supplies, were slow and reluctant to recognize the need for money to handle and distribute supplies efficiently. The twenty-one commissioners worked without compensation except travel expenses, but the commission at times had as many as five hundred agents, inspectors, doctors, cooks, and teamsters on its payroll. Inspections and preventive actitivies, which the commission regarded as its particular contribution and which were costly to perform, lacked the emotional appeal of relief work. Other agencies competed for public sympathy and financial support, and at least two, the Christian Commission and the Western Sanitary Commission (an independent organization that conducted large-scale relief operations west of the Mississippi) were serious rivals. Bellows and Olmsted, stressing the constructive and scientific aspects of their commission's program, looked to insurance companies for assistance; they found a valuable ally in Thomas Starr King, a popular and influential San Francisco preacher who was able to channel the lion's share of the Far West's exuberant contributions to the United States Sanitary Commission. Pope Pius IX's gift of $500 for suffering soldiers found its way, after a roundabout journey, into the treasury of the commission. English and European branches raised some money abroad, and a rich American dentist who lived in Paris paid for the commission's prize-winning exhibit at the Paris World's Fair of 1867. Contributions to the Sanitary Commission and its branches amounted to an estimated $25,000,000, a sum considerably larger than that raised by any of its rivals. Money gifts made up about $7,000,000 of the total, and the remainder represented the value of supplies and services furnished the commission.

While the Sanitary and Christian commissions organized assistance for fighting men, other groups, including many prewar abolitionists, sought means to help the Negro, for the "fundamental and astounding" result of the war, apparent long before victory had been won, was the ending of slavery. From the beginning of the war fugitive slaves had made their way to Fortress Monroe and other Union-held positions in the South, and as northern armies occupied portions of the Confederacy the number of refugee, abandoned, and captured slaves in or on Union hands rapidly increased. The status of these Negroes was at first uncertain, but step by step in 1862 actions of both the Congress and the president conferred immediate freedom on some and made it clear that emancipation awaited all. Early in 1862 societies were organized in Boston, New York, and Philadelphia to send money, clothing, books, teachers, missionaries, and plantation supervisors to destitute Negroes in the Sea Islands. In the next three years these original societies swelled into regional and national freedmen's aid associations that undertook to relieve the physical and spiritual wants of Negroes in conquered parts of the South and to train them for citizenship.

The relief and other assistance provided by these associations were desperately needed. Military officers and treasury agents had dealt with the freedmen as best they could, occasionally in an enlightened manner. But investigations conducted in 1863 by Robert Dale Owen, Samuel Gridley Howe, and James McKaye of the Freedmen's Inquiry Commission and James Yeatman of the Western Sanitary Commission revealed shocking conditions in the "contraband" camps and on plantations taken over by the government and leased to private individuals. McKaye estimated that neglect and disease had killed one-fourth of the Negroes herded in the contraband camps. Yeatman warned that unless the conditions of the freedmen were drastically bettered "one-half are doomed to die in the process of freeing the rest." The freedmen's aid associations redoubled their efforts and were able to report substantial progress in religious uplift and education. To their credit, however, they realized that the job was too big for private philanthropy. In December 1863 a joint committee representing the freedmen's aid societies of Boston, New York, Philadelphia, and Cincinnati urged Lincoln to recommend establishment of "a regularly constituted government bureau, with all the machinery and civil powers of the government behind it," to supervise and care for freedmen. Voluntary agencies, they said, simply could not carry out such a gigantic task "were their resources ten times what they are, and ten times what they can be made."

It took more than a year of further agitation by the freedmen's aid societies and other interested groups before Congress, in March 1865, authorized establishment in the War Department of a Bureau of Refugees, Freedmen, and Abandoned Land. Lincoln died before naming a commissioner for the bureau. His successor, Andrew Johnson, acting on the advice of Secretary of War Stanton, gave the post to Major General Oliver O. Howard, a West Pointer of distinguished piety. The novelty of the federal government's assuming responsibility for the welfare and protection of large numbers of people whose rights had been little regarded either in the North or in the South assured the bureau of a troubled existence. The act establishing the agency gave it wide but vaguely defined powers, and few of the bureau's critics—numerous both during and after Reconstruction—charged Howard or his subordinates with failing to interpret their authority broadly or to exercise it vigorously. As a relief agency the bureau operated on an unprecedented scale, assisting whites as well as Negroes. It leased land to freedmen, helped them find work, and supervised labor contracts with employers. It maintained courts to hear minor civil and criminal cases involving Negroes, and established hospitals, orphan homes, schools, and colleges. The relief activities of the bureau brought the usual fears of pauperization, but Howard's policies in this sphere were prudent to the point of harshness. He decreed that help should go only to the "absolutely necessitous and destitute." In theory, at least, the bureau attempted only to put the freedmen on the road to self-support in a free labor system.

The relation of the Freedmen's Bureau to the freedmen's aid societies (of which there were nearly thirty) provided an example, unfortunately soon forgotten, of the possibilities for fruitful cooperation between a government welfare agency and private philanthropy. The bureau's relief activities eventually made it possible for the societies to concentrate their energies on education, the work in which they were really most interested. The Freedmen's Bureau was also interested and active in education, but such competition as developed was not between it and the private societies but between rival groups within the philanthropic ranks. Some, like the American Missionary Association in which the Tappans were active, used education to spread religion and strengthen denominational interests. On the other hand, the Freedmen's Union Commission, a coalition of nonsectarian aid associations, stressed education pure and simple and reminded its teachers that they were not "missionaries, nor preachers, nor exhorters." The Freedmen's Bureau did not succeed in getting these rival groups to unite, and it could not ease the friction between them; but it discouraged duplication of effort in communities already supplied with schools, and it stimulated further philanthropic interests in the education of the freedmen by calling the attention of charitable organizations to those areas where need for teachers and schools was still great.

The Freedmen's Bureau did more than point out that education, prohibited under slavery, was the most urgent want of the freedmen: it provided about half the money spent on Negro education between 1865 and 1870. The bureau leased, repaired, built, and helped build hundreds of schoolhouses. It protected schools maintained by benevolent societies, furnished transportation and quarters for teachers employed in the schools, and, although not specifically authorized to pay teachers' salaries, found means to assist the societies in meeting this expense. By the late 1860s teachers were in shorter supply than school buildings. The bureau therefore suggested that the philanthropists establish teacher-training institutions for Negroes, and it encouraged this work by making grants to twenty normal schools, colleges, and universities. The assistance rendered by the bureau in starting Fisk, Atlanta, and Howard Universities, as well as other institutions of higher learning for Negroes, constituted one of its most important and lasting contributions. General Howard was interested in quality as well as quantity and at one point he declined to help the American Missionary Association found more normal schools on the ground that the association was already trying to operate more schools than it could support well.

By 1870, when the Freedmen's Bureau ceased its educational activities, the idea of Negro education had taken root in the South. The real question was not whether Negroes should be educated, but how and under whose control. Southern whites resented the Freedmen's Bureau and detested the northern teachers imported by the benevolent associations. They were not willing to allow the education of Negro children to remain permanently in the hands of persons who believed in racial equality and radical Republicanism. However, with few exceptions, such as the devoted women who spent their lives among the Negroes of the Sea Islands, Yankee teachers had gone home before the end of the Reconstruction. Recognizing that the South was not yet in a position to make adequate provision for instructing any of its children, northern philanthropists such as George Peabody, John F. Slater, and Robert C. Ogden continued their efforts on behalf of Negro and southern education. But after the 1870s this assistance was accepted, and, as a matter of fact, given, with the understanding that it would not violate southern institutions and traditions.

6

"Scientific Philanthropy"

In the bestowal of charity and in prevention of misery, the world has reached a new epoch.
DANIEL COIT GILMAN

The twenty-five or thirty years after the Civil War seemed, to Americans living at the time, an era of stunning achievement in all fields of philanthropy. Later generations, accustomed to smile or wince at the social crudities of the Gilded Age, have been slow to recognize that generosity and altruism were as characteristic of the period as acquisitiveness and self-seeking. Granted that philanthropists and those who write about them have a tendency to dwell on what has been done and to pass over things left undone, there was a certain foundation of fact in Robert Treat Paine's boast, made in 1893, "This last quarter of a century has witnessed a noble outburst of the energies of good men to help suffering brethren." Charitable directories published in the 1880s needed as many as a hundred pages to list and describe the numerous agencies alleviating misery and combating disease, pauperism, ignorance, and crime. At least a part, and sometimes a generous part, of vast fortunes made by fair means or foul found its way back to the community in gifts to hospitals, libraries, art museums, churches, relief societies, orphan asylums, homes for the aged, seminaries, colleges and universities, and specialized institutions for training engineers, farmers, businessmen, physicians, dentists, pharmacists, and nurses.

When charity reformers and civic leaders of the post–Civil War generation spoke of the arrival of a new epoch in philanthropy they had something more fundamental in mind than the quantity and variety of their countrymen's giving. The magnitude and multiplicity of the outpouring for benevolent purposes rather alarmed than pleased them. What they hailed was the development of a more scientific spirit and method in philanthropy. And it was the spread of this scientific approach, bringing reforms in public welfare and private charity, that impressed them as the great humanitarian achievement of their day. At long last, or so they thought, the charitable impulse was being disciplined, the head was triumphing over the heart, the "machinery of benevolence" was coming to be understood and usefully operated, and "philanthropology," the study of the scientific principles of philanthropy, would soon be as well recognized as any other branch of learning.

The basic principles of the "new charity" would hardly have struck Joseph Tuckerman or Benjamin Franklin as novel, and the almoner who said in 1874, "I can ruin the best family in Boston by giving them a cord of food in the wrong way," spoke in the accents of Cotton Mather. The new charity was actually quite traditional in its point of view and already outdated in some of its assumptions and attributes. The scientific philanthropists of the late nineteenth century took the "do's" and "don'ts"—especially the latter—handed down from generations of charity reformers, organized them into a comprehensive system of rules, and applied them more rigorously than ever before in American history.

Although the ultimate sources of scientific philanthropy were remote, experience during and just after the Civil War provided the immediate background for its emergence. The relative success of the Sanitary and Christian commissions gave new prestige to voluntary action. The Sanitary Commission, in particular, with its emphasis on visitation, inspection, and advisory functions, influenced the development of both official and voluntary agencies in the postwar years. The public health movement benefited from the wartime interest in camp and hospital improvement. A committee of sanitarians, which likened the poor population of New York City to "an immense army in camp, upon small territory, crowded into old filthy dwellings, and without the slightest police regulations for cleanliness," secured a reorganization of health services in the metropolis that was ultimately copied in other cities. Similarly, the belief that veterans were involved in the wave of crime and disorders that followed the war revived enthusiasm for prison reform and stimulated fresh interest in all branches of social science. War commissions and relief associations gave countless men and women of philanthropic disposition a taste for service and an experience in authority they were reluctant to surrender after hostilities were over.

One of those who was not ready to quit was Reverend Henry W. Bellows of the now defunct Sanitary Commission. Another was Miss Clara Barton, who had conducted her battlefield relief operations independent of the Sanitary Commission or any other authority. In 1866 Bellows and some of the men who had worked with him in the Sanitary Commission organized the American Association for the

Relief of Misery on the Battlefield. For five years they sought unsuccessfully to obtain American ratification of the Geneva Convention of 1864 providing for neutralization of aid to the wounded in time of war. The connection between the Sanitary Commission, the Association for the Relief of Misery on the Battlefield, and the Red Cross movement is plain, but it was Miss Barton, not the Bellows group, who eventually established the American Red Cross and secured the adherence of the United States to the Geneva treaty.

Clara Barton was a unique character in her own or any generation. Had she chosen to do so she might have qualified for Dorothea Dix's corps of Civil War nurses, for she met the standards of maturity and plainness. She was born in North Oxford, Massachusetts, on Christmas Day, 1821, and once said of herself, "I was never what the world would call 'even good looking.'" Yet she was, by her own account, and despite a stature of little more than five feet, an "imposing figure." She had a magnetism that commanded loyalty and an imperiousness that led one of her close and devoted associates to call her "the Queen." Miss Barton had a remarkable talent for dramatizing herself. "I wrung the blood from the bottom of my clothing before I could step, for the weight about my feet," she wrote in one of her Civil War letters. She took herself and her work very seriously. These are useful qualities for leadership in any public enterprise— and Clara Barton had in addition the *sine qua non* of all the great humanitarians: "What is nobody's business is my business," she said, and believed.

After the Civil War Miss Barton occupied herself for several years in lecturing on her battlefield activities, in checking hospital and burial records to obtain information for answering inquiries from relatives of missing prisoners of war, and in identifying and marking the graves of thousands of soldiers. She happened to be in Switzerland in 1870 and there met officials of the International Committee of the Red Cross. Work with the German Red Cross in the Franco-Prussian War brought her new laurels and popular identification with the Red Cross movement. In 1877 the Russo-Turkish War summoned her out of semiretirement and fired her ambition to found an American Red Cross society that would centralize and systematize relief activities in such emergencies. It was an uphill struggle, but in 1881 she incorporated the American Association of the Red Cross, and in the following year she had the immense satisfaction of seeing the long-delayed American ratification of the Geneva Convention become a reality.

Clara Barton's success in these campaigns stemmed in part from her ability to explain the provision of the Geneva treaty and the functions of the International Committee of the Red Cross in such a way as to allay American suspicions of foreign involvements even in humanitarian undertakings. But more important, both in the short and the long run, was her conception of the American Red Cross as an agency for rendering assistance in times of peace as well as war. In her propaganda as well as in the constitution of the new society she emphasized opportunities and responsibilities for service in plague, fire, flood, drought, and accident. As the historian of the American Red Cross has pointed out, her idea of what the Red Cross could and should do in peacetime made sense to people who saw no danger of war but who had recently raised large funds for victims of the Chicago and Boston fires and who were all too familiar with the havoc wrought by natural disasters, epidemics, and appalling railway and mine accidents. For most of the twenty-five years that Miss Barton dominated the American Red Cross, disaster relief was the organization's major activity. Although sixty years old in 1881 when her service with the Red Cross began, she administered relief in person and on the spot both in domestic catastrophes such as the Johnstown flood of 1889 and the Sea Island hurricane of 1893, and in foreign crises such as the American massacres of 1896.

The peculiar nature of disaster relief, not to mention Miss Barton's vigorous personality and individualistic methods of operation, put the American Red Cross, in its formative years, outside the mainstream of late nineteenth-century philanthropy. To say this implies no discredit to Miss Barton or to the organization she founded. The Red Cross, which in practice meant Clara Barton, was not engaged in charity as the word is usually interpreted. Miss Barton had a sensible aversion to pauperizing recipients of Red Cross aid, but she was not as hagridden by the fear of pauperism as so many of her contemporaries were. She wanted to give temporary help to normal people who were victims of abnormal misfortune and to render such assistance as she could to restore them to their normal way of life. That, it must be said, was all that those she aided seem to have wanted or expected. As Miss Barton's critics within the Red Cross were to point out, she had no taste and small talent for organizational or administrative refinements. But surely her singular and endearing characteristic was lack of interest in reforming anything or anybody. She did not launch crusades to end wars, famine, plagues, fires, or floods; she simply met emergencies as they arose and to the best of her abilities. Thus, although the comparison is somewhat strained, she belongs in the tradition of Stephen Girard rather than of Benjamin Rush.

Miss Barton once served briefly as superintendent of a women's reformatory in Massachusetts, but her Red Cross work hardly touched the problem of greatest concern to advocates of scientific philanthropy. This was the treatment of people who, even in normal times, were dependent on public or private bounty for all or part of their support. Massachusetts, the pioneer in so much nineteenth-century social legislation, took a step toward more intelligent handling of the problem in 1863 by creating a Board of State Charities. In the next decade ten other states followed Massachusetts' example. As a general rule the members of these state boards had no administrative responsibilities; they served without pay (in order to make the offices unattractive to spoilsmen); and their duties were to inspect, report upon, and make recommendations for improving public welfare institutions and such private ones as received state assistance. In an era not notable for the excellence of its public servants, the members and secretaries of these boards—Samuel G. Howe, Franklin B. Sanborn, Josephine Shaw Lowell, and Frederick H. Wines, to mention but a few of a distinguished company—set high standards of integrity and competence.

The task of bringing greater efficiency and more humanity into state welfare services required persistent effort. In New York and New Jersey the state boards of charity received strong backing from State Charities Aid Associations, voluntary organizations whose membership and program had some resemblance to the wartime auxiliaries of the Sanitary Commission. The National Conference of Charities and Correction, a creation of the state boards, grew into a late-nineteenth-century version of the Benevolent Empire of the 1830s and became one of the most powerful agencies for spreading the doctrines of scientific philanthropy. Even so, progress was slow. The boards and their allies represented informed opinion, but legislatures were not bound to follow their recommendations, and they exercised only shadowy supervision over local poor-relief officers. Nevertheless the boards began the work of policing almshouses, insane asylums, orphanages, and schools for the blind and deaf. They resumed the struggle to obtain state care for the pauper insane and secured establishment of new asylums, training schools, and reformatories. They worked diligently to get dependent children out of almshouses and into state schools, county or private orphanages, or foster homes.

The care for the dependent classes, burdensome enough in normal times, became an even more serious problem when periods of depression vastly increased the number of people needing and demanding assistance. The hardship and destitution caused by the depression of 1873–78 were like the effects of a nationwide natural disaster. Private citizens, the older charitable organizations, and public authorities responded by setting up soup kitchens, breadlines, and free lodging houses, and by distributing coal and food to the poor in their homes. In the emergency little attention was paid to investigation of need, tests of destitution, or safeguards against the possibility that some of the needy might be receiving help from several sources at the same time. First come, first served, was the rule.

Persons of substantial means and enlightened opinion who worried in normal times about the financial cost and social consequences of improper care of the dependent classes were horrified by the excess of "kindly but mistaken charities" during the depression. They deplored the "profuse and chaotic" distribution of private charitable assistance to the "clamorous and impudent," and they complained that much of the municipal expenditures for poor relief went to impostors or grafting politicians and that such doles as did reach the needy had a bad effect on their character and willingness to work. This "peevish fault finding," as contemporary critics called it, was little appreciated in the early stages of the depression. "Are we to let people starve because the means of relief which are attainable are such that we may not regard as altogether the best possible?" asked the New York *Daily Graphic* in 1874. When charity reformers criticized James Gordon Bennett's gift of $30,000 to a soup kitchen, the *Graphic* pointed out that Bennett's scheme gave "all soup and no salary," whereas professional philanthropy proposed "all salary and no soup."

It was not salaries that the so-called professional philanthropists demanded (although paid charity agents began to be employed during the depression) but something better than soup and alms for the poor. They wanted better organization of relief operations, more discrimination in the bestowal of assistance, and more attention to the individual needs of the persons helped. Much of their emphasis, it must be admitted, was negative. They did not urge improved administration of public relief but cessation of all public aid to the poor outside of the institutions. Outdoor relief, defined by one of its opponents as "the paying out of funds raised by taxation from provident men to support the improvident in their homes" had long been in ill repute, and toward the end of the depression taxpayers in Brooklyn and Philadelphia were sufficiently aroused and well organized to put an end to it. The saving of money effected by this action in the two cities, and the beneficent results it was thought to have in compelling would-be paupers to become self-supporting, confirmed charity reformers in the belief that outdoor relief was both undesirable and unnecessary. Private charity, properly organized and administered, could do all that needed to be done for the poor who did not require institutional care.

First, however, private charity must be purged of its sentimentality and organized into an effective force. Jewish welfare agencies had joined in Philadelphia in 1870 and in New York in 1874 to form the United Hebrew Charities, and during the depression charitable societies in the larger cities made some efforts to cooperate in detecting impostors and rounders. But it was the example of the London Charity Organization Society, founded in 1869, that most impressed those Americans who were seeking (as a Philadelphia group said) "a method by which idleness and begging, now so encouraged, may be suppressed and worthy self-respecting poverty be discovered and relieved at the smallest cost to the benevolent." Societies patterned after the London COS began to be organized in the United States in the late 1870s and multiplied rapidly in the 1880s. For the rest of the century, "charity organization" and "scientific philanthropy" were virtually synonymous.

Charity organization meant just that. As originally conceived it emphatically did not mean the granting of relief by the charity organization societies. The founders of these societies believed that there were already too many agencies engaged in giving alms and old clothes to the poor. "NO RELIEF GIVEN HERE," announced signs at the entrance to the Buffalo COS, and Josephine Shaw Lowell of the New York COS did not hesitate to advise prospective donors that all the organization's funds went for administrative expenses and not one cent to the poor.

The basic idea of the charity organization movement was to promote cooperation and higher standards of efficiency among the older relief-dispensing agencies. This objective was regarded as presumptuous by some firmly intrenched agencies who were well satisfied with their own methods and jealous of their prerogatives. With varying degrees of success, therefore, the charity organization societies acted as clearinghouses and bureaus of information. They maintained registries of all applicants for relief, with detailed records of the assistance given or refused by cooperating societies, and they undertook searching investigation of the need and worthiness of the "cases" referred to them. When they discovered a "helpable" applicant, they attempted to find employment for him, or referred him to the relief-dispensing agency best suited to meet his particular need. Through force of circumstances, and not without qualms of conscience, some of the charity organization societies actually became purveyors of relief. Usually, however, they preferred to help the poor by providing such services as penny savings banks, coal-saving funds, provident wood-yards, day nurseries for the children of working mothers, and workrooms where women could be trained to become nursemaids, laundresses, or seamstresses.

In theory, "friendly visiting" of the poor in their homes by volunteers working under the supervision of paid agents was the core—or better, the heart—of charity organization. By this means ties of sympathy and personal interest were to be established between the rich and the poor, and the poor were to be permanently improved and uplifted. The visitors were not to be almoners, for almsgiving was counterfeit philanthropy. Instead of stray coins, visitors were to bring encouragement and advice to the people they visited. From the writings of Octavia Hill, an English philanthropic worker, American COS leaders culled the following suggestions for volunteer visitors:

You want to know them, —to enter into their lives, their thoughts; to let them enter into some of your brightness; to make their lives a little fuller, a little gladder. You who know so much more than they, might help them so much at important crises of their lives. You might gladden their homes by bringing them flowers, or, better still, by teaching them to grow plants; you might meet them face to face as friends; you might teach them; you might collect their savings; you might sing for and with them; you might take them into the parks or out for quiet days in the country, in small companies, or to your own or your friends' grounds, or to exhibitions or picture galleries; you might teach them and refine and make them cleaner by merely going among them.

Miss Hill conceded that the poor, in their turn, might teach the visitors patience, vigor, and content. But in general hardly anyone active in the movement at the start questioned that the visitors were morally as well as materially superior to the visited.

This conviction of superiority, like most of the original charity organization program, rested on certain assumptions about the causes of poverty and dependency. As a rule the charity reformers were so preoccupied with pauperism that they gave little serious thought to poverty. To the extent that they did think about poverty they accepted the view that it was caused by weakness of character, body, or intellect, and curable by reform of the individual. Josephine Shaw Lowell (1843–1905), the principal founder of the New York COS, is a case in point. As she saw it, building character rather than relieving need was the true aim of the society's work. It is not "the poor" but "our brothers" who are our concern, she said. She took it for granted that those brothers were a young and untutored lot who needed stern discipline and careful training.

Mrs. Lowell was a woman of the leisure class who devoted forty years of her life to public service. But to say this does scant justice to the force of character and sturdy good sense that won the respect of her contemporaries. Born into a family of wealth, culture, and liberal leanings, she was the sister of one war hero and the wife of another. All the circumstances of her life, from fortunate birth to tragic widowhood, thrust her into a career of service. She brought to her work self-discipline, matter-of-factness, and a kindness which, if not indulgent, was all embracing.

Kindness in her case was based not on sentimentality but on a religious conviction that each human being deserved good from every other because all were sons of God and had an eternal future. Mrs. Lowell was made of sterner stuff than some philanthropists. Although she wrote often of the duty of charity, she did not make a point of stressing, as Cotton Mather, Amos Lawrence, and many others had, the pleasures and privileges of giving.

As Mrs. Lowell saw it, the world was made up of two classes: workers and idlers. Workers might do or be many things, provided their activities were useful; idlers, in her succinct definition, were people who lived off the workers. Unfortunately, workers had a natural inclination to become idlers. The mass of men and women, Mrs. Lowell maintained, needed the pressure of necessity to force them to exercise their faculties. Hence it was dangerous to do too much for anyone lest he lose the ability and appetite for work. Like other charity reformers of her generation Mrs. Lowell also believed that certain undesirable social traits were transmitted from generation to generation and that some groups had a hereditary tendency toward pauperism and crime. Neither Mrs. Lowell nor her coworkers accepted the conclusion of the extreme Social Darwinists that all acts of mercy to the weak in body and mind tended to degrade the human race, but they did advocate putting chronic paupers into strictly supervised institutions so that the vicious and degraded would not perpetuate their kind.

It is not surprising that Mrs. Lowell and other founders of the charity organization movement should have been influenced by the notions of political economy and natural science current in the 1870s and 1880s. More significant is the fact that those ideas seem to have had little effect on the actual working of the societies. Charity organization best demonstrated its claim to be scientific by allowing the demands of reality to override the hypotheses with which it began. Investigations, originally undertaken as a species of detective work to discover fraud, came to be regarded as diagnoses to ascertain facts needed to treat distress intelligently. Salaried workers, although outnumbered by volunteer friendly visitors, played an increasingly important part in the work of the societies. These paid workers, who supervised and trained the volunteers, were already numerous enough in the 1890s to suggest that a new profession was in the making. In practice, charity organization societies became centers to which people in trouble applied for help in locating agencies that could assist them. Odd and indirect as this service sounds, it was a useful one in large cities where the very abundance of specialized benevolent associations made for confusion. The societies never gave up their efforts to improve and coordinate charitable work, and they proved their value in the depression of 1893–97, when new societies were founded, faltering ones revived, and flourishing ones took on new vigor.

Because scientific philanthropy insisted on gathering the facts about the specific causes of each applicant's need, COS case workers had to report and deal with poverty-producing factors that had little to do with the sufferers' characters. The caseworkers attributed as many as possible of these situations to moral lapses, but even before the gray nineties they were well aware of the environmental causes of distress. The labor disputes of the eighties and nineties made some leaders of the "new charity" wonder whether the newest might not be justice in work and wages. Mrs. Lowell resigned from the New York State Board of Charity in 1889 because she felt that the interests of the working people were of paramount importance. "It is better to save them before they go under, than to spend your life fishing them out when they're half drowned and taking care of them afterwards!" she said. "I must try to help them, if I can, and leave the broken down paupers to others."

For at least three-quarters of a century charity reformers had been seeking to prevent pauperism. They had often expressed the opinion that the first duty of the community was not to feed the hungry and clothe the naked but to prevent people from becoming hungry and naked. By 1893 Robert Treat Paine, president of the Associated Charities of Boston since its founding, was of the opinion that the social order itself needed housecleaning. "Pauperism cannot be wisely considered alone," he said, "but the problem of how to uplift the general level of life must be studied as *one whole problem.*" The remedies proposed were still less fundamental than the language of those who advanced them suggested. Scientific philanthropy and social reform had not yet quite joined forces but they were drawing closer together.

7

Benevolent Trusts and Distrusts

> If a combination to do business is effective in saving waste and in getting better results, why is not combination far more important in philanthropic work?
>
> JOHN D. ROCKFELLER

The most famous document in the history of American philanthropy—although the word philanthropy does not appear in it—is an article entitled "Wealth" published in the *North American Review* in June 1889. The author was the "Star-Spangled Scotchman," Andrew Carnegie. Born in a weaver's cottage in Dunfermline, Scotland, in 1835, Carnegie had come to the United States in 1848. As the eldest son of a poor family, he was old if not large for his years, and at the age of twelve cheerfully and self-confidently assumed the responsibilities of breadwinner. "Anybody can get along in this Country," he wrote in 1852. "If I don't it will be my own fault." Andrew Carnegie, likable, alert, shrewd, and able, got along famously. By 1889, thirty times a millionaire, he had been a rich man for more than twenty years. For him the question had long been not how to gain wealth but what to do with it. He had reached some conclusions on the problem as early as 1868 and in 1887 had told his friend William E. Gladstone that he considered it a disgrace to die rich. Now, in his famous essay, he proposed that millionaires, instead of bequeathing vast fortunes to heirs or making benevolent grants by will, should administer their wealth as a public trust during life.

The year of Carnegie's birth was also the year in which Tocqueville published *Democracy in America*. Of all the changes that had swept over American society in the fifty-odd years since 1835, one of the most striking was the arrival of that race of rich men whose absence Tocqueville had noted. Carnegie certainly did not doubt that there was a "millionaire class" in the United States. It was to this class that he addressed himself. In assumption of superiority Carnegie went far beyond the charity reformers. His view resembled that of John Winthrop and William Penn, except in one important respect. Carnegie did not say, as those men had, that the great ones owed the distinction to peculiar arrangements ordained of God. He attributed the eminence of the millionaire class to fitness to survive and triumph in the competitive struggle. The trusteeship Carnegie proposed thus differed from traditional doctrines of stewardship. The millionaire, a product of natural selection, was an agent of the public, of the forces of civilization, rather than a servant of God. Trusteeship devolved on the man of wealth because he was fittest to exercise it. In the exercise of his trust he was responsible only to his own conscience and judgment of what was best for the community.

An English critic, astounded by the brashness of Carnegie's scheme, named it the gospel of wealth to distinguish it from the gospel of Christianity. With customary good humor Carnegie accepted the label, and, as usual, he won the encounter; for who can deny that "the gospel of wealth" sounds better and stronger than "wealth"? As a matter of fact there were religious overtones in Carnegie's gospel. He was willing to have the scriptural passage about the difficulty of rich men entering the kingdom of Heaven interpreted strictly, and he believed that laboring for the good of one's fellows was the essence of Christ's teaching. But, as Carnegie frankly admitted, he did not believe that under modern conditions much good could be accomplished by imitating the life or methods of Christ. Let the laws of accumulation and distribution be left free; let the able and energetic dispose of their surplus as they saw fit; the millionaire class, working toward the same objectives as Christ, but (as Carnegie said) "laboring in a different manner," would someday bring "Peace on earth, among men good will."

According to the gospel of wealth, philanthropy was less the handmaid of social reform than a substitute for it. Wise administration of wealth was an antidote for radical proposals for redistributing property and a method of reconciling the poor and the rich. Carnegie spoke of "the temporary unequal distribution of wealth"; however, like his mentor, Herbert Spencer, he thought that it would take eons, an overturn of natural laws of economics, and an almost inconceivable revolution in human nature to erase that inequality. He believed it was a waste of time to challenge evolutionary processes, and he was firmly convinced that the only alternative to the system that rewarded millionaires with palaces and laborers with cottages was one that would condemn all to hovels. But Carnegie was no less convinced that "administrators of surplus wealth"—his term for philanthropists—had it in their power to bestow benefactions of lasting benefit on their weaker and poorer brethren.

Clara Barton. (From Clara Barton, *The Red Cross*. Washington, D.C.: American National Red Cross, 1898.)

Dorothea Dix. (From a portrait in the New Jersey State Hospital, Trenton; reproduced by permission.)

Andrew Carnegie. (From *Life Magazine*, April 13, 1905.)

Had Carnegie chosen to do so, he might have said simply that men possessed of more wealth than they could possibly use would be well advised to employ it for the public good. Possibly that was all he really meant. The arrogance of his language and the despotic tendencies of his philosophy should not blind us to the fact that his solution for the problem of surplus wealth was neither entirely new nor inconsistent with American traditions. Although Carnegie preached and practiced giving on an undreamed-of scale he did not propose that philanthropy should shoulder the whole burden of welfare. Far from it. Recognizing the responsibility of the state to care for the destitute and helpless, he urged the millionaire class to concentrate its philanthropic efforts on the able and industrious. His advice suited the temper of the times and the inclinations of self-made men. Coming after so many years of emphasis on the cause and cure of pauperism it infused new vigor into philanthropy.

Carnegie was as contemptuous of almsgiving and as fearful of impulsive generosity as the most doctrinaire charity reformer. "To assist, but rarely or never to do all," was the rule he laid down. Although he made a few bows in the direction of reforming the character and improving the morals of the poor, the assistance which had seemed most valuable to many nineteenth-century philanthropists, he was not really interested in those who needed this kind of help. The uplift he favored was of a different and less direct variety: libraries, parks, concert halls, museums, "swimming baths," and institutions such as Cooper Union and Pratt Institute, both of which he greatly admired. Significantly he called these agencies "ladders upon which the aspiring can rise."

At the start of the 1890s the New York *Tribune* figured the number of persons in the millionaire class at 4,047. Few of these men and women seem to have taken literally Carnegie's assertion that it was a disgrace to die rich. Some of them, however, already were and long had been distributing a part of their surplus during life. Just how many were so disposed and exactly how much they gave it is not now possible to say. An investigation of their giving habits made by the *Review of Reviews* in 1893 reached the sensible albeit equivocal conclusion that cities would be poorer without the parks, museums, libraries, and technical institutes provided by generous millionaires, and considerably richer if more men and women of wealth followed the example of those who gave. This interesting, although not necessarily reliable, survey indicated that the percentage of millionaires who "recognized their obligations" varied from city to city. Baltimore, with 49 percent of her millionaires listed as active givers, ranked highest on the list and New York, where millionaires were most numerous but apparently least generous, was at the bottom. Donors in different cities had distinct preferences: Cincinnati's millionaires supported musical and artistic ventures; those in Minneapolis gave to the state university and the public library; and Philadelphians were interested in overseas relief, Arctic exploration, and the education of Indians and Negroes. Boston, surprisingly, made a poor showing. "Our Boston millionaires," reported the local investigator, "give money when it is solicited (properly), and they all include in their wills some bequests to Harvard and to Massachusetts General Hospital. That is all."

Of all the ladders for those who aspired, free libraries and educational institutions with a practical slant struck capitalists of the 1880s and 1890s as most inspiring. Carnegie's own benefactions, like those of so many philanthropists, began with the donation of a library to his hometown, and he ultimately gave a library building to almost every community which provided a site and promised to maintain the building. He regarded Enoch Pratt, donor of the Pratt Free Library in Baltimore, as "the ideal disciple of the gospel of wealth." Carnegie and other businessmen gave generously to Negro industrial schools, such as Hampton and Tuskegee, which elevated manual and domestic training into character-building disciplines. They were much less generous toward Negro institutions of higher learning. Only a trickle of philanthropic aid, mainly furnished by church groups, went to these struggling, poorly housed and equipped colleges, but, meager as it was, this assistance helped keep them alive. Students at Fisk University took financing into their hands. Through concert tours in Europe and America the Fisk Jubilee Singers raised funds which permitted the institution to move from dilapidated army barracks to a new building appropriately named Jubilee Hall.

Although some business leaders thought higher education almost as detrimental to whites as to Negroes, colleges and universities continued to be beneficiaries of the millionaires' surplus wealth. "Here is a noble use of wealth," Carnegie said of Leland Stanford's audacious plan to build a university in the Far West, a project which in 1889 was believed to involve the greatest sum ever given by an individual for any purpose. Stanford's avowed purpose was to create a new kind of university which would give a practical rather than a theoretical education. Albert Shaw observed admiringly that the donor was going about the task in the same businesslike fashion he had employed in building the great stock farm where his fast horses were bred.

John D. Rockefeller (1839–1937) was an old hand at giving when, in May 1889, a month before the appearance of Carnegie's "Wealth," he made an initial contribution of $600,000 toward founding the new University of Chicago.

He was then approaching fifty and had been rich, and getting richer, for twenty-five years. But Rockefeller did not wait until he had a surplus before beginning to give. His account book for 1855, the year he went to work, recorded small but frequent contributions to charity, Sunday school, and missions. In the 1850s the amounts sometimes totaled a tenth of his income, and they increased over the years. Even so Rockefeller's benefactions were hard-pressed to keep up with his accumulations. Thus in 1888, when he donated $170,000 to various good works, dividends from the Standard Oil combination were returning millions. Not even the rising University of Chicago, to which he gave $1 million in 1890 and a like sum in 1892, the latter "as a special thank-offering to Almighty God for returning health," could drain off his surplus.

The responsibility of wealth pressed as heavily on Rockefeller as on Carnegie. If possible, Rockefeller felt the burden even more than Carnegie, since he adhered to the old-fashioned religious doctrine of stewardship rather than to the new gospel of wealth. Amos Lawrence might have said, as Rockefeller did, "The good Lord gave me the money," but Carnegie certainly did not. As archaic as the sentiment sounds, there is no reason to doubt that Rockefeller sincerely believed it. He thought that the good Lord had given him the money for a purpose and expected him to handle it with care. The steward was faithful to his trust. Rockefeller was quite willing to give, but he felt an obligation to inquire into the worthiness of the causes to which he was asked to contribute. By 1891 he complained that these investigations were taking as much of his time and energy as the affairs of Standard Oil. Help came in the person of a thirty-eight-year-old Baptist clergyman, Frederick T. Gates, who agreed to assist Rockefeller in his benefactions by interviewing supplicants, making inquiries, and suggesting action. As a former fund-raiser Gates was wise in the ways of money-seekers. In his charge, as Gates himself recalled, Rockefeller soon found himself "laying aside retail giving almost wholly, and entering safely and pleasurably into the field of wholesale philanthropy."

Rockefeller's entry into the field of wholesale philanthropy set off a controversy—mainly one-sided, since Rockefeller did not reply to the attack—that continued for at least a quarter of a century. In 1895 Washington Gladden, minister of the First Congregational Church in Columbus, Ohio, and a leader of the social gospel movement, published an article, "Tainted Money," in which he outdid Emerson and antedated Thorstein Veblen in denouncing the ways of trade. Although Gladden did not mention any multimillionaire by name, his attack on the benefactions of "robber barons," "Roman plunderers," "pirates of industry," and "spoilers of the state" was thought to be directed at the Rockefeller philanthropies. Gladden had stated in a sermon delivered to the National Conference of Charities and Corrections in 1893 that the central consideration of charity should be the effect of the gift upon the character of the recipient. Now he raised the question whether a church or university could take offerings of money made in morally reprehensible ways without condoning the methods and accepting the standards of the donor. "Is this clean money?" he asked. "Can any man, can any institution, knowing its origin, touch it without being defiled?"

This was a hard question and it was taken seriously in the 1890s and 1900 when nearly every issue seemed at bottom a moral one. It came up again in 1905 when Gladden and other liberal clergymen objected to the acceptance by the Congregational Board of Foreign Missions of a $100,000 gift from Rockefeller. The controversy simmered down after it was revealed that the board had solicited Rockefeller for the money. Moral questions are notoriously difficult to resolve and in this case no consensus could be reached because Rockefeller's character was defended as ardently as it was attacked, and eminent moralists pointed out that the purpose of the gift was as worthy of consideration, and easier to judge, than the origin of the money.

Jane Addams (1860–1935) of Hull House, who was already beginning to occupy an unenviable distinction as "the conscience of the nation," was one of the few public figures who viewed the tainted-money issue with detachment. In the 1890s she rejected an offer of $20,000 for a Hull House project on the grounds that the donor's bad record as an employer made it unthinkable to accept his sponsorship of the undertaking, a cooperative boarding house for working girls, but she refused to become embroiled in the public debate over tainted money. Her conscience was sensitive and she was accustomed to drawing fine ethical distinctions. As a rule, however, she avoided passing moral judgments on people. It was the unrighteousness of conditions that troubled her, and movements for the fulfilment of democracy that excited her.

Miss Addams had founded Hull House, the best known of the early settlement houses, in the same year—1889—that Andrew Carnegie enunciated the gospel of wealth. Like him, she hoped to establish ties of sympathy between rich and poor, but her purpose and methods differed from his. She made those differences clear when she confessed that the settlement movement was based on emotion as much as conviction, that it represented an outlet for sentiments of universal brotherhood, and that it appealed to persons who had "a bent to express in social service and in terms of action the spirit of Christ." While Carnegie proposed building ladders upon which the ambitious poor could rise, Miss Addams and other settlement leaders went to live with the poor. The settlement houses were designed to offer educated young men and women a means of getting in touch with the "starvation struggle" of the masses. Once the settlement workers had established friendly relations with their underprivileged neighbors and learned their needs, they could join with them in efforts to improve the common life. Perhaps this was a species of uplift. Jane Addams called it "the arousing of social energies."

Settlement houses were only one manifestation of the current of religious humanitarianism stirring in churches and among individuals of all faiths. Around the turn of the century other forces and a host of voluntary associations were at work or organizing to strengthen the social framework of democracy and to restore and extend the principles of self-government. But settlement residents, as Miss Addams pointed out as early as 1892, were "bound to see the needs of their neighborhoods as a whole, to furnish data for legislation, and to use their influence to secure it." Uncommitted to any particular program except flexibility and experimentation, the settlements contributed to nearly all the social movements of the early twentieth century. Settlement leaders, including Miss Addams, Lillian Wald, Mary McDowell, Eleanor McMain, Mary Kingsbury Simkhovitch, and others of equal prominence, were formidable champions of the interests of women, children, and immigrants, and effective campaigners for improved housing, health, and recreation. The common attribute of these women was ability to reduce abstract issues to human terms and to translate high ideals into prosaic practice. In working with and for their neighborhoods they came to realize that "prevention," so long the watchword of the reformer, was not enough. There were unsatisfied needs in every community, whether for playgrounds, nurseries, or some closer approximation of social justice, that could be met only by positive action.

It was a sign of new ways of thought that after the 1890s

the term "social work" began to replace "scientific philanthropy." The change was related to the growing number of paid workers in welfare agencies and to the development of training courses in applied philanthropy that, by 1910, had become schools of social work. Meanwhile new leaders such as Mary Richmond (1861–1928) and Edward T. Devine (1867–1948) had assumed direction of the charity organization movement. Miss Richmond, who occupied important positions in the Baltimore and Philadelphia charity organization societies and the Russell Sage Foundation, strove to put casework on a professional basis. Through her book *Social Diagnosis* (1917), she exercised a dominant influence on both the philosophy and methods of social work. Devine, as secretary of the New York C.O.S. and editor of the influential social work magazine *The Survey,* brought the new profession into the forefront of the social reform movements of the Progressive Era. In the 1900s social workers retained the old dislike of relief and cautious attitude toward charity. But where scientific philanthropists of an earlier generation had deplored charity seekers, social workers criticized the conditions that made charity necessary. Poverty rather than pauperism was now the bugaboo, improvement of the general standard of living the remedy.

Inspired by new hopes and visions, but still struggling with the old problem of misery, social workers sometimes expressed misgivings about the nature and tendencies of philanthropy. Was the benefactor-beneficiary relationship a denial of the equality democracy implied? Did charity perpetuate the conditions that created poverty? Could philanthropy, tied as it was to the purse strings of the classes who benefited most from the existing order, accomplish anything of importance in building a better society? The same or similar questions were being raised by critics outside of social work, although not so much in inquiry as in condemnation. To practicing philanthropists who were also democrats and social reformers these were matters of grave import. If answers were not immediately forthcoming, the very fact that the questions were raised and thoughtfully considered had a wholesome influence on philanthropic developments.

Developments of great significance were under way. Rockefeller and Carnegie had retired from business in 1897 and 1901, respectively, but they still faced the problem of what to do with mounting fortunes. By 1901 even wholesale philanthropy of the sort each had been practicing for a decade was inadequate to dispose of accumulations totaling not tens but hundreds of millions. Some more effective method of organizing and conducting what Rockefeller called "this business of benevolence" must be devised. To Rockefeller the answer was plain. Put your surplus money in a trust, he advised the "men of worth and position" gathered to celebrate the tenth anniversary of the founding of the University of Chicago: "Let us erect a foundation, a trust, and engage directors who will make it a life work to manage, with our personal co-operation, this business of benevolence properly and effectively."

In the dozen years after 1901, as if to prove that philanthropy could be made a successful venture, Rockefeller, Carnegie, and other donors established a series of foundations that made earlier philanthropic ventures seem somewhat amateurish. The Rockefeller Institute for Medical Research (1901), General Education Board (1902), Carnegie Foundation for the Advancement of Teaching (1905), Milbank Memorial Fund (1905), Russell Sage Foundation (1907), Carnegie Corporation of New York (1911), and Rockefeller Foundation (1913) do not exhaust the list of foundations organized during the period, but their number, and even the size of their capital assets, was less significant than the boldness of the enterprise to which they were committed. Most earlier charitable trusts had been established for some narrowly defined purpose. The smaller Carnegie funds, designed to promote the donor's particular philanthropic interests, continued in this tradition. The major trusts founded by Carnegie and Rockefeller, however, were limited only to the advancement of knowledge and human welfare. Relieving the needy was not their objective. They would attack misery at its source through the weapon of research.

The advent of the foundations coincided with the era of muckracking and trustbusting, with a leftward trend in politics, growing militancy in the ranks of labor, and a general fear of bigness. According to popular legend John D. Rockefeller, alarmed by muckracking attacks such as Ida M. Tarbell's *History of the Standard Oil Company* (1904), employed a public relations counselor, Ivy Lee, who advised him to increase his benefactions in order to buy public favor. Actually Lee did not become associated with Rockefeller until 1914, more than twenty years after Rockefeller had become a wholesale philanthropist. Frederick T. Gates, the principal architect of Rockefeller's benefactions, was aware of and presumably not averse to allaying popular animosity toward his employer. Gates, however, was a clergyman and businessman rather than a public relations expert. He was mainly concerned with helping Rockefeller administer a vast fortune wisely and beneficently.

Interestingly enough, the organization of large philanthropic trusts aroused little opposition until 1910. In that year a bill to incorporate the Rockefeller Foundation was introduced in Congress. By this time anything bearing Rockefeller's name or financed by Standard Oil money was bound to provoke controversy. Opponents revived the slogans of the tainted-money debate and likened Rockefeller's gifts to the Trojan horse and the kiss of Judas. The move was all the more resented because the federal government was prosecuting the Standard Oil combination for violation of the Sherman Antitrust Act. In 1911 the Supreme Court ordered dissolution of Standard Oil of New Jersey, the center of the Rockefeller empire. The decision made it unlikely that Congress would charter a new Rockefeller trust, even a benevolent one. The opposition of the Taft administration further weakened the foundation bill's chances for passage. Attorney General George Wickersham called the measure "an indefinite scheme for perpetuating vast wealth." President William Howard Taft also expressed disapproval of "the proposed act to incorporate John D. Rockefeller." In 1913, rebuffed by the federal government, Rockefeller incorporated the foundation under the laws of New York State.

The next two years were difficult ones for the foundations. In 1914 several members of the United States Senate attempted to prohibit the Department of Agriculture from accepting grants provided by the General Education Board for farm demonstration work in the South. Meanwhile, the United States Industrial Relations Commission, a body established by Congress to study the underlying causes of industrial unrest, broadened its investigation to include the operation of philanthropic foundations. The newly organized Rockefeller Foundation was a particular target of attack, but in 1915 the commission's director of research arraigned all foundations for their wealth, loosely defined powers, exemption from federal taxation, freedom from public control, subserviency to donors, and benumbing effect on smaller philanthropic agencies and individual giving. None of this criticism led to legislative action against the foundations. But since the attitudes of beneficiaries are as important in philanthropy as the desires and purposes of benefactors, it is significant that the early foundations began their work in a somewhat hostile atmosphere.

The fear, however, was mainly of possible abuse of power in the future. Even as this suspicion was expressed, other voices were calling attention to the present need for the foundations and to their possibilities for good. The Russell Sage Foundation had already proved its usefulness to social work and social reform by financing the Pittsburgh Survey and by assisting the National Tuberculosis Association begin its educational exhibits. The Rockefeller Sanitary Commission, organized in 1909 and later absorbed by the Rockefeller Foundation, demonstrated that hookworm disease could be eradicated. In the course of this campaign the commission advanced the entire movement for public health. The General Education Board cooperated with the Department of Agriculture in efforts to increase the productivity of southern agriculture. The board made valuable contributions to secondary education in the South and to higher education in all parts of the country. The Carnegie Foundation for the Advancement of Teaching inaugurated pensions for college teachers which furthered interest in pensions for other workers, and it sponsored and published Abraham Flexner's epochal *Medical Education in the United States and Canada* (1910). As early as 1912 Edward T. Devine denied that foundations would inhibit the normal springs of benevolence. On the contrary, said Devine, the effect of the foundations had been to stimulate both public appropriations and private giving for education, health, and welfare.

"You have had the best run for your money I have ever known," Elihu Root once told Andrew Carnegie. Carnegie, a cheerful and impulsive giver in spite of theories, managed to dispose of $350 million. John D. Rockefeller, less impulsive than Carnegie, also had a good run for the $530 million he conferred on benevolent causes. "We must always remember that there is not enough money for the work of human uplift and that there never can be," he said in 1909. "How vitally important it is, therefore, that the expenditure should go as far as possible and be used with the greatest intelligence!" The advice, although sound, was commonplace. It was the application that was difficult. Rockefeller's and Carnegie's chief contribution to philanthropy was to found institutions capable of distributing private wealth with greater intelligence and vision than the donors themselves could hope to possess. The great philanthropic trusts they established climaxed the long effort to put large-scale giving on a businesslike basis.

8

The Business of Benevolence and the Industry of Destruction

> I suppose we had to do it, and I suppose it was worthwhile, but think of the creative job we could have done with that money in a world of reason and sanity!
>
> GEORGE E. VINCENT

While administrators of great wealth were devising new methods to dispose of surplus millions, promoters of good causes offered the general public unparalleled opportunities for relieving pockets and bank accounts of spare dollars. And what a variety of goods "retail philanthropy" displayed! Churches, home and foreign missions, temperance organizations, church-related or nonsectarian colleges, hospitals, orphanages, and homes for the aged always needed money. The plight of newsboys, working girls, distressed immigrants, tenement dwellers, and southern mountain children was held up for all to see. Disasters at home or abroad brought appeals for aid from the Red Cross and special relief committees. In good times and bad local relief associations, charity organization societies, settlement houses, babies' milk funds, free dispensaries, children's aid societies, societies for the prevention of cruelty to children and animals, the YMCA, YWCA, YMHA, Salvation Army, and Volunteers of America advanced their respective, and separate, claims for support.

Opportunities and importunities for giving, already numerous in 1900, increased enormously in the next decade and a half. The continuing vitality of the voluntary principle and a broadening sense of responsibility for improving the social environment led to the formation of a host of new national organizations maintained by dues, donations, and subscriptions. These were the years when the Boy Scouts, Girl Scouts, Campfire Girls, National Tuberculosis Association, American Cancer Society, Goodwill Industries, the Lighthouse, National Association for the Advancement of Colored People, National Urban League, American Association for Labor Legislation, National Child Labor Committee, and a hundred other leagues, associations, and committees came into being. Incomplete as the listing is, the names suggest the diversity of interests supported by private giving. After 1914 the situation was further complicated by the necessity of relieving war-sufferers in Europe.

In 1914 American philanthropy, if judged by the standards of a Rockefeller, Carnegie, or Morgan, was still conducted in a distressingly unbusinesslike way. This was less true of the internal operation of philanthropic agencies, many of which were professionally managed and efficiently organized, than of the relations of the different societies to each other. Both locally and nationally benevolent activities were poorly coordinated. Partly because of the rapid expansion in the prewar years, partly because of the nature of voluntary enterprise, there was duplication or overlapping of effort, rivalry for public favor, competition for funds. Fund-raising in particular was in a chaotic condition. As Matthew Carey had pointed out many years earlier, those who gave were solicited time and again, while many potential givers were either ignored or approached in ways not calculated to stimulate generosity.

These defects were obvious to social workers, and progress toward correcting them was being made before the war. Even in a nation of joiners social workers displayed remarkable ability to find or create organizations to join. They formed conferences within conferences, and established federations, councils, and committees to improve and promote special fields and methods of social work. In a few cities representative councils of welfare agencies took over the task, earlier attempted by charity organization societies, of raising standards and coordinating charitable efforts. Federated fund-raising, first tried in Denver in 1888, realized among Jewish charities in Boston in 1895, and adopted on a broader scale in Cleveland in 1913, was shortly afterward put into effect in fifteen other cities. Meanwhile a Danish innovation, the sale of special stamps at Christmas time to "stamp out" tuberculosis, had been taken up in the United States. After 1910 when the Christmas seal campaign became a joint responsibility of the Red Cross and the National Tuberculosis Association, it proved a relatively painless method of raising money and also demonstrated the possibility of cooperation between national voluntary agencies. Sums raised in Christmas seal campaigns ($450,000 in 1913) were small, however, compared to those garnered each year by the YMCA. The YMCA's leadership in fund-raising went back to the days of the evangelist, Dwight L. Moody, but in the decade after 1905 practice made near-perfect the hard-hitting, highly publicized "Y" drive to attain a specific dollar goal in a limited period through professionally directed teams of volunteer collectors.

Of all American philanthropic organizations the American Red Cross, by tradition, the terms of its charter, and international agreements, was most directly concerned by the outbreak of war in Europe. In 1914 the Red Cross had fewer than 150 chapters and only about twenty thousand members; but even these modest figures reflected an appreciable growth in size and strength in the decade since the reorganization that accompanied Clara Barton's resignation. Its unofficial leader from 1905 to 1915 was Miss Mabel Boardman, a woman of inherited wealth, established social position, high ideals, and fixed opinions who, in making the Red Cross a national organization, shaped it after her own comely image. When war came, Miss Boardman and Red Cross officials promptly offered assistance to sister societies in Europe and called on the chapters to raise funds for war relief. At the time (August 1914) and for more than a year thereafter, Miss Boardman and her advisers interpreted Red Cross charter obligations strictly and assumed that war relief could legally be extended only to sick and wounded combatants. In September 1914 amid fanfares of publicity, a Red Cross "mercy ship" sailed for Europe bearing 170 doctors and nurses and supplies and equipment to establish hospital units in the warring nations. Partly because of the expense involved in maintaining these units, they were withdrawn in October 1915, but, to the extent that the Allied blockade permitted, the Red Cross continued to send medical and hospital supplies to the fighting forces of both sides.

In fact, as events in the very first months of the war proved, medical assistance for combatants was much less needed than relief to civilians in occupied countries, to refugees from war zones, and to sufferers from disease and famine caused by military destruction, blockade, and the disruption of normal life. Belgium was the immediate problem. There, in the space of a single month, an industrious, thriving, populous nation was reduced to destitution, its industry, trade, and transportation destroyed. By autumn, with stores and warehouses empty, and factories closed, almost the entire population, numbering some 7,500,000, was in desperate straits. On October 16, 1914, Brand Whitlock, the American minister in Brussels, cabled President Wilson, "In two weeks the civil population of Belgium, already in misery, will face starvation." That Belgium did not starve was due almost entirely to the efforts of an unofficial, unincorporated organization set up in London about a week after Whitlock sent his message to Wilson.

The Commission for Relief in Belgium grew out of an attempt made by a Belgian relief committee to buy food in England. The Belgian group sent Millard K. Shaler, an American mining engineer then living in Brussels, to London to make the purchase. In London, Shaler sought out another mining engineer, Herbert Hoover, who had recently won fame by directing the relief and repatriation of thousands of American travelers stranded in Europe at the start of the war. When British officials refused to grant Shaler a shipping permit for the goods he had bought, Hoover and Shaler appealed for assistance to Ambassador Walter Hines Page. In cooperation with other neutral diplomats, Page obtained a guarantee from Germany that Belgian relief supplies would not be requisitioned by the occupation forces and arranged with Allied governments to allow those supplies to pass through the blockade. And, with the help of a Quaker conscience, Hoover made a wise decision. He exchanged a $100,000-a-year business career for the difficult and unremunerated post of chairman of the

Commission for Relief in Belgium, a step which was to lead him, leap by leap, into positions of helpfulness and power such as few men have known.

The task of the CRB was to acquire, by purchase or gift, the tons upon tons of food and clothing needed to sustain the people of Belgium, and later of German-occupied portions of northern France; to assemble and transport these supplies from all over the world; and, as a neutral agency, to oversee their distribution or sale (to those who could afford to buy) by Belgian and French relief committees. In the best of circumstances the task would have been immense, and the difficulty of performing it in the midst of war can scarcely be imagined. Fortunately, in addition to the brilliant leadership of Hoover and his staff—which included, among others, a contingent of Rhodes Scholars—the CRB had the cooperation of the belligerents and the warm support of world opinion. In the two and a half years of American neutrality no philanthropic cause found wider favor in the United States; but supplies and money came from other countries, too, and in proportion to population New Zealand made the largest contribution. The commission could not have accomplished its work, however, had it depended solely on voluntary contributions of philanthropic individuals or groups. All told these amounted to about $52 million, while the monthly expenditures of the commission ran from $5 million at the outset to a high of $30 million in 1918. By far the greater part of the approximately $1 billion spent by the CRB between November 1914 and August 1919 came from Belgian government funds on deposit abroad, subsidies by the British and French governments, and, after 1917, United States government loans. After the United States entered the war the work of the commission continued under Dutch and Spanish sponsorship.

One of the agencies that assisted the CRB at the start

of its operations was the Rockefeller Foundation. The Foundation, just beginning its mission of promoting "the well-being of mankind throughout the world," had not contemplated entering the field of direct relief. It had intended to "go to the root of individual or social ill-being or misery" and had assumed that its proper work lay in the advancement of public health through medical research, education, and demonstration. Nevertheless, in the autumn of 1914 the Rockefeller Foundation provided a depot for the use of the CRB, purchased almost a million dollars' worth of food for the commission, chartered ships, and advanced funds for freight charges. Meanwhile, the Foundation appointed a War Relief Commission, headed by Wickliffe Rose, who had been in charge of the Rockefeller Sanitary Commission's campaign against hookworm, and including Ernest Bicknell, on leave from his position as national director of the American Red Cross. This commission investigated relief needs in all the nations at war, established a European headquarters in Switzerland, conducted a variety of relief programs on its own, and provided funds to assist other agencies in their work.

In all, one hundred and thirty American agencies were participating, directly or indirectly, in war relief at the end of the period of American neutrality. They had sponsored activities ranging from sewing classes for Belgian refugees in Holland to educational, recreational, religious, and welfare services of YMCA secretaries in prisoner-of-war camps. The Red Cross conducted a successful campaign against typhus in Serbia in 1915 and, at the end of that year, reversing its earlier policy, became active in civilian relief. The American Committee for Armenian and Syrian Relief raised money to feed and shelter refugees in Turkey, Persia, and Russia; and the American Jewish Relief Committee attempted against insuperable odds to get aid to Poland, where hundreds of thousands of civilians—facing the same problem as the Belgians—perished from disease and starvation. Nowhere were humanitarian efforts conducted on as large a scale or as generously supported as in Belgium. Even there, and to a much greater extent elsewhere, the tightening Allied blockade—which at last declared contraband even such items as rubber gloves for surgeons—interfered with the flow of supplies. Voluntary philanthropy was at best but a feeble weapon to oppose the engines of war, and all that could be done by American agencies met but a minute part of an overwhelming need.

James T. Shotwell, general editor of the *Economic and Social History of the World War* (a 150-volume work which was not completed until the eve of World War II), observed in 1929 that the most remarkable thing about the war was not that it involved so many people but that it involved them so completely. For Americans the period of total involvement was far shorter than for other major participants. Brief though the experience was, it accelerated and accentuated tendencies that were to give twentieth-century American civilization a distinctive character. This was as true of philanthropy as of other aspects of American life.

The changes worked by war were most obvious in the American Red Cross. In April 1917 President Wilson summoned a conference of businessmen and financiers to discuss the financing of the Red Cross program. These men promised the Red Cross increased support from the business community, providing its administration was strengthened by appointment of a War Council. In May 1917 the War Council occupied the newly completed national headquarters building and transformed the Red Cross from an agency of neutrality and humanity into an auxiliary of the United States armed forces. The War Council selected as its chairman Henry P. Davison, a member of J. P. Morgan and Company, and he in turn named other leading bankers, corporation executives, and, inevetibly, a public relations expert, to top positions in the organization. At the time of Davison's appointment it had been said that he was the kind of man who could make the Red Cross a "50 million dollar proposition instead of a 5 million dollar one." Davison did more than that. One of his first decisions was to set the goal for the 1917 fund drive at $100 million.

This figure—a sum fifty times as large as the Red Cross had spent for war relief between 1914 and 1917, and much larger than any voluntary organization had ever before attempted to raise—is as good a symbol as any of the daring and vision Davison brought to the Red Cross. The campaign to obtain it was no simple appeal to chapters for funds. It was a carefully planned undertaking to convince the public that every dollar given to the Red Cross was a demonstration of patriotism and a contribution to victory. To assist in conducting the campaign the Red Cross borrowed Charles S. Ward, the YMCA's most successful money-raiser, and seventy-five experienced YMCA secretaries. Campaign leaders, working with amazing speed, assigned quotas to individual cities and towns, rallied community and business leaders to the cause, and organized thousands of volunteer workers, and prepared the countless forms, posters, advertising layouts, and publicity releases to be used in the drive. Conducted in June, hard on the heels of the First Liberty Loan, the campaign not only achieved but exceeded the goal. Similar methods applied with more time for planning carried the 1918 drive to the astonishing total of about $175 million. In all the Red Cross collected $400 million during the war and postwar years, and membership, which stood at about a quarter of a million at the start of 1917, had reached twenty-one million by the start of 1919.

With vastly increased funds and members the Red Cross was in a position to render effective assistance both to American troops and to civilians and fighting men in the Allied countries. From the outset aid to the Allies, especially France, loomed large in Davison's program for the Red Cross. The organization ultimately spent considerably more in assisting refugees, children, the families of French soldiers, and the French antituberculosis campaign than in services for the American Expeditionary Force. In World War I the Red Cross supplemented army and navy medical departments much more directly than in World War II. It recruited men for the ambulance corps and nurses for the army, navy, and Public Health Service; and set up, equipped, staffed and sent overseas numerous base (1,000-bed) hospitals and smaller hospital units.

While the Red Cross had exclusive responsibility for supplementary relief for the sick and wounded, it shared responsibility—that is, competed with—a number of other philanthropic agencies in serving able-bodied soldiers and sailors. The Commission on Training Camp Activities maintained some semblance of order in the United States by permitting the Red Cross to distribute supplies and perform social work through field directors attached to military units, and authorizing the YMCA, Knights of Columbus, Jewish Welfare Board, War Camp Community Service, and YWCA to develop educational and recreational services in camps and surrounding communities.

Overseas, however, the situation was more confused because the army did not attempt to coordinate the work of the private societies engaged in military relief. The agencies themselves, eager to be helpful and anxious to prove the worth of their services, set up hotels, clubs, canteens, "huts," and "dugouts" wherever they could, jockeyed for position and favor, and became embroiled in unwholesome

American Philanthropy

religious and institutional rivalries. The result was spotty
and uneven service, some areas being oversupplied with
facilities, while others received not so much as a baseball,
chocolate bar, or magazine from the societies. Agencies like
the YMCA that attempted to do most suffered criticism for
sins of omission and commission; those like the Salvation
Army that attempted relatively little won extravagant
praise. In the long run the confusion and competition
produced by what Raymond Fosdick of the Commission on
Training Camp Activities called "the present policy of
laissez-faire" was to convince the army that the morale
services attempted by the societies should not be left to
private agencies. "Morale," as Fosdick stated in his final
report to the secretary of war, "is as important as ammu-
nition and is just as legitimate a charge against the public
treasury."

The competition of the private agencies extended from
the field of action to the crucial area of fund-raising. Here,
however, the pressure of public opinion and the influence of
Secretary of War Newton D. Baker and John D.
Rockefeller, Jr., eventually forced the seven national
organizations (other than the Red Cross) that were
participating in soldier relief at home and abroad to join in a
united fund drive. The United War Work campaign of
November 1918, although inaugurated amid impressive
demonstrations of unity, was conducted under peculiarly
difficult conditions. The great influenza epidemic, which
reached its peak in October, was still in progress and
incapacitated both solicitors and contributors. More important, the war was coming to an end. John R. Mott, the saintly
secretary general of the YMCA, stepped into the breach
with the startling message that peace was more dangerous
than war. "We need not be solicitous for our soldiers and
sailors when they are drilling and fighting and confronting

the great adventure of life and death," he announced. The real danger and need lay ahead when relaxation of discipline and more leisure would expose the troops to increased temptations. A nation in the process of adopting the Prohibition amendment responded enthusiastically to this and similar moral arguments. Moreover a 1917 amendment to the income tax law encouraged individual giving by permitting deduction of charitable contributions up to 15 percent of taxable income. This provision, combined with the 60 percent surtax levied on high incomes, enabled the very rich to give generously of money that would otherwise have gone to the Collector of Internal Revenue. Once again the goal was oversubscribed. In what was then called "the largest voluntary offering in history," the United War Work Fund raised $200 million "to prevent the period of demobilization becoming a period of demoralization."

Peace in truth did present problems, and problems much graver than the leisure-time activities of American soldiers and sailors. The chief problem was to get food, clothing, and medicine to millions of men, women, and children in central and eastern Europe who were suffering from the worst famine in three hundred years. Fortunately the United States had quantities of agricultural commodities which it was more than willing, for humanitarian, economic, and political reasons, to send abroad. If helping suffering humanity also helped American farmers dispose of surplus corn and wheat, so much the better. The important thing was that assistance was needed and provided in enormous quantities.

Throughout most of 1919 European relief needs were far greater than voluntary agencies could meet. This was the period when Mr. Hoover, simultaneously head of the United States Food Administration, Grain Corporation, American Relief Administration, and also director-general of relief for the Allied governments, performed his most remarkable feats of financing and executing international aid. Toward the end of 1919, while governmental relief agencies were being liquidated, American philanthropy assumed the task of feeding and caring for millions of European children left orphaned, crippled, homeless, and undernourished by war and attendant catastrophes. At the suggestion of Mr. Hoover, who had transformed the once-official American Relief Administration into a private charitable organization, the numerous groups interested in this field organized the European Relief Council; the council conducted a joint fund drive in the winter of 1920–21 to which foundations, schoolchildren, and community chests contributed $30 million.

Cotton Mather's observation that the reward of doing good is an increase in opportunities to be helpful was borne out later, in 1921, when the Russian writer, Maxim Gorki, appealed to "all honest European and American people" for food and medicine for famine-stricken Soviet Russia. Previous proposals to send aid to postrevolutionary Russia had come to naught because of suspicion on both sides. However, in the summer of 1921 Mr. Hoover, now secretary of commerce but acting in the capacity of chairman of the unofficial American Relief Administration (the beneficiary of the assets of the Grain Corporation, which Hoover had headed during the war), was able to negotiate an agreement with Russia. The Soviets agreed to give ARA personnel freedom, protection, and assistance in relief operations, and the ARA undertook to extend such assistance as it could and guaranteed that its workers would not participate in political activities. The Russian and American governments, the ARA, the Red Cross, and organizations as various as the Volga Relief Society, Southern Baptist Convention, American Friends Service

Committee, and Laura Spelman Rockefeller Memorial helped finance the program. A businesslike undertaking conducted to the mutual satisfaction of both the Soviet government and the ARA, Russian famine relief constituted a hopeful precedent for the future as well as a successful capping of the international relief activities of the war era.

Nearly all the foundations contributed heavily to the war and postwar fund drives. In the sentence quoted at the head of this chapter George E. Vincent of the Rockefeller Foundation expressed the point of view of foundation executives: war relief was necessary and presumably worthwhile, but it was not the creative job that the foundations hoped to perform. Education and research were the real concerns of foundations, and even during the war they continued active in these fields. Public health, medical research, and medical education—all three, of course, closely related—were the particular interests of the Rockefeller philanthropies. Between 1913 and 1929 the International Health Commission of the Rockefeller Foundation, operating on a worldwide scale and always working in cooperation with governmental agencies, lent its assistance to campaigns against hookworm, yellow fever, pellagra, malaria, and tuberculosis. Foundation philanthropy is often regarded as impersonal, but four scientists serving the Rockefeller Foundation, including the renowned bacteriologist Hideyo Noguchi, died of yellow fever while fighting that disease in Africa or South America.

The Rockefeller Foundation and the General Education Board, in what was perhaps their most important service, made large grants to medical schools in the United States and abroad. The key figure in obtaining and distributing the $50 million which Rockefeller contributed to the cause was Abraham Flexner (1866–1959), secretary of the General

Education Board for a decade after 1917. Funds supplied by Flexner, whom Hans Zinser dubbed "the uncle of modern medical education in America," were not free gifts, but hardheaded investments, made on condition that the recipient would raise an equal or larger sum from other sources and institute improvements in facilities and instruction. The emphasis was on improving the quality rather than on expanding the number of medical schools. Through the assistance of these grants, and as a result of the stimulating effect they had on giving by other donors and appropriations by state legislatures, medical education—backward and neglected in 1910—had been virtually revolutionized by the end of the 1920s.

A more difficult task, and one much less completely effected, was improvement and expansion of educational facilities for southern Negroes. "The only purpose for which the Negro has asked or received philanthropic aid has been for the support of education," said Booker T. Washington in 1912. Northern philanthropists had been furnishing this aid ever since emancipation. At the turn of the century, interest in the education of Negores merged with the efforts of the Southern Education Board and the General Education Board to promote the public school movement in the South. "We have no thought of colonizing northern teachers in the South, or of propagating northern ideas at the South," said Wallace Buttrick of the General Education Board to a joint session of the Georgia legislature; "quite the contrary; we believe that . . . your schools must be organized and maintained by you in harmony with your institutions and traditions." This approach was based on the philosophy that progress in the education of Negroes depended on further education of southern whites. In practice it meant acquiescing, at least for the time being, in the development of segregated and unequal school systems. But Negro education, although subordinated to white, was not entirely neglected. Philanthropy continued to provide opportunities for Negro youth that southern states and communities could not or would not undertake on their own initiative. In the two decades after 1911 Julius Rosenwald of Sears, Roebuck, and Company, through various personal gifts and grants made by the Rosenwald Fund, contributed to the building of more than five thousand rural schools. Toward the end of the 1920s the Rosenwald Fund, the General Education Board, the Carnegie Corporation, several other foundations, and Negro philanthropists (such as James and John Burrus of Nashville) displayed greater interest than formerly in higher education for Negroes.

Two events at the end of the war—the doubling of Yale's endowment through the Sterling bequest and Harvard's successful, professionally directed campaign to raise $14 million—augured well for higher education. In the next decade foundations and individual donors, including Edward S. Harkness, George Eastman, and James B. Duke, made conditional or outright gifts to colleges and universities that enlarged endowments, created new departments, altered the appearance of campuses, and (in the case of Duke) changed the name of the institution. The Carnegie Corporation gave so exuberantly in the early 1920s that by 1924 it had pledged $40 million in future income to various institutions. Conditional grants made by the General Education Board had by 1925 added an estimated $200 million to the endowments of three hundred institutions. A newer development, fostered by the growth of foundations, was the promotion of scholarship by means of fellowships and grants for advanced research. Some foundations were operating agencies, conducting investigations and performing services through their own staffs. The larger number, however, were fund dispensers and used part or all of their income to finance studies undertaken by individuals or groups independent of their control. The latter course, as the Rockefeller Foundation early learned, was especially necessary in controversial areas, such as the social sciences, where the objectivity of the investigation must be clearly demonstrated.

Even in the 1920s questions were raised whether foundation-financed research could be objective and whether institutions accepting aid from foundations and corporations could maintain their integrity. There was a flare-up of the old tainted-money debate in 1925 when the board of regents of the University of Wisconsin, in an action both praised and derided, resolved not to accept gifts from "incorporated educational endowments"—although it continued to accept donations from the Wisconsin Manufacturers' Association, public utility companies, and other corporations. Generally speaking, however, scholars were more interested in securing adequate support for research than in quibbling about its source; and obtaining funds from foundations for fellowships, grants-in-aid, and other research subsidies became one of the tasks of the American Council of Learned Societies and the Social Science Research Council. In addition to research projects of individual scholars, foundations supported such large-scale cooperative ventures as the *Encyclopedia of the Social Sciences* and the *Economic and Social History of the World War*. It was not a foundation, however, but the New York Times Company that financed preparation and publication of the original twenty volumes of the *Dictionary of American Biography;* and it was a private citizen, John D. Rockefeller, Jr., who gave the Library of Congress $500,000 to begin the enormous task of reproducing material relating to American history in the archives of foreign countries.

Whether performed by great donors such as Mr. Rockefeller, Jr. (whose personal benefactions included gifts for the resurrection of Colonial Williamsburg and toward the restoration of Versailles, Reims Cathedral, and Fontainebleau), or by men and women of lesser means, individual giving remained the mainstay of philanthropy. Foundations had increased to two hundred by 1930 and annually poured millions of dollars into selected channels of benevolence. Their aggregate endowment, however, approximately $1 billion, was only about half what Americans gave each year for philanthropic purposes. Habits of giving and techniques of raising money developed during the war continued in the 1920s. Each year the springs of charity poured out a golden flood: $1.75 billion in 1921, $2 billion in 1924 and 1925, almost $2.5 billion in 1928.

During the 1920s the business of benevolence developed professionals, not only in the arts of casework, but in the specialty of fund-raising. The former were notoriously underpaid; the latter were well rewarded for their services. Social workers, influenced by contemporary trends in psychiatry and interested in techniques of helpfulness, became increasingly concerned with complex problems of individual adjustment to social stress. Professional fund-raising companies counseled and otherwise assisted fund-seeking institutions to reach their goals, charging a flat fee or a percentage of the collection. By the end of the 1920s there were twenty firms of this sort in New York City alone; their clients included leading colleges, churches, and community chests.

Spurred by the success of the war drives, the community chest movement spread from 40 cities in 1919 to about 350 a decade later. At the outset federated financing had been opposed both by strong agencies which had no difficulty in raising money and by those who saw in it another example of business domination. Acceptance of the community chest idea, which of course was by no means complete, reflected the force of the "New Era" concept of cooperation in all areas of enterprise. The community chest reduced competition and promoted rational distribution of charitable profits. It expanded the number of givers, increased the amount of money available for social work, and ultimately released social agencies from dependence upon a few well-to-do givers. The chest, sometimes called "the budget plan of benevolence," made giving less an act of personal charity than a form of community citizenship, almost as essential as the payment of taxes.

The outpouring of money for philanthropy was matched only by the praise heaped on it. From time to time, it is true, doubts were expressed about the wisdom of undue reliance by society upon private benefactions. But critics of business civilization seldom questioned American generosity and defenders frequently boasted of it. In 1928, a year which saw five hundred lump-sum gifts of $1 million or more, the *Saturday Evening Post* characterized the charitable zeal of business leaders as a "practical application of the golden rule." "We work, and we work hard, not for the money itself but for the good that may be done with it," said the *Philadelphia Inquirer* early in 1929. And a sober historian, Marcus W. Jernegan, writing in a learned journal in March 1929, affirmed the popular view: "Never in the world's history have such unprecedented amounts of money been granted by private and public agencies to alleviate human suffering."

Professor Jernegan's inclusion of public agencies was significant. Even before the depression public expenditures for welfare were growing more rapidly than private contributions to charity. State after state had adopted special relief programs for dependent children, the blind, and the aged. State appropriations for mental hospitals and schools for blind and deaf children increased; so also did local outlays for public health nursing, baby clinics, dispensaries, hospitals, and sanitoriums. Nevertheless, at the very crest of prosperity, aid to the needy was already straining the budget of family welfare societies. In April 1929 the *Survey Graphic* devoted an entire issue to problems raised by what was then called technological unemployment. All too soon—although not soon enough— the normal business of benevolence would yield the stage to the grim business of relief.

9

A Time to Remember

The effort to make voluntary charity solve the
problems of a major social crisis . . . results only
in monumental hypocrisies and tempts selfish
people to regard themselves as unselfish.

REINHOLD NEIBUHR

Almsgiving, a practice long out of fashion in philanthropic
circles, came back into style in the first two years of the
Great Depression. Little was heard in 1930 and 1931 of the
old warning that an excess of benevolence would debauch
and pauperize the poor, although a great deal was said about
the soul-destroying effects of governmental doles.
Financiers and corporation executives threw themselves
into the work of raising funds for the unemployed and
discovered, as one of them said, "There's a spiritual side to
helping those who must have help this winter."
Industrialists lent warehouses for use as shelters for the
homeless. Al Capone, YMCAs, newspaper publishers, and
Catholic nuns supported breadlines. A society woman—so
the story went—admiring the breadline run by Mrs. X,

"Lady Bountiful of the Bowery," said to a social worker: "Please find out what it costs. I'd love to have one."

These charitable labors were carried on with the blessings of the president of the United States. No one was more disturbed by the paradox of poverty in the midst of plenty than Herbert Hoover. No earlier president recognized as fully the responsibility of the federal government to take vigorous action to promote economic recovery. And none of his predecessors was more firmly convinced that responsibility for relieving distress lay with individuals, voluntary organizations, and local governments. In speech after speech Hoover sought to drive home the obligation of individuals and communities to prevent those "in honest difficulties" from suffering hunger and cold. Time and again he attempted to stimulate the nation's spiritual energies to greater charitable efforts. "Charity is the obligation of the strong to the weak," he said in February 1930. "Works of charity are the tests of spiritual development of men and women and communities." As the months and years passed, Hoover's praise of charity, "the loftiest of all spiritual qualities," became more fulsome. His speeches usually included some reference to "community service" or "mutual self-help" through the responsibility of local government, but he never waxed as eloquent about tax-supported assistance as about voluntary benevolence.

The president's approach placed heavy burdens on community chests and the American Red Cross. The former, in Hoover's opinion, stood for the sense of charity in individual cities; the latter, which he called "one of the most beautiful flowers of the American spirit," represented "our people in their most generous, unselfish and spontaneously warm-hearted character." Both institutions, to the best of their abilities, lived up to the trust the president imposed in them. Community chests in a number of cities, including hard-hit Detroit, reached their goals in the autumn of 1930 and in some instances raised larger sums than in previous years. "In every city," reported the Association of Community Chests and Councils in November 1930, "a large part of the increase has come directly from job-holders—persons who may at any time have to turn to the chest for aid." Meanwhile, in one of the most curious and characteristic episodes of the early depression period, the American Red Cross spurned a proposed congressional grant of $25 million and undertook to relieve two and a half million drought sufferers in twenty-three states with $5 million from its disaster reserve funds and $10 million raised in a special campaign. "All we pray for is that you let us alone and let us do the job," the chairman of the Red Cross central committee told Congress in January 1931.

President Hoover enthusiastically indorsed the Red Cross's rejection of the government's tainted money. The immediate problem was famine, but, as he saw it, the basic moral issue involved was vastly more important. "We are dealing with the intangibles of life and ideals," Hoover said. "A voluntary deed by a man impressed with the sense of responsibility and brotherhood of man is infinitely more precious to our National ideals and National spirit than a thousandfold poured from the Treasury of the Government under the compulsion of law." Statistically minded critics estimated that the Red Cross drought-relief program, the largest peacetime operation in which it had ever engaged, brought those aided an average of 42 cents of assistance per week.

As the depression worsened and the nation, in the president's words, passed through another Valley Forge, the administration launched its most ambitious effort to alleviate distress through benevolence. In August 1931 Hoover announced the appointment of Walter S. Gifford as head of the Organization for Unemployment Relief. Gifford, described by *Time* as "a 'clean desk' executive" whose only hobby was charity, was president of the American Telephone and Telegraph Company and also of the New York Charity Organization Society. To assist Gifford in the task of mobilizing and coordinating the charitable resources of the country Hoover enlisted the services of one hundred leaders of business, industry, finance, and philanthropy. The organization distributed model relief plans to cities and towns across the nation and prepared a nationwide campaign to raise an undisclosed sum—unofficially reported to be $175 million—for community chests and other private relief agencies. By an unfortunate coincidence United States Steel, Ford, General Motors, and other large corporations— many of whose executives were members of the president's Unemployment Relief Organization—announced wage cuts of 10 percent or more just before the campaign was scheduled to begin. In the circumstances Hoover's speech opening the fund drive sounded even more cloistered than usual. He dwelt on the "God-imposed responsibility of the individual man and woman to their neighbors" and urged Americans to be their brothers' keepers.

No fund appeal since the war drives of 1917 and 1918 received wider publicity or had a more professional flavor than the campaign of October–November 1931. Movie theaters and college football teams gave benefit performances. Radio broadcasts carried messages of inspiration and hope to millions of homes. Advertising agencies contributed a series of high-powered advertisements which appeared, free of charge, on billboards and in newspapers and magazines. If anything the campaign was oversold. Although there were no representatives of the unemployed in the president's Relief Organization the first advertisement purported to be an open letter from "Unemployed,

1931." Tightening his belt, as well he might, "Unemployed, 1931" said, "I'll see it through if *you* will!" The second proclaimed, "Between October 19th and November 25th America will feel the thrill of a great spiritual experience." Give liberally, the copywriter urged, "And know that your gift will bless yourself; it will lift your own spirit." Another advertisement, which looked very much like those for toothpaste, declared, "The world *respects* the man who lives within his income. But the world *adores* the man who *gives* to the LIMIT of his ability." Finally, "In one month . . . every city and town in the land will raise the funds that will be necessary to banish from its borders the fear of hunger and cold. . . . Just one month, and our biggest job will be over."

Twenty years later Hoover recorded in a volume of his *Memoirs* that the drive was a success both in raising funds and in "awakening" a sense of national responsibility for being "'my brother's keeper.'" Contemporary evidence and opinion, although divided, was less reassuring. The campaign did raise a great deal of money, but the total was closer to $100 million than $175 million, and this was nowhere nearly enough to banish from the nation either the fear or the actuality of hunger and cold. Those who chose could take comfort from the fact that 200 community chests, reached or slightly exceeded their quotas and 179 increased previous totals by 14 percent. On the other hand, those who were so inclined, and they included the executive director of the Association of Community Chests and Councils, could point out that one-fourth of the chests had failed by 10 percent or more; that only 35 percent of chest funds would be spent for relief and that this represented only 30 percent of the total conservatively estimated need for relief in the chest cities. The other 70 percent was supposed to come from tax-supported agencies. Chest success did not accurately reflect a community's ability to meet the crisis, since exhausted resources or limitations on taxing and borrowing powers made it impossible for many cities to raise the public share of relief funds. In practice a chest goal was more likely to be an estimate of the amount which could be raised than an indication of the sums really needed by welfare agencies. Moreover, the campaign had no effect on sorely distressed rural areas, mining villages, and mill towns where there were no local charities and only the most rudimentary public provisions for poor relief.

While the campaign receipts were still being totaled, a Senate committee began hearings on two bills proposing federal appropriations for unemployment relief. Mr. Gifford was unable to provide the committee with definite information on the extent of unemployment, the number of persons in need, the number receiving aid, or the standards of assistance furnished the needy. He gave the impression, however, that matters were well in hand. With unintended humor he observed that federal appropriations might be a disservice to the unemployed, since "Individuals would tend to withdraw much of the invisible aid they are now giving."

A number of social workers also appeared before the Senate committee. These witnesses, in close touch with the relief situation in their communities, were much less confident than Mr. Gifford that matters were well in hand, and they were less disturbed by the prospect of federal aid. Two years of depression had wrought changes in social workers' thinking. There was no tendency now to magnify the extent of private benevolence or to dwell on the superiority of charity to public relief. On the contrary, witness after witness maintained that even in normal times private organizations relied on public agencies to carry the major burden of assistance and that in the present emergency it was public responsibility and public appropriations, not private giving, that required stimulation. Walter West, executive secretary of the American Association of Social Workers, testified that the country's existing relief system was primitive. It forced the jobless and their families to bear almost the entire cost of unemployment, since neither public nor private agencies relieved them until they were destitute. One advantage of federal relief, said West, would be to "take off some of the curse of charity." Another witness, J. Prentice Murphy of Philadelphia, advised the committee: "If the modern state is to rest upon a firm foundation, its citizens must not be allowed to starve. Some of them do. They do not die quickly. You can starve for a long time without dying."

Hoover's speech opening the emergency fund drive had implied that philanthropy was on trial. Actually the trial was over. Philanthropy stood condemned, convicted not only of bankruptcy but of more heinous offenses. The fact that private relief organizations, Red Cross chapters, and religious groups such as the American Friends Service Committee were doing what public bodies found it impossible or inconvenient to do received little notice. Philanthropy, according to its critics, was a dodge of the rich to escape taxes and hold on to power. This was an old charge that gained new force each time business tycoons asked others to be their brothers' keepers. "Riot insurance" was the name scoffers gave the businessmen's and bankers' relief efforts. Theodore Dreiser, who had once written with weird objectivity of the curious shifts of the poor, now, in *Tragic America* (1931), denounced all charity as a racket, controlled like everything else by Wall Street. Paul Douglas, Stuart Chase, and other liberal economists marveled at the mentality of men who abhorred the "dole" of unemployment insurance and cherished breadlines, handouts, and relief drives as the American Way. It remained for Abraham Epstein, a pioneer crusader for public old-age insurance, to commit the supreme heresy. He denied that Americans were generous. In a widely quoted article published in the *American Mercury* in 1931 Epstein declared: "The myth of our unparalleled generosity has no firmer base than the benevolence of a very few men who have distributed small parts of their extraordinary large fortunes."

That Hoover's homilies on charity should have contributed to bringing philanthropy into disrepute was unfortunate, ironic, and understandable. History abounds in examples of humanitarians who were ahead of their times. Hoover belonged to a different breed: the humanitarian behind the times. In his public addresses he seemed to envisage American society as a sentimental jungle in which the overflowing hearts and tender consciences of the strong would minister everlastingly to the wants of the weak. He revered charity too highly and attached too much virtue to casual giving—so much, in fact, that he was tempted to place the interests of the benevolent before the needs of the necessitous. Possibly because of experience in war and famine relief he tended to equate philanthropy with succor of the suffering. This was an old and respectable view, and tenable in time of war or natural disaster. In was not adequate or appropriate, however, in an era of economic crisis; and it conflicted with a long-established tendency in American philanthropy. For years Americans had boasted of their generosity but almost in the same breath they had decried the need for charity. The constant effort of American humanitarians since the days of Cotton Mather had been to restrain and discipline, not to expand, the charitable impulse. With the assistance of great givers like Carnegie and Rockefeller they had sought and all but succeeded in turning the mainstream of philanthropy from ameliorative to preventive and constructive tasks. It was too late to reverse the direction. As the governor of New York observed in August 1931, the time for platitudes had passed.

To the despair of friends and foes Franklin D. Roosevelt usually managed to avoid either getting too far ahead of or lagging too far behind public opinion. In his attitudes toward charity, as in so many other matters, he revealed an understanding of abiding tendencies in the national character. Instead of exaggerating the moral significance of neighborly kindness, he attempted to prove, as Tocqueville would have said, that virtue was useful. Even in acknowledging gifts to a favorite charity, the Warm Springs Foundation, Roosevelt went to some pains to point out that every disabled person restored to useful citizenship added to the assets of the nation. "By helping this work," he said, "we are contributing not to charity but to building up of a sound nation." Similarly, in calling for state aid to the unemployed in 1931, Roosevelt declared that such help should be offered "not as a matter of charity, but as a matter of social duty." Subsequently he was to defend vast federal appropriations for unemployment relief as a means of promoting business recovery; and still later he argued that federal minimum wage, maximum-hour, and child-labor laws were necessary to conserve manpower, increase purchasing power, stabilize markets for farmers' products, and make business more profitable. Ironically enough, Roosevelt's insistence—sometimes strained and occasionally comic—on finding practical justifications for humanitarian action appears to have been an important factor in convincing an adoring electorate that his heart was in the right place.

Under Roosevelt's leadership New York became the first state to offer assistance to local governments in the financing and administration of unemployment relief. A number of other states followed New York's example but in others timidity, disinclination to burden taxpayers, constitutional prohibitions, and in some cases sheer lack of resources precluded effective state action. Nevertheless a break had been made with the outdated assumption that relief was a purely local responsibility. After that not even the Chamber of Commerce of the United States and an organization called Sentinels of the Republic (which sponsored a series of radio broadcasts in which prominent conservatives addressed the nation on "Too Much Government," "Government Interference in the Home," "The Menace of Paternalism," and "Our Vanishing Freedom") could block the drift toward federal participation in relief. Hoover stood firm as long as he could. But in the spring of 1932 he asked the Red Cross to supervise the processing and distributing of surplus wheat and cotton to the needy—a task which the organization accepted and performed with dispatch and credit—and in July he gave his approval to a measure authorizing the Reconstruction Finance Corporation to make grants thinly disguised as loans to states for unemployment relief and public works. After Roosevelt entered the White House the tentative steps already taken in the direction of greater governmental responsibility for welfare turned into something resembling a march. The tempo varied from time to time but generally the movement went forward.

When the emergency was over—it lasted for the better part of ten years and was ended only by the greater crisis of World War II—the nation had not only survived but in doing so had entered into a new social era. The ransoming of capitalism had cost more money than any government had ever before spent in time of peace. Enormous expenditures for public welfare required borrowing on a scale that only war had previously justified, and the adoption of a revenue program that compelled wealthy persons and large corporations to carry a larger share of the tax burden than they were accustomed to bear. As a result of grants-in-aid to states and federally administered work and relief projects the unemployed were better provided for than in any previous depression. Admittedly this was not saying much. Social workers, not to mention the unemployed and the so-called unemployables, recognized needs that if they had been met, would have required still larger appropriations than Roosevelt and his oddly assorted supporters were willing to sanction. It is significant that both at the time and later the New Deal was as often criticized for attempting too little as for doing too much. In all likelihood a comparable emergency in the future will be met by prompter and more, rather than less, governmental action.

Incomplete though the New Deal relief and security programs were, they registered a striking advance over the inhumane, archaic, and unsystematic methods of treating distress practiced before the depression. By 1941 the United States had a start toward social insurance systems that would protect workers against some of the hazards of age and unemployment. It had a considerable start toward federal-state partnership in caring for the aged, the blind, and dependent children. Federal leadership, supervision, and financial assistance had strengthened the states' welfare services and had encouraged states to adopt measures such as unemployment insurance which they had previously been hesitant to put into effect. Preventive measures to forestall or minimize dependency and promote security had been inaugurated, had been approved by the Supreme Court, and had seemingly become accepted as permanent obligations of government. Most surprising of all, in the midst of depression, organized labor had grown in numerical strength, legal status, and aggressiveness. Assisted by the generally sympathetic attitude of the federal government, larger numbers of Americans than ever before had won and were vigorously exercising the right to improve their economic conditions through collective bargaining.

The entry of the federal government into relief financing

and the consequent expansion of public welfare activities at all levels of government took some of the pressure off philanthropy. Throughout the 1930s there remained ample need for the services private agencies could offer millions of families on relief and the millions more who, although hard-pressed, were not yet receiving relief. No one pretended, however, that private charity played more than a subordinate and supplementary role in the alleviation of distress, and the common assumption was that its responsibilities in this area would continue to decline. Philanthropy was almost rid of the unwelcome task of relieving destruction and almost free to return to more congenial occupations: "pioneering," development of experimental programs, promotion of research, enrichment of cultural life, and improvement of techniques of helpfulness applicable to individuals and families at any income level.

The only problem was money. "Where are the millions of the 1920s?" was a familiar lament. The springs of charity by no means dried up, but they ran at only about half their usual volume. The stock market crash reverberated through the corridors of art galleries and music halls, for even in normal times museums, symphony orchestras, and opera companies operated at a deficit, and relied heavily on a few very rich and generous patrons. Proud organizations like the New York Philharmonic and the Metropolitan Opera Company now had to pass the hat to ordinary music lovers. Saving the "Met" became almost a yearly event, nearly as exciting as opening night. The Red Cross, the National Tuberculosis Association, and hundreds of private agencies represented in local community chests retrenched.

Even richly endowed foundations felt the squeeze of hard times. The Julius Rosenwald Fund, for example, could not meet pledges made when the market was high; its endowment was invested in common stock of Sears, Roebuck, and Company, which dropped from $200 a share in 1928 to $10 in 1932. The fund was saved from premature liquidation by the cooperation of the General Education Board and the Carnegie Corporation, which took over some of its responsibilities, and by changing its program from making grants to engaging in research. Other major foundations, although not as seriously affected by the depression, also adjusted programs to meet the emergency. Grants became smaller and more varied and were directed more toward fellowships and support of specific research projects than to increasing institutional endowments.

The Carnegie Corporation, like the Rosenwald Fund, operated under the burden of commitments made in freer spending days. Nevertheless, the corporation was able to contribute almost $2 million to emergency relief and social service agencies in 1932–33, and throughout the depression period it found the means to assist art museums and to promote art and musical education. The Carnegie Corporation also supplied the American Foundation for the Blind with funds to develop recorded or "talking books" for those of the blind who could not use braille (about 80 percent). The venture offered a classic example of the way philanthropy is supposed to work, because in 1935, after the foundations had perfected the program, Congress began to appropriate money to the Library of Congress to permit nationwide extension of the service.

The depression caught the Rockefeller Foundation in the throes of reorganization and in the midst of replacing old leaders with new. The new officials were less medical-minded than their predecessors, more willing to support research in the social sciences and humanities, and less averse to "scatteration," the foundation expression for retail philanthropy. In 1933 the trustees appropriated a million and a half dollars to expedite discovery of remedies for the depression. No very striking results flowed from this emergency measure, but the grants the foundation made to the National Bureau of Economic Research and similar agencies contributed to advances in methods of studying economic problems as well as to the accumulation of more precise knowledge of income distribution and related issues. Hardly less valuable, in a time of increasing governmental responsibilities, was the foundation's aid to the Public Administration Clearing House. This agency, still operating in Chicago, brought together organizations representing public officials in city management, welfare, public works, finance, and personnel administration. The Rockefeller Foundation bore out its claim to be a pioneering institution by lending support to the extension and improvement of instruction in the Russian, Chinese, and Japanese languages in the early 1930s, long before the necessity for such work was popularly recognized.

Despite the scaling-down of benefactions as the economic crisis became more serious, some of the millions and some of the millionaires of the 1920s remained active in the 1930s. Several of today's larger foundations, including the A. W. Mellon Charitable and Educational Trust (1930) and the Kellogg (1930) and Sloan (1934) foundations, came into being during the darkest years of the depression. The great individual givers, Edward S. Harkness and John D. Rockefeller, Jr., while contributing generously to emergency relief drives, also gave on an even more generous scale to the kinds of projects in which they had long been interested. Harkness, like the younger Rockefeller, devoted his life to disposing of the fortune his father had made in Standard Oil. His princely gifts went to princely institutions: Harvard, Yale, Columbia, Phillips Exeter, Lawrenceville School, the Metropolitan Museum of Art, and great hospitals and medical centers. Rockefeller's benefactions rivaled his father's in size and outdid them in variety. The restoration of Williamsburg, the colonial capital of Virginia, International House at the University of Chicago, the Cloisters Museum, and preservation and development of park sites from Mt. Desert Island and New York City to the Grand Tetons were among his philanthropic interests in the early 1930s.

Restoration projects also appealed to the master tinkerer, Henry Ford. His attitude toward charity—"Give the average man something and you make an enemy of him"— smacked more of the cracker barrel than of the gospel of wealth, and it was a cracker-barrel world that Ford attempted to reincarnate at the Ford Museum and Greenfield Village in the industrial city of Dearborn, Michigan. The museum was a replica of Independence Hall that spread over acres and contained relics of old-fashioned ways of doing business, making things and going places. Surrounding the museum was Ford's reproduction of an early American village. It revealed, in one fascinating, inharmonious whole, the birthplaces of Ford, Noah Webster, William A. McGuffey, and Luther Burbank, a seventeenth-century stone cottage from England, a steamboat from the Suwannee River, the schools Ford had attended as a boy, a tintype studio, a windmill from Cape Cod, a village green, a colonial church, Thomas A. Edison's workshop and laboratory, the Wright brothers' cycle shop, and the building in which Ford had built his first automobile. Opened in June 1933, the museum and village enshrined themselves in the hearts of countless visitors whose country was even then moving ahead, so Franklin D. Roosevelt said, toward the goal of a self-supporting and self-respecting democracy.

Philanthropy could survive the depression. But could it survive the New Deal? That was the question conservatives worried about, especially after the advent of the new and more aggressive New Deal labor, social security, and tax policies of 1935. Community chest leaders scored a victory that eventually proved to be important when, over

MORALE

It wins wars.
It beats depressions.
It lays the firm foundations for prosperity.

AMERICA is engaged in a mighty enterprise of morale building. In one month—October 19th to November 25th—every city and town in the land will raise the funds that will be necessary to banish from its borders the fear of hunger and cold.

Just one month, and our biggest job will be over. Just one month, and we shall have met the worst threat the Depression can offer; and we shall have won!

You can help. Give to the funds that your community is raising. Give generously.

Feel the thrill that comes with victory. Go forward with America to the better days ahead.

The President's Organization on Unemployment Relief

Walter S. Gifford
Director

Committee on Mobilization of Relief Resources

Chairman

The President's Organization on Unemployment Relief is non-political and non-sectarian. Its purpose is to aid local welfare and relief agencies everywhere to provide for local needs. All facilities for the nation-wide program, including this advertisement, have been furnished to the Committee without cost.

Advertisement of the President's Organization on Unemployment Relief. (From *The Saturday Evening Post*, November 14, 1931.)

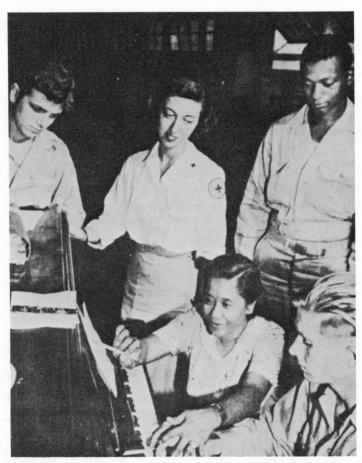

Scene in ARC Roosevelt Club, Manila, 1946. (Reproduced by courtesy of American National Red Cross.

Roosevelt's mild objections, they amended the Revenue Act of 1935 to permit corporations to deduct charitable contributions up to 5 percent of taxable income. Those who professed to believe that business was conducted for no other purpose than to support charities continued to express grave doubts about the effect of higher estate, income, and corporation taxes on giving, and about the implications for philanthropy of the New Deal's allegedly leveling tendencies. Soon there will be no more millionaires, ran the argument. With the goose will go the golden egg. And then what will happen to churches, colleges, museums, and hospitals? The *Saturday Evening Post* warned that government might go on piling up taxes but it need not expect benefactions to pile up too. As if to prove the point the widely publicized will of Jesse Isidore Straus, president of Macy's department store and former chairman of the New York State Temporary Relief Administration, contained a codicil revoking gifts to eighteen philanthropic institutions because of high estate taxes levied by the state and federal governments.

As events were to prove, it was possible for both benefactions and taxes to pile up. Since the days of Amos Lawrence large donors had been in the habit of describing their charitable gifts as investments; in the face of higher income and inheritance taxes, the richer the donor, the sounder his charitable investments became. The economic uses of philanthropy were not exploited to the full until the war prosperity of the 1940s. Even in the 1930s, however, it was recognized that a person in the higher income brackets, if so inclined and properly advised, could make useful contributions to philanthropy with little sacrifice of spendable income, and occasionally to his own advantage. In making income tax returns donors could deduct charitable gifts up to 15 percent of taxable income; they could avoid the capital gains tax by giving appreciated stock to a foundation or recognized philanthropic institution (and, as trustee, continue to vote the stock); and they could reduce the amount of inheritance taxes their heirs would have to pay by bequeathing judicious portions of their estates to incorporated foundations. It was also possible, as Edsel and Henry Ford demonstrated, to arrange matters so that the foundation would pay the inheritance tax imposed on the portion of the estate left to members of the family.

Philanthropy remained in bad repute in liberal and radical circles throughout the 1930s, and for reasons which, if not new, were vigorously and cogently argued. "Philanthropic and business interests are not merely complementary, they are identical," observed one critic in 1938. "Just as you can't run a steel mill without machine guns, so you can't run a capitalist democracy without a pretense of philanthropy." Eduard C. Lindeman, of the New York School of Social Work, whose *Wealth and Culture* (1936) was a study of the operation of one hundred foundations during the 1920s, offered an economic interpretation of modern philanthropy: it was disintegrating capitalism's way of distributing, in its own interest, wealth which could not be spent on luxuries, was not needed for reinvestment, and could not profitably be employed for speculation. Foundations, and by implication all large-scale benefactions, denoted the development of a rudimentary social consciousness in the donors, but they also represented the donors' determination to control social thought and expression. Lindeman's judgment of the trustees of the great philanthropic foundations was even more damning than his interpretation of the motivation of donors. Taken as a group the trustees represented "social prestige, financial success, and middle aged respectability." These were exemplary attributes, but were they adequate or proper qualifications for leaders of organizations supposedly dedicated to pioneering, pathfinding, opening-up of new frontiers of social well-being? Lindeman did not think so. "Nothing," he said, "is so repugnant as the arrogance of those who presume to impose cultural norms upon a society on no basis of warrant other than . . . pecuniary success under . . . a competitive economy."

Since Americans have seldom been disposed to obey the proverbial advice to refrain from looking gift horses in the mouth, it is not surprising that in the 1930s, of all times, they should have cast wary and suspicious eyes on the benefactions of millionaires. The gifts were accepted but with slight thanks. In 1936 the *Christian Century*, recalling Charles Lamb's fable, reflected that to perpetuate the present system in order to keep up the flow of million-dollar gifts would be like burning down a house to roast a pig. The *Nation* observed in 1934 that the best thing that could happen to American universities would be an inability to find rich men to beg from and to put on their governing boards. The broker Charles Hayden's bequest (1937) of $50 million to endow a foundation for educating American youth mentally, morally, and physically prompted the *New Republic* to remark, "If these are the best uses to which vast fortunes can be put it might be better not to permit such accumulations at all." "It is a good thumping gift but it is not enough to justify the existence of swollen fortunes," Heywood Broun said in 1937 of Andrew Mellon's offer to give the federal government both his collection of old masters and the money to house the collection.

Mellon's gift, announced in December 1936, was a thumping big one indeed, the biggest single benefaction of the decade, and the largest gift that had ever been made to the United States government. The grand total for the collection, the National Gallery building, and an endowment fund contributed by the Mellon Educational and Charitable Trust was in the neighborhood of $80 million. There was no disposition to reject Mellon's offer but the fact that the aging financier had made it while a suit involving his 1931 federal income tax return was pending received due, or perhaps undue, notice. In the spirit of the time critics deplored the conservative design of the gallery building and worried lest the self-perpetuating board of trustees might discriminate against living American artists. The National Gallery, which opened in 1941, *was* classic in style, but its permanent collection contained works by living American artists as well as masterpieces by dead Europeans. The Index of American Design, a gift of the federal government, comprised 20,000 water colors and drawings of folk and decorative arts perpared by artists employed on WPA art projects.

There were other evidences of the New Deal's patronage of the fine arts, music, drama, scholarship, education, and recreation. Not only in relief but in many other fields the taxpayer of the late 1930s was supporting activities once regarded as primary concerns of the philanthropist. But larger governmental expenditures, instead of stifling neighborly kindness, seemingly stimulated it. As early as 1935 the nation's total contribution to private benevolence, estimated as $2.5 billion, slightly exceeded the prede-pression peak. By 1938, in spite of conservative fears and radical jeers, philanthropy again ranked as one of the leading American enterprises.

If material as well as spiritual considerations contributed to the revival of private giving, it was nevertheless true that philanthropy emerged from the depression decade with a stronger base of popular support. The number of contributors to community chests rose even when chests failed to reach their goals. Annual Mobilizations for Human Needs, the nationally conducted publicity campaigns for community chests, were carried out with all the fervor and dedication of war drives—which in fact they soon became. The Red Cross experienced no difficulty in raising a $25 million relief fund at the time of the Ohio-Mississippi floods of 1937, and, in furnishing assistance, did not hesitate to work with numerous federal agencies, including the WPA and the CCC. The president's Birthday Balls and the March of Dimes campaigns of the National Foundation for Infantile Paralysis brought philanthropy into the hearts and price range of the multitudes. Those who disdained traditional charity had abundant opportunity to contribute time and again to committees, leagues, and alliances fighting militarism, fascism, racial injustice, and violations of workers' rights.

As the 1930s drew to a close, philanthropy still faced difficult problems. It had lost its sentimental aura and it remained to be seen whether the public could be induced to give as generously for preventive and constructive tasks as for emergency relief of suffering. It also remained to be seen whether philanthropy could, in fact, provide the leadership, imagination, and understanding necessary to devise happier social relationships. Meanwhile, as Roosevelt observed in paying tribute to the work of volunteer and official agencies in the floods of 1937 and the New England hurricane of 1938, there was no conflict between private and governmental welfare service. There was more than enough work for both, he said, not only in meeting disasters, but in "our national effort to lift up the lower one-third of our nation to a standard of living that will conform with decency and comfort and self-respect." Before that task was completed another war and a continuing emergency widened the horizons of both government and philanthropy. The problem was not one-third of the nation, but something like one-half of the globe.

10

A Voyage Is Now Proposed

A Voyage is now proposed to visit a distant people
on the other side of the globe; not to cheat them,
not to rob them, . . . but merely to do them good,
and make them, as far as in our power lies, to live
as comfortably as ourselves.

BENJAMIN FRANKLIN

World War II was an expected war in which the United
States was not expected to participate. War had been so
often forecast and so long anticipated that the German
invasion of Poland in September 1939 came almost as an
anticlimax. A decade of crises had familiarized the world
with the politics of terror, violations of treaties, subversion
of established governments, seizure of foreign territories,
and bombing of civilians. In the prewar years and continuing
at least until the middle of 1940, American policy, as
expressed in neutrality legislation, official statements, and
public opinion polls, was to deplore aggression and to affirm
that the mistake of 1917 would not be repeated. Whatever
happened American boys would not be sent overseas to fight

other nations' battles. Munitions makers, international bankers, and foreign propagandists would not again be permitted to draw the United States into a war to save democracy.

In this climate of opinion philanthropic efforts to relieve victims of war and oppression multiplied but rarely flourished. Throughout the 1930s American Jews gave unstintingly to finance the Joint Distribution Committee's far-flung, desperate labors to save Europe's persecuted Jewry from extinction. Pacifist, youth, and church groups tirelessly solicited for China and Spain. "We dance that Spain may live," read placards announcing dances sponsored by college students sympathetic to the Loyalist cause. There was no lack of organizations seeking funds for overseas relief. The trouble was that they all appealed to the same relatively small segment of the American people who were genuinely concerned about Fascist aggression. Attempts to obtain broader popular support made little headway. In 1938 the American Red Cross tried and failed to raise $1 million for Chinese relief. The Committee for Impartial Civilian Relief in Spain had even less success in attempting to collect $300,000 so that the Red Cross and the American Friends Service Committee might supply limited quantities of surplus American foodstuffs to both sides in the Spanish civil war. The events of 1939 brought little change in public attitudes except to heighten suspicion of actions that might conceivably endanger the neutrality of the United States.

The Neutrality Act of 1939, adopted shortly after the outbreak of the war, recognized the possibility that the overseas operations of American relief organizations might affect the foreign policy and national interests of the United States. The act, in addition to numerous restrictions on American economic activity in nations officially declared to be at war, required voluntary agencies which wished to engage in civilian war relief in belligerent countries to register with and submit monthly reports to the Department of State. The act specifically excluded the American Red Cross from the registration and reporting provisions and it did not apply to agencies operating in nations such as China, the Soviet Union, and Finland, which were not technically belligerent. During 1940 and 1941 the number of both registered and unregistered foreign relief agencies increased rapidly as the war spread to more and more countries. In the approximately two years of American neutrality in World War II, about seven hundred American organizations raised a total of $90 million for civilian and refugee relief overseas, and Congress appropriated an additional $50 million for distribution to refugees by the Red Cross. The fall of France in the summer of 1940 made assistance to nations still fighting the Axis powers seem less a form of charity than one of the measures "short of war" contributing to the defense of the United States.

At the same time that agencies for overseas civilian relief were increasing in number (there were seventy for Great Britain alone), national defense measures at home brought a boom in domestic welfare services. Aid to American armed forces, only recently in bad repute, regained its traditional popularity after adoption of the Selective Service Act of 1940. "Swing into patriotic note," the vice-chairman of the Red Cross advised chapter leaders in the autumn of that year. Early in 1941 the Red Cross swung into the blood donor program, its major contribution to national defense and one of the notable achievements of voluntary activity in the war years. Meanwhile, profiting from experience in World War I, the YMCA, YWCA, National Catholic Community Service, National Jewish Welfare Board, Salvation Army, and National Travelers Aid Association combined their military welfare programs and fund appeals in the United Service Organization for National Defense (USO).

Unfortunately the cooperative approach represented by USO was the exception rather than the rule in 1941. Groups in every community wanted to do something for the draftee and were determined to do it by themselves. There were no bottlenecks in the organization of war charities. The president's Committee on War Relief Agencies, appointed in 1941, studied the problem of duplication and encouraged combination of agencies engaged in the same or similar lines of work. The committee, however, lacked authority to exercise effective supervision. The war relief picture, confused before Pearl Harbor, became chaotic afterward. By the summer of 1942 the president's committee reported that the number of war relief agencies could only be estimated, that those operating in the domestic field were subject to no coordination, supervision or control, and that the public was therefore subjected to far too many solicitations by agencies which duplicated work performed by others. "We were fairly falling over each other in a complex and undirected effort to organize, to publicize, to solicit, and to give," recalled Winthrop Aldrich, who was president of the British War Relief Society and active in USO.

By an executive order issued in July 1942, President Roosevelt transformed the earlier Committee on War Relief Agencies into the President's War Relief Control Board and greatly increased its authority. The board now had power to control all solicitations for voluntary war relief, both foreign and domestic; only the American Red Cross, church, and other nonwar charities remained outside its jurisdiction. It had power to license and withdraw licenses from war relief agencies and, in the interest of economy and efficiency, to eliminate or merge organizations. The board scheduled the various national fund appeals and prevented competing campaigns during the periods set aside for the Red Cross, National War Fund, United Jewish Appeal, and War Bond drives. The staff of the Control Board sharply scrutinized overhead costs and made reasonable economy of operation a requirement for continued licensing. It found that in a few agencies overhead costs consumed 50 percent, 70 percent, and in extreme cases, all of the funds raised for relief. When the members of the board (Joseph E. Davies, Charles P. Taft, and Charles Warren) made their final report in 1946, they could point to impressive achievements: the board had cut the number of war relief agencies from seven hundred to ninety, had promoted a remarkable degree of cooperation among the survivors, and had improved the services they offered. It had played a part in reducing overhead costs from an average of 10 percent in 1942 to just over 3 percent in 1945; and it had helped bring the National War Fund into existence.

The National War Fund, a private nonprofit corporation established late in 1942, was the most ambitious venture in united fund-raising the United States had yet seen. In three national campaigns conducted in 1943, 1944, and 1945 the fund combined the appeals of local nonwar charities (mainly community chests) and the major war-related service and relief agencies including USO, British War Relief, United Service to China, and American Aid to France. The union of war and nonwar charities was fortunate for all concerned. Local welfare organizations, which might otherwise have suffered from the competition of the more glamorous war agencies, received considerably more than half of the $750 million total raised in the three War Fund drives. "The chests had the organization, and the war agencies had the appeal," the general manager of the National War Fund later remarked; "as long as the war lasted it was a winning combination."

Even while this winning combination was operating, it was obvious that larger funds than voluntary organizations could muster would be required for postwar relief. In November 1943 fifty governments organized the United Nations Relief and Rehabilitation Administration (UNRRA) in a cooperative effort to meet the immediate postwar needs of war-devastated countries. At the close of the war this international agency sold or gave the governments of liberated countries immense quantities of food, clothing, medical supplies, livestock, and other relief materials. To the extent that it was possible to do so UNRRA returned exiles, prisoners, and refugees to their homes. For those who could not or dared not go home it operated displaced persons camps. UNRRA was financed by the noninvaded countries which provided commodities and cash to the extent of 2 percent of their national incomes in 1943. The United States share of the $4 billion expended by UNRRA was $2.6 billion. In addition to money and goods from governments UNRRA received $210 million in cash, clothing, food, and livestock from individuals and associations in the United States, Canada, Australia, and New Zealand. Needless to say, this hopeful experiment in sharing resources on the basis of "from each according to his means and to each according to his needs" did not survive very long in a divided, distrustful world. UNRRA lasted long enough, however, to tide nations in bitter need over the worst of the postwar crisis and to help avert widespread famine and epidemic.

Neither the work of UNRRA nor the lend-lease and economic recovery programs launched by the United States government during and after the war diminished the eagerness of the American people to extend sympathetic assistance to people in foreign countries. After 1943 the American Council of Voluntary Agencies for Foreign Service, comprising the larger foreign relief agencies registered with the President's Control Board, planned and coordinated nongovernmental programs. CARE, the Cooperative for American Remittances to Europe (later Everywhere), which began sending food parcels from Americans to designated recipients overseas in 1946, was one of the council's creations; CRALOG (the Council of Relief Agencies Licensed to Operate in Germany), LARA (Licensed Agencies for Relief in Asia), and ARK (American Relief for Korea) were others. All of these alphabetical agencies, as their names indicated, were federations of numerous organizations which pooled their energies for a common cause.

The bureaucratic character of postwar relief was the product of several factors: the number of people and organizations wishing to help, the hard realities of fundraising, and the extraordinary complexities of relief operations after 1945. Programs had to be approved by and correlated with those of official agencies. In occupied areas clearance had to be obtained from military authorities. Elsewhere, agreements had to be negotiated with governments regarding protection of property, exemption of relief supplies from customs duties and other taxes, and freedom from ration control. These difficulties, however, did not prevent fifty or more voluntary agencies from entering the field. Between September 1939 and December 1945 American voluntary agencies sent more than $500 million in goods and funds to war sufferers overseas; in the six years after the war private philanthropy raised approximately $2 billion for relief, reconstruction, and social services abroad. The aid furnished by voluntary organizations, impressive though it was, was insignificant in comparison to the appalling need. Nevertheless it reflected the light of American kindliness and goodwill, a candle if not a beacon in the stormy night.

Philanthropic contributions to postwar relief supplemented the much larger expenditures made by official agencies. In the period immediately after the war the American army spent as much as $500 million a year for civilian relief in countries where United States troops were stationed. Under the Marshall Plan, or European Recovery Program, which began in 1948 and continued until 1951, the United States helped nations of western Europe bolster their economies by means of grants and loans totaling $12.5 billion. The Marshall Plan was a form of prudent investment rather than a display of loving kindness and even ardent supporters of tax-supported foreign aid acknowledged that "person to person" giving possessed virtues that "government to government" assistance could never attain. Parcel post packages sent to friends and relatives in foreign countries accounted for a large share of personal giving. CARE and religious organizations such as the Roman Catholic War Relief Services and the Protestant Church World Service provided additional channels through which private citizens contributed relief supplies to individuals, churches, and charitable institutions overseas. In 1946 American Jews, numbering less than five million, collected $105 million for the United Jewish Appeal, and in 1948 they raised $150 million for it. With funds supplied by UJA the Joint Distribution Committee, United Palestine Appeal, and United Service for New Americans took European Jews out of displaced persons camps, assisted Jewish emigration and resettlement, and helped the new state of Israel in its fight for life.

War needs and war prosperity contributed in about equal measure to the generous support accorded assorted philanthropic causes in the 1940s. War taxes, although reaching levels which might reasonably have been expected to inhibit voluntary giving, did not in fact have that result. Charitable contributions reported in income tax returns were five times as large in 1945 as in 1939; corporation gifts increased nine times during these same years. Possibly the amounts given to charity might have been larger if taxes had been lower, but in the opinion of J. K. Lasser, the nation's favorite income tax adviser and author of *How Tax Laws Make Giving to Charity Easy* (1948), the taxing system fostered "the natural impulses to give to charity." The tax laws recognized the necessity and desirability of private contributions to charitable, religious, and educational institutions by permitting individuals and corporations to make tax-deductible gifts for philanthropic purposes. Progressive rates virtually assured that persons whose incomes were subject to surtaxes and corporations in the excess profit bracket would make contributions at least up to the limit of tax deductibility. For wealthy people and profitable corporations charity was a bargain, because what was given was mainly forgiven taxes. In the upper income brackets the question became not whether one could afford to give but whether one could afford not to give. It was not necessary for large givers to seek "tax loopholes" in order to take advantage of the inducements the revenue code offered donors. Their benefactions, although hard on the Treasury Department and presumably burdensome to other taxpayers, accorded with the letter and spirit of the law.

Income, inheritance, and corporation taxes, which continued at a high level in the decade after World War II, also contributed to a great increase in the number of foundations, one of the striking philanthropic developments of the postwar and cold war era. Out of consideration for the social utility of foundations the revenue code conferred various privileges upon them. Subject to certain restrictions, foundation income from investments was tax exempt; contributions to foundations were deductible; and the gifts and bequests they received were subject neither to gift nor estate taxes. Quite aside from tax benefits, the foundation provided a convenient method of channeling the gifts of large individual and corporate donors to beneficiaries; with tax advantages, and in the face of high income and estate taxes, the foundation was irresistible. In the late 1940s there was evidence that some foundations served the donors' business interests better than they served philanthropy. In 1948 a congressional investigation conducted by Senator Charles W. Tobey of New Hampshire uncovered some of the curious uses to which foundations might be put. They could and were being used to provide venture capital for industry, to safeguard dynastic control of business enterprises, and to permit ruthless operators to plunder and wreck going concerns. Of course the unscrupulous businessman could not pocket the foundation's tax-free profits but, as trustee, he could use them for further piratical ventures. As one observer noted, there might even be something left over for occasional gifts to charity.

Separating foundation goats from foundation sheep was not easy, and eradicating those which were simply tax-evasion schemes without hurting legitimate foundations was even more difficult. A complicated revision of the revenue code adopted in 1950 dealt with the worst abuses. Under the new law, foundations might lose tax-exempt status if their records showed they existed mainly for the accumulation of capital or if they engaged in certain transactions which diverted income or principal to the donor or his associates. In any case income obtained by conducting a business unrelated to the foundation's ordinary purpose was subject to taxation. Nevertheless the legal or not yet prohibited forms of tax benefit enjoyed by foundations remained sufficiently appealing to encourage further growth. By the mid-1950s their number exceeded 5,000 by conservative estimate and approached 7,500 by some counts.

In the early 1950s the larger and more reputable foundations whose financial affairs were conducted with such probity that they expressed willingness to operate in a fishbowl, were subject to a different kind of scrutiny. Had they made grants to support un-American or subversive activities? If so to whom? When? Why? How much? Since government offices, universities, public schools, churches, motion picture studios, and radio and television networks were under attack for harboring subversive elements, and since philosophical systems, methods of scholarship, textbooks, folktales, and works of art were widely suspected of spreading un-American attitudes, it was only natural that foundations should also be subjected to congressional investigation.

There were two probes. The first, held in 1952 under the auspices of the Select (Cox) Committee of the House of Representatives, asked the larger foundations to answer a searching 100-item questionnaire, and through public hearings, interviews, and correspondence gathered additional material on foundation operations. The committee reported that in a few instances foundations had made grants to individuals or associations subsequently "cited or criticized" by congressional committees, but that the general record of the foundations was good. The second or Special (Reece) Committee investigation of 1954 was less judiciously conducted. Its chairman, paid staff, and practically all the witnesses permitted to testify reiterated that foundations, educational institutions, and research organizations were involved in a "diabolical conspiracy" to

foist socialism on the American people. By a majority vote
the committee ended the hearings without permitting the
foundations to reply, except through written statements. In
a minority report two members of the committee called the
proceedings "an ugly stain" on the record of the House of
Representatives. Whatever disservice the committee
rendered the House, it did no serious harm to foundations.
Editorial reaction to the Reece Committee was distinctly
unfavorable. Foundations were already unpopular with
extreme rightists; nobody else took the majority report
seriously—least of all, apparently, one of the members of
the committee who accompanied his signature of the report
with a statement expressing disapproval of its principal
findings and conclusions.

Foundation officers have long maintained that it is
extremely difficult to give money away wisely. In the late
1940s and 1950s they did not suffer from lack of advice.
Edwin R. Embree, formerly president of the Rosenwald
Fund and an old Rockefeller Foundation hand, warned the
foundations against "scatteration." William H. Whyte, Jr.,
the anti-organization man, reminded them of their
obligation to support the individual researcher. The Cox
Committee made it plain that foundations were expected to
check on the "loyalty" of scholars, musicians, artists, and
research institutions before making grants to them.
Seymour Harris, a distinguished economist, advised
foundations and nonprofit research organizations to avoid
public policy issues and to concentrate on collecting and
organizing facts. Congressman B. Carroll Reece, who
regarded "empiricism" as a dangerous, un-American "ism,"
wanted to know why foundations did not support "pro-
American projects" such as "studies regarding the
excellence of the American Constitution, the importance of
the Declaration of Independence, and the profundity of

the philosophy of the Founding Fathers"? William H. Whyte, writing in *Fortune*, a comparatively safe platform from which to make the suggestion, urged foundations to exercise "their ability and will to contribute to changes in the status quo of American life." All these recommendations implied dissatisfaction with current foundation practices. The most serious was Edwin Embree's charge that foundation giving was becoming "conventional and stereotyped" and that there was "an ominous absence of that social pioneering that is the essential business of foundations."

The principal recipient and target of this advice and criticism was the Ford Foundation, which was the newest face and had the fattest purse in the foundation world. Although organized in 1936, the Ford Foundation concentrated on local and family affairs until after the death of Henry Ford in 1947 and did not become active nationally until the early 1950s. Then, in possession of 90 percent of the stock of one of the nation's greatest corporations, it was in a position, and necessarily obligated, to spend on a larger scale and broader front than any other foundation. Its resources, counted in billions rather than millions, comprised one-third of the combined assets of all foundations, and by 1954 its annual appropriations represented between a fourth and a fifth of total foundation spending.

The most striking thing about the Ford Foundation was its announced decision to spend money "in the difficult and sometimes controversial task of helping to realize democracy's goals." This meant problem solving, not in the relatively safe and approved areas of medical and biological research, but in the social sciences, education, and the field of international understanding. To solve its own problem of rapidly accumulating funds the foundation set up a number of autonomous organizations such as the Fund for the

Advancement of Education, Fund for Adult Education, Fund for the Republic, Resources for the Future, Center for Advanced Study in the Behavioral Sciences, and the National Merit Scholarship Corporation. Some of the foundation's direct grants for research in the social or behavioral sciences supported teams of scholars engaged in efforts to solve problems which, in the opinion of critics, were scarcely problems and hardly worth solving. On the other hand the foundation's largest gift—the largest ever made by a foundation—was universally praised. This was a special appropriation of $560 million announced in December 1955 to assist privately supported colleges and universities to raise teachers' salaries, to help privately supported medical schools strengthen instruction, and to enable privately supported nonprofit hospitals to extend and improve services. Toward the end of the 1950s in addition to conducting foreign aid and fellowship programs, supporting experiments in educational television, and supplying venture capital to both the more and less venturesome areas of scholarship, the foundation began to make grants to novelists, poets, artists, musicians, composers, and dramatists.

Even after the advent of the Ford Foundation individual donors continued to provide roughly 75 percent of the nation's total contribution to philanthropy. The foundations' share was about 8 percent, which was slightly more than the percentage from charitable bequests and somewhat more than that of corporation gifts. The total—half of which went to religion—was unprecedentedly high: $5.4 billion in 1954, $6.7 billion in 1957, and proved to be well in excess of $8 billion in 1960. Of course these amounts would not buy as much in the 1950s as in earlier decades, and they were drawn from and had to be spread over a constantly growing population. On the other hand, some charitable obligations were declining because social insurance, buttressed by industrial health and welfare programs, pension plans, and unemployment benefits had strengthened the economic security of workers and their families. Neither governmental nor private welfare programs actually assured the American people against want, but it was certain that never again would voluntary benevolence be expected to play the dominant role in relieving sheer economic need. For this very reason philanthropy's role became more complex, and its responsibility for devising and demonstrating helpful services was heavier than ever before.

Private welfare agencies were no longer supported only by the rich and they no longer catered only to the poor. They were community enterprises offering counsel, guidance, and opportunities for growth to people at all economic levels. In a real but new sense the old charity organization motto, "Not alms but a friend," was the program of philanthropy in the 1950s.

Alms, if not being distributed to the needy, were still being collected by a variety of organizations through house-to-house and direct mail solicitations. Some of these were frauds which, in the 1950s, took an estimated $120 million a year from unwary givers. The vast majority, however, were legitimate and a great many had to do with health—or rather disease. It was a rare week (some said night) which did not find mothers marching up and down Main Street armed with collection kits supplied by one or another of the fifty national and innumerable local disease-combating associations. The National Foundation for Infantile Paralysis set the pace, not only in fund-raising but in accomplishing its mission. After scoring a brilliant victory over paralytic polio with the Salk vaccine in 1955, the agency shortened its name to the National Foundation and turned toward the conquest of rheumatic diseases, birth defects, and disorders of the central nervous system.

Social workers and public health experts, without disputing the great service rendered by the National Foundation, American Cancer Society, American Heart Association, and similar groups, questioned whether separate attacks on different ailments added up to an effective program for fighting disease and promoting health. As long as salesmanship and emotional appeal were the tests of support, comparatively rare diseases received as much or more attention than the more serious and prevalent ones. Meanwhile businessmen, labor leaders, newspaper editors, and housewives became resentful of the ever-recurring drives. At the end of the 1950s it seemed probable that the United Fund (a combined community chest and national agency campaign) or some variation of it (such as one drive for local agencies and another for national organizations) would sooner or later cut down the number of separate solicitations by agencies in similar lines of work.

At midcentury the most difficult, vital, and in many ways most traditional tasks of American philanthropy lay in the field of foreign aid. Helping those in need wherever they might be was no new experience for the people of the United States. The obligation was as old as belief in the stewardship of wealth and the gospel of doing good. Distance was no barrier to neighborly kindness in an era of instantaneous communications and swift travel; and even if Americans had been less disposed toward benevolence than they were, considerations of self-interest and national security would have required them to pay serious attention to the plight of the three-fifths of the world's population living in near-misery. The poverty of these people, as President Harry S. Truman warned in 1949, was a handicap and a threat both to the sufferers and to the rest of the world.

The "Point Four" program whose outlines President Truman sketched in his inaugural address of January 20, 1949, envisaged a cooperative attack on world poverty through technical assistance and capital investment in underdeveloped or overexploited areas. In 1950 Congress implemented the technical assistance features of this "bold new program" by adopting the Act for International Development. In the Mutual Security Act of 1957 Congress provided for the establishment of a new and potentially important lending agency, the Development Loan Fund. Meanwhile, supported in part through funds supplied by the United States, United Nations' agencies such as the Food and Agriculture Organization, World Health Organization, International Children's Fund, and International Bank for Reconstruction and Development expanded their efforts to help undeveloped areas increase the productivity of their soils and workshops and improve the health and living standards of their people.

This was the kind of work in which American missionaries had been active for a century or longer. At the start of the Point Four program religious organizations and other voluntary agencies were operating approximately 2,500 social service, medical, educational, agricultural, and even industrial projects in Latin America, Africa, the Middle East, and Asia. In the 1950s organized philanthropic efforts overseas (as distinguished from assistance sent by individuals to relatives, friends, and strangers abroad) were coordinated by the American Council of Voluntary Agencies for Foreign Service, and mildly supervised by the Advisory Committee on Voluntary Aid (successor to the President's War Relief Control Board), which operated under the United States International Cooperation Administration. In one fairly typical year, 1956, private gifts for foreign relief totaled $535 million or about 8 percent of all American philanthropic expenditures. The money was used to sow corn and dig wells in Mexico, develop improved varieties of wheat in Columbia, plant trees in Italy, take mason jars to

Greece, found a library school and an institute of business administration in Turkey, set up social work demonstrations in Indian villages, and send fishing equipment to cooperatives in Hong Kong. All these and many other projects undertaken by philanthropy continued in the familiar pattern of encouraging self-help and building ladders for the aspiring. The Rockefeller and Ford Foundations were engaged in this work. So was CARE. But it was significant that a great deal of foreign relief and technical assistance was sponsored by religious groups and conducted by employees and volunteers in the service organizations of the various denominations and faiths.

Quantitatively, American philanthropy played only a minor role in the crusade to promote the economic and social development of the poorer half of the world's population. Attempts to measure philanthropy by monetary standards, however, result either in cynicism or complacency and are bound to be misleading. The relatively small share of foreign aid expenditures borne by voluntary agencies did not accurately indicate either the actual or the potential contributions of philanthropy to the work at hand. Limited budgets, as organizations like the American Friends Service Committee regularly proved, were no barriers to useful service. Voluntary agencies supervised the distribution of American food surpluses. They participated, sometimes on a contractual basis, in technical training and agricultural demonstrations. But, as always, the contribution of philanthropy lay less in specific deeds than in a tendency to influence social policy toward responsible action and humane goals. Religious organizations and periodicals were among the most vocal and vigorous champions of Point Four, and the churches were perhaps the most important influence in building up popular support for foreign economic aid.

During the 1950s, partly as a result of the Korean War and the intensification of the cold war, governmental spending for "mutual security," or military assistance to foreign countries, consumed the lion's share of appropriations for foreign aid. The Point Four program, however, was not abandoned. In 1957, when the total outlay for foreign aid was $8 billion, roughly 20 percent or about $1.7 billion was designated for economic and technical assistance. Critics denounced Point Four as a "giveaway," "global charity," and "compulsory benevolence." Supporters viewed economic assistance as an endeavor in which national self-interest coincided with national idealism and asserted that appropriations for it should be doubled. Others, sympathizing with the objectives of the program, questioned its organization and methods of operation. There was room for wide difference of opinion on these points. Some observers, consciously or unconsciously adopting the point of view of scientific philanthropy, suggested that the multiplicity of governmental, intergovernmental, and voluntary agencies participating in technical assistance, the short term, project-by-project approach followed by most of the operating agencies, and the confusion caused by lack of central leadership and direction were more serious handicaps than inadequate financial support. At the end of the decade the whole foreign aid program, military as well as economic, was under review by Congress.

The voyage Franklin proposed in 1771 was still, almost two centuries later, a very chancy venture. In addition to and quite as important as the question of support or opposition at home, there was the problem of reception abroad. If those who supplied the money were restless, those who received the assistance were proud, suspicious, fearful of being bought. Since technical assistance was essentially an effort to help people help themselves, its effectiveness depended as much on the initiative of the recipients as on the generosity of benefactors. Yet even with the best of intention on both sides there were complicating factors. Every improvement in health and reduction in mortality in undeveloped areas increased the pressure of population on food supplies. Unless production of food kept pace with increasing population, achievement of decent levels of consumption would be impossible. In spite of problems of this sort one school of thought maintained that modern knowledge made human want obsolete. According to other experts the gap was widening, poorer countries growing relatively poorer, hungry continents becoming still hungrier.

Everyone agreed that the extraordinary needs of the age demanded knowledge as well as goodwill. It was frequently said that fostering economic growth under conditions of freedom was the most challenging task of the twentieth century. Certainly it was one of the most difficult assignments modern man had consciously attempted. The outcome was admittedly a gamble. Whether the risks involved in the undertaking were greater than the possible consequences of failure to act was an unsettled issue.

As the United States entered the second half of the twentieth century, problems that had formerly troubled a few wealthy philanthropists had become the common concern of all citizens. This was true not only because services previously supported by private benevolence were now maintained by taxation but also because the United States had the largest national and per capita wealth of any nation. In facing the problems of a revolutionary epoch the American people had the advantage of great material resources wrested by labor and intelligence from a once underdeveloped continent. They could draw upon the knowledge and skills acquired, and profit from the mistakes made in three and a half centuries of hard-fought struggle to win justice, education, security, and opportunity for all. The American record abounded in men and women sensitive to the misfortunes of their fellows and willing to make others' causes their own. Americans had a long experience in founding voluntary agencies to perform tasks which individuals could not accomplish alone and which public bodies, for one reason or another, were not able to undertake. They had had long experience with charity, too. They knew that charity was subject to abuse, by the giver as well as the taker, and that the most effective and acceptable form of benevolence was not endless, soul-satisfying almsgiving but sensible efforts to help people become independent and prepared to work out their own destinies.

I I

Looking Backward, 1980s–1960s

... the difference between the age of
individualism and that of concert was well
characterized by the fact that, in the nineteenth
century, when it rained, the people of Boston
put up three hundred thousand umbrellas over
as many heads, and in the twentieth century they
put up one umbrella over all the heads.

"We might, indeed, have much larger incomes,
individually, if we chose so to use the surplus of
our product, but we prefer to expend it upon
public works and pleasures in which all
share. . . . You have not begun to see how we
live yet, Mr. West. At home we have comfort,
but the splendor of our life is on its social side,
that which we share with our fellows."

EDWARD BELLAMY

Edward Bellamy's *Looking Backward, 2000–1887* (1888)
contrasted the harsh and depressing reality of urban
existence in late nineteenth-century American with the
more gracious and genial life he believed Americans might

enjoy in the latter part of the twentieth century if they replaced competition and individualism with cooperation and socialism. In the 1980s, despite revolutionary advances in technology and communication, no American city had installed the kind of shelter against inclement weather Bellamy described in his book. Not only when it rained, but in dealing with numerous other problems, Americans continued to rely on individualistic, voluntary solutions. Since the big change in values Bellamy anticipated had not come about, Americans in the 1980s were chary of expenditures for public pleasures or needs other than those related to national defense. They ranked the private side of life above the social, and, as a matter of principle, fostered the former and stinted the latter.

"But," to repeat a question Bellamy posed about Americans in the 1880s, "did they think only of themselves?" The answer in the 1980s, as a century earlier, was an emphatic "no." In a society that encouraged private spending and accumulation, private giving and voluntary association for public purposes enjoyed popular and official favor. Each year for more than a quarter century after 1960 recorders of American philanthropy reported that total giving by individuals, foundations, corporations, and charitable bequests had reached a new high. The total for 1985—approximately $80 billion—was more than two and one-half times as large as a decade earlier, almost four times as large as in 1970, and more than seven times the amount—roughly $11 billion—raised in 1960. Of course a dollar contributed to charity did not buy as much in the 1980s or 1970s as in 1960 and so the real increase in giving was more modest than current dollar figures indicate. As the table below shows, when the changing value of the dollar is taken into account, the total for 1985 was a little more than twice as large as the total for 1960.

ESTIMATED TOTAL GIVING, 1955–1985

Year	Amount in Billions Current Dollars[a]	Amount in Billions 1986 Dollars[b]	Index (1955 = 100.0)[b]
1955	7.70	31.53	100.0
1956	8.33	33.61	106.6
1957	9.26	36.07	114.4
1958	9.50	36.03	114.3
1959	10.37	39.01	123.7
1960	10.92	40.43	128.2
1961	11.36	41.64	132.1
1962	11.88	43.06	136.6
1963	13.21	47.31	150.0
1964	13.70	48.43	153.6
1965	14.75	51.26	162.6
1966	15.80	53.38	169.3
1967	17.04	55.96	177.5
1968	18.95	59.72	189.4
1969	20.79	62.18	197.2
1970	21.02	59.35	188.2
1971	23.44	63.46	201.3
1972	24.48	64.16	203.5
1973	25.70	63.41	201.1
1974	26.98	59.99	190.3
1975	28.61	58.28	184.9
1976	32.06	61.75	195.8
1977	36.34	65.75	208.5
1978	38.95	65.46	207.6
1979	43.69	66.00	209.3
1980	48.74	64.86	205.7
1981	55.49	66.90	212.2
1982	60.04	68.20	216.3
1983	64.96	71.49	226.7
1984	73.70	77.80	246.7
1985	79.84	81.38	258.1

[a]American Association of Fund Raising Counsel, *Giving USA: Estimates of Philanthropic Giving in 1985 and the Trends They Show* (New York, 1986), 41.

[b]Computations supplied by Independent Sector on basis of *Economic Report of the President* (Washington, D.C., 1987), 307.

The favorable official attitude toward philanthropy was expressed in state and federal laws that exempted charitable, religious, and educational organizations from property and income taxes and encouraged taxpayers to make contributions to them. During the 1960s the federal tax code allowed individuals to deduct a maximum of 30 percent of gross income for contributions to exempt organizations; corporations had the right—although few of them chose to exercise it—to deduct charitable contributions of up to 5 percent of income; and bequests to exempt organizations paid no federal estate tax. In 1960 the Internal Revenue Service recognized 45,124 exempt organizations including churches, foundations, community funds, and associations active in many different fields and serving the public interest in diverse ways. Supporters advanced numerous justifications for the organizations' privileged tax status: they performed public services not available from government or not appropriate for government to offer; they assured a variety of sources of support for activities benefiting the common welfare; and tax deductible gifts to them, unlike other deductions such as interest payments, encouraged money to be spent in the public interest rather than for private gain.

How the Tax Laws Help You to Help Others was the title of a leaflet produced by United Community Funds and Councils of America for use in the 1965 fund drive. The issue that attracted increasing attention from reporters, members of Congress, and bureaucrats throughout the decade was the extent to which rich people were using tax laws to help themselves, their families, and their businesses. The approximately 15,000 private charitable foundations whose numbers had enjoyed spectacular growth in the 1950s and were being augmented at the rate of 1,200 a year in the early 1960s were particularly suspect. Friends as well as critics of philanthropy pointed to the abuses of family and company foundations where (in the words of Julian Levi of the University of Chicago) "sweet charity began at home by first locking the door to the Internal Revenue Service and then considering a remote, intangible, delayed benefit to society at large."

In May 1961 Congressman Wright Patman of Texas, a Democratic member of the House of Representatives since 1929, urged Congress to take a close look at foundations to determine which of them were flying under false colors. In the following years, as chairman of a subcommittee of the House Committee on Small Business, Patman issued reports and conducted hearings highlighting his views that foundations, by and large, were tax dodges, instruments promoting the concentration of wealth and power in the hands of a few rich families, detrimental to competition and small business, and subject to only lax and sporadic control by public authorities. Reporting on the alleged machinations of one foundation Patman asserted, "If this mixture of high finance and tangled directorate and officers appears baffling, it is because it is baffling."

Early in 1963, announcing plans for an expanded audit system not only for foundations but for all tax-exempt organizations, the commissioner of Internal Revenue acknowledged that Patman's investigations had been of assistance in and had provided the impetus for IRS audits disclosing violations of the letter and spirit of the tax laws. A Treasury Department report prepared at the request of the Senate Finance Committee and the House Ways and Means Committee, issued in 1965, stated, "The preponderant number of private foundations perform their functions without tax abuse," but noted major problems in six areas of foundation practice: self-dealing, delay in benefit to charity, involvement in business, family use of foundation to control property, financial transactions unrelated to charitable functions, and need for broadening the base of foundation management.

The Treasury Department recommendations for dealing with these problems, although endorsed by President Johnson, were not acted on by Congress until after the election of 1968. By that time the number of foundations had grown to about 22,000, with assets of $20.5 billion and annual grants totaling $1.5 billion. The Tax Reform Act of 1969, a measure of such complexity it was sometimes called the Lawyers Relief Act, devoted about one-third of its considerable length to charitable tax deductions in general and to rules and regulations—forty-six pages of them— regarding foundations. The law increased the allowable deduction for contributions to charitable organizations other than foundations from 30 to 50 percent of income while retaining the 20 percent deductibility limit on gifts to foundations. This decision was in keeping with the act's underlying assumption that charitable organizations dependent upon the public for support were less suspect and less in need of supervision than private foundations endowed by a single individual or family. Misdeeds of the former could be corrected by loss of public favor and, if necessary, withdrawal of tax exemption and deductibility; the latter needed stricter sanctions to prevent or punish misbehavior. Accordingly, the law charged foundations an "audit-fee tax" of 4 percent of net income, limited foundation stockholding in any one company to 25 percent, prohibited grants to donors or their relatives, and placed restrictions on grants to individuals. Foundations were required to distribute at least 6 percent of income annually and were forbidden to use their funds for influencing legislation or the outcome of elections. The law directed foundations to make fuller reports on their activities and financial status than had been required in the past and imposed stringent penalties on foundations, their managers, and major contributors for violation of the terms of the act.

The law did not include harsher restrictions such as a twenty-five- or forty-year limitation on the life of foundations, which had been proposed and considered in congressional debate. Testimony in favor of foundations by Jonas Salk, discoverer of the polio vaccine; Theodore Hesburgh, president of Notre Dame University; and James R. Killian, Jr., science adviser to President Eisenhower, and vigorous lobbying by other leaders in science, education, and the arts seem to have had a moderating influence on the legislation.

The Tax Reform Act of 1969 capped a decade of political liberalism, economic growth, racial strife, urban violence, and expansion of governmental activity in education, civil rights, and social welfare. For philanthropy it was a turbulent but hopeful period marked not only by increases in resources but by shifts in program and direction. Giving rose modestly in the first half of the decade, sharply in the second half. Of the estimated $148 billion donated to charity in the 1960s, just under 80 percent came from individuals; foundations and bequests contributed about 8 percent each; and corporations gave 5 percent of the total. Religion, the only part of the philanthropic sector entirely dependent on voluntary giving, received almost half the total, but its share (46 percent) was lower than in earlier decades. One-third went in approximately equal portions to education (mainly colleges and universities) and health (including hospitals and research). Welfare received less than either education or health and, like religion, a smaller part of the total (7 percent) than formerly. The amount given for civic and cultural activities and for support of the arts, although comparatively small (5 percent), was substantially larger than in the past.

Gathering and dispensing the nation's annual philanthropic yield involved a good deal of competition and controversy in ordinary times and probably more than usual in an era of increasing affluence and heightened social awareness. Federated fund-raisers in 2,200 United Way communities resented the separate fund drives conducted by "go-it-alone" health agencies, deplored the possibility of a consolidated campaign by national health agencies, and opposed initiation of a combined federal campaign for government employees. Donors, facing an avalanche of appeals, had to decide which agencies and causes to support, and to what extent. Individuals could pick and choose with impunity but the decisions posed hard problems for associated, corporate, and foundation givers who could expect recriminations whether they gave only to conventional causes or included radical, unpopular ones in their largesse. Under the pressure of black protest and federal civil rights legislation, and to the consternation of established supporters and clients in some communities, philanthropic organizations moved to desegregate services, facilities, and employment practices, and to involve minorities and the poor in volunteering and decision making. Church debates on the rival claims of brick-and-mortar or blacktop projects versus social action programs hardly prepared members and clergy for a 1969 demand from James Forman of the National Black Economic Development Conference for $500 million in reparations for past injustice to black Americans.

To some observers government intrusion into areas formerly the preserve of voluntary activity comprised a more serious threat to philanthropy than internal rivalries.

In social welfare the primacy of government had been acknowledged for a quarter century before the new programs and increased spending entailed by the War on Poverty. The Civil Rights Act and federal aid to education brought "Washington" into close contact with public and private schools, colleges, and universities. Adoption of Medicare and Medicaid in 1965 suggested that government was on the way to becoming as dominant in health care as it was in welfare and the financing of hospital construction. Creation of the National Endowments for the Arts and the Humanities (1965), although initial appropriation for both agencies were miniscule, foretold a larger public role in the support of culture and scholarship. With the Peace Corps (1961), VISTA (1965), Teacher Corps (1965), and a variety of Office of Economic Opportunities programs for both young and old, even volunteering seemed to be evolving into a federally supported function. In view of the "lopsided availability of tax dollars over voluntary dollars," a concerned social worker raised the question, "Are voluntary agencies necessary?"

The government, at least, seemed to find voluntary agencies helpful in extending social services to new fields and a broader clientele. In the 1960s, to a greater extent than at any time since the New Deal, government agencies, instead of providing services directly through their own offices, entered into contracts with, purchased services from, or made grants to private agencies. Some of the latter were new organizations created to carry out provisions of the Economic Opportunity Act of 1964; others were established agencies glad to use federal funds to make up for declining receipts from private donors. The 1967 amendments to the Social Security Act, authorizing a greater variety of services than had been provided under previous amendments, encouraged their purchase from private sources. By 1968, when numerous United Way agencies reported they were receiving substantial government grants, the system of using voluntary agencies to deliver service paid for by public funds was taking shape. Opinion differed on whether the new relationship threatened the autonomy of philanthropy by subordinating it to government or represented a sensible collaboration that strengthened society's ability to cope with human problems.

While public pressure kept most voluntary agencies on well-worn, socially approved paths, a few foundations—or a portion of foundation grants—supported innovative and controversial activities. The Field Foundation, small in comparison to giants like Ford and Rockefeller, declared in its report for 1965: "Great opportunity exists for experimentation to devise methods by which private resources may be used to supplement public resources for the benefit of both the community and the individual. Private foundations have an opportunity and a responsibility in this direction." Few foundations had been more active than Field, organized in 1940 by Marshall Field III, in searching out such opportunities. Concerned for many years with promoting child welfare and interracial and intercultural relations, Field joined in the early 1960s with the Stern Family Fund and Taconic and New World foundations in supporting militant black organizations in voter registration drives in the South. Later in the decade Field Foundation grants made it possible for a coalition of women's organizations to study the operation of the federal school lunch program and issue a report pointing out inadequacies in its coverage, financing, and administration. In 1966 and 1967 Leslie Dunbar, director of the Field Foundation, and a group of physicians associated with the foundation inspected preschool health conditions in Mississippi; one of the physicians, Milton J. E. Senn,

Sterling Professor of Pediatrics at Yale University, was the first witness at the Congressional Hearings on Hunger and Malnutrition in America that ultimately led to the calling of the 1969 White House Conference on Food, Nutrition, and Health.

Ford Foundation resources assured that its presence would be felt in whatever field of philanthropy it entered. During the 1960s Ford made significant grants affecting education, the arts, educational and public television, civil rights, civil liberties, law and the administration of justice, race relations, poverty, and the disadvantaged. The foundation's challenge grants, totaling about $350 million to private colleges and universities, produced an additional $1 billion in matching grants to the fortunate institutions; matching requirements of $80 million in challenge grants to twenty-six symphony orchestras taxed (some said overtaxed) the philanthropic resources of the communities in which the orchestras were located. Ford's Public Affairs Program turned from efforts to bring research and scholarship in the social sciences to bear on contemporary urban problems toward demonstration of "action" projects addressing education and deliquency in the slums and mobilizing the electoral strength of minority communities. Paul N. Ylvisaker, the head of the program, asserted in 1963 that because of the gravity of the urban crisis "philanthropy will have to start doing business with City Hall."

In *The Big Foundations* (1972) Waldemar A. Nielsen charged that the major foundations lagged behind black leadership and government in dealing with the racial and social upheavals of the 1960s. By the latter half of the decade, however, foundations large and small were deeply involved in social issues. A survey of foundation giving in 1968 showed that 18 percent of all foundation grants were directed to urban problems, poverty, and race relations.

Ford doubled the budget of its Public Affairs Program in 1966 and over the next four years made grants to promote action by minority groups to improve housing, employment, and education, to support legal aid to the poor, and to establish public interest law centers serving the interests of consumers, the environment, and minorities. In 1968 the foundation announced that it would invest part of its portfolio in minority-owned businesses and in low-income and racially integrated housing. In the same year Ford grants established the Center for Community Change to "enhance the voice of the poor in their own destiny." Some of Ford's grants went to established organizations such as the National Association for the Advancement of Colored People and the Urban League, others to inexperienced groups and even to street gangs. "Never in the history of American philanthropy," declared Nielsen in *The Golden Donors* (1985), "had anything comparable in scale and aggressiveness to the Ford Foundation's assault on the problem of race and poverty been seen."

At least some of the Ford Foundation's action, including support of school decentralization in New York City, aid to voter registration drives in different sections of the country, and experimental programs in juvenile delinquency, received critical attention in Congress when the Tax Reform Act of 1969 was under consideration. At the time of the act's passage foundation supporters wondered whether its punitive provisions would limit foundation grants to safe, noncontroversial areas. Whether the prohibition on use of foundation funds for influencing legislation or the outcome of elections would be strictly or liberally interpreted was a matter of particular concern to those who believed philanthropy had a legitimate role to play in advocacy and the shaping of public policy.

I 2

Giving for Home and Overseas

People give to help people, but they give, too, to
reduce their tax burden.
AAFRC SPOKESMAN, FRED SCHNAUE

In 1970 Boys Town, one of America's favorite and best-
supported charities, raised $17.7 million in response to its
requests for small gifts to "bring happiness to homeless and
unwanted boys." This information was contained in information filed with the Internal Revenue Service in compliance with the financial disclosure provisions of the Tax
Reform Act of 1969. The report also revealed that Boys
Town had an endowment of $200 million, larger than all
but a few universities, and annual expenditures of $9 mil-
lion, one-third of which went for fund-raising. During the
next few years Boys Town's board of directors took steps to
put the institution's embarrassment of riches to productive
use.

In the mid-1970s estimates of the cost of raising a
charitable dollar ranged from 26 cents in Illinois to 13.8
cents in New York State. Throughout the decade charges of

questionable uses of funds and excessive fund-raising and administrative costs continued to be leveled against charitable organizations. Just as the conduct of foundations had seemed to require corrections in the 1960s so, in the 1970s, according to many state and local officials, the activities of charities that solicited money from the public needed to be brought under closer scrutiny. By the end of the decade twenty states and numerous county and local governments had adopted laws or ordinances limiting charity solicitations to organizations that could prove a sizable proportion of the collection went for charitable purposes rather than for salaries and administrative costs.

Foundations felt repercussions from the Tax Reform Act of 1969 for a number of years after its passage. The *Foundation Directory* observed in 1975, "The law tends to inhibit birth of new foundations and encourages dissolution of small ones." About 400 foundations with assets of at least $1 million were established in the 1970s, roughly half as many as in the 1960s and one-third as many as in the 1950s. Since only foundations with assets of more than $10 million were in a position to make grants of significant size, universities and other organizations seeking support for research or new programs found their options limited. In 1971 $25.6 million of foundation funds that might otherwise have supported grants went to the federal government in payment of the tax on foundation assets. In 1978 Congress reduced the excise tax from 4 to 2 percent. The total collected between 1971 and 1985 exceeded $1.2 billion, about three times the actual cost to the IRS of monitoring foundation operations.

An explanation of the Tax Reform Act issued in 1970 by the staff of the Congressional Joint Committee on Internal Revenue Taxation stated that while the intent of the act was to prohibit and punish foundations for lobbying, electioneering, or attempting to influence legislation by efforts to affect public opinion, the act did not prevent foundations from supporting "the examinations of broad, social, economic, and similar problems of the type the government could be expected to deal with ultimately." This qualified assurance was accompanied by a warning that Congress believed foundations must take responsibility "for the proper use of the funds they give away." In the circumstances, foundation boards, traditionally deemed conservative, tended to be more than ordinarily cautious, to pay strict heed to the advice of lawyers and accountants, and to award grants to well-established institutions and organizations rather than to inexperienced or controversial ones. During the Nixon administration the tax-exempt status of civil rights, welfare rights, environmental, and antiwar groups, and public interest law firms received censorious attention from the Internal Revenue Service. In 1974 Alan Pifer, president of the Carnegie Corporation of New York, called the situation "paradoxical": foundations were advised they could engage in activities bearing on public policy development but given to understand that it would be unwise to do so.

The economic climate of the 1970s was even less favorable for foundations than the political atmosphere. The recession that began in 1973 sharply reduced the market value of foundation assets—losses of 30 to 40 percent were not uncommon and in some cases exceeded 60 percent—and caused Ford, Carnegie, and other foundations to reduce the number and size of grants awarded. Grant totals, when adjusted for inflation, were smaller in 1979 than in 1969; in the latter year for the first time since 1950 corporate gifts to philanthropy were slightly larger than foundation grants. This was more the result of foundation weakness than a surge of generosity on the part of corporations. The latter contributed a smaller percentage of pretax income in 1979 than in 1971 when *The Wall Street Journal* commented that the richest corporations were "skinflints" in their charitable behavior; in both years the amount donated to philanthropy was closer to 1 percent of pretax income than to the 5 percent permitted by law.

Philanthropic giving as a whole grew at a sluggish pace in the 1970s and in some years failed to keep pace with inflation. For a decade after 1969 private giving declined as a percentage of gross national product, and when measured against government spending for nondefense purposes was relatively smaller in the mid-1970s than in 1960. In the face of higher food, fuel, housing, and other costs, individual donors—the most important source of philanthropic contributions—economized on gifts to church and charity. Personal giving as a percentage of total personal income, which had stood at around 2 percent in the 1960s, began to fall in 1973 and by 1980 was below the level of 1970 and 1960. The fall-off in giving seemed most pronounced in the large section of the population with incomes from $10,000 to $25,000 a year.

The feeling on the part of leaders of the nonprofit community that philanthropy was not keeping pace with the economy and that its significance in American life was not sufficiently recognized by either government or business led to the establishment in 1973 of a privately supported Commission on Private Philanthropy and Public Needs. The commission, chaired by John Filer of Aetna Life and Casualty Company, utilized the help of scholars and other experts in law, economics, health, education, sociology, and history to collect and analyze data on the current state and characteristics of the nonprofit sector, its relations with government and private enterprise, and the impact of charitable giving on American society. The five volumes of research papers assembled for the commission revealed more clearly than ever before the scope and ramifications of the philanthropic, nonprofit sector: it involved a total of about 6 million voluntary organizations including 350,000 religious groups, 37,000 human service organizations, 6,000 museums, 5,500 private libraries, 4,600 private secondary schools, 3,500 private hospitals, 1,514 private colleges and universities, and 1,100 symphony orchestras. In 1974, according to the commission's estimate, the philanthropic ledger included not only about $25 billion in gifts, but also $32 billion in service charges and endowment income, and $23 billion in government funding (conversely some private giving went to public institutions such as state colleges and universities). In a report published in 1975 the commission called for the establishment of a permanent national commission on philanthropy, expansion of corporate giving, changes in the tax laws to encourage further giving, and removal of restrictions on efforts to influence legislation by charitable organizations other than foundations.

The commission's report was accompanied by a counterstatement issued by the Donee Group, a coalition of minority, women's, public interest, and social action voluntary organizations that had acted as an advisor to the commission. The Donee Group, as its name indicated, represented the recipients (actually would-be recipients since their applications were so often rejected) rather than donors of philanthropy. Using the research assembled for the commission the Donee Group came to different conclusions about the relevance and vitality of mainstream philanthropy. It charged that philanthropy's resources were seldom accessible to groups striving to cope with emerging social problems and that, far from providing the venture capital for social change, philanthropy had become bureaucratic, conservative, and even less willing than government to take risks. The Donee Group, adopting the name Committee for Responsive Philanthropy, continued in existence after the demise of the Commission on Private Philanthropy and Public Needs, serving, in the words of Waldemar A. Nielsen, as "a useful gadfly on the foundation rump." The committee also provided leadership for the growing number of nontraditional charitable organizations in their efforts to participate in fund drives involving payroll contributions.

Rules against lobbying by tax-exempt organizations, criticized in the reports of both the commission and Donee Group, went back to 1934 and had been reiterated in 1954 and strengthened in 1969. Efforts at relaxation of the rules began in the latter year when the American Bar Association, citing an act of Congress adopted in 1962 that allowed business firms to claim expenditures for lobbying and trade association dues as deductible business expenses, charged that the neutrality of the tax laws with respect to lobbying had been upset in favor of business interests against charitable organizations. In the next seven years measures proposing correction of the situation came before Congress on several occasions. In addition to the fairness issue advocates of relaxation questioned the constitutionality of the restrictions and charged that the Nixon administration used IRS audits to harass groups that criticized or opposed its policies. Beginning in 1973 the Coalition of Concerned Charities, representing eighty national voluntary associations with millions of members throughout the country, gave vigorous assistance to the efforts of Congressman Barber Conable of New York and Senator Edmund Muskie of Maine to obtain corrective legislation and gradually overcame the assumption of members and staff of congressional tax-writing committees that the matter was "not considered a high-priority issue." By 1976 the Muskie-Conable bill had strong bipartisan support; as adopted in the summer of 1976 the act permitted charitable organizations other than private foundations, churches, and church groups to spend a part of their budgets up to a maximum of $1 million a year on lobbying at all levels of government. The exclusion of private foundations accorded with the recommendations of the Commission on Private Philanthropy and Public Needs and the exclusion of churches and religious organizations was at their request.

One result of the cooperation among voluntary organizations to persuade Congress to adopt the Public Charities Lobbying Act was merger of the National Council on Philanthropy, founded during the congressional investigations of foundations in the 1950s, and the successor to the coalition of voluntary associations organized in 1973. The new group, which went into operation in 1980, took as its name Independent Sector. It faced the formidable tasks of developing coherent policy objectives and common action programs for the large number and diverse kinds of fundraising and grant-making organizations comprising the nonprofit sector. Its stated purpose was to preserve and promote the national traditions of giving, volunteering, and not-for-profit initiative. Since 1980, while representing the interests of philanthropy in current policy debates, Independent Sector has also played an important part in encouraging academic research and teaching on the past and present role of voluntarism in American life.

In 1961 the economist John Kenneth Galbraith wrote that twelve years after President Truman's promulgation of the Point Four program "provision of assistance to other countries for their economic development" had become "a settled arrangement for helping the less fortunate countries of the world to escape from poverty and to place themselves on a path to self-sustaining growth." Despite the considerable sums the United States government invested in foreign economic assistance, which in 1960–61 totaled more than $3 billion, there was a widespread feeling that much of the assistance had been ineffectively employed and that the results were disappointing. Galbraith's explanation of the failure was that too much reliance had been placed on providing capital and technical assistance and not enough help and encouragement given developing countries to promote education, social reform, and effective government.

During the 1960s, while Americans struggled to end poverty and racial unjustice at home and became involved in a costly war in Indochina, the United States government maintained its own programs to assist friendly and nonaligned nations and increased its contributions to international development institutions. The result, even before the end of the decade, was further recognition on the part of experts "of the difficulty of speeding up the growth process in the less developed countries," and disgruntlement in some quarters because foreign aid had seemingly not aroused gratitude toward the United States or enhanced its popularity and influence. In the early 1980s Landrum Bolling, surveying 150 years of American response to overseas need, concluded that, in spite of "the problems, disappointments, and frustrations of foreign aid, both public and private," the record was "fundamentally a success story" and "proof of the positive results that can be obtained through cooperation between the private and public sectors."

The engines of cooperation between public and private sector efforts in overseas aid were the Food for Peace Program, orginating in 1954, and the Agency for International Development (AID), founded in 1961. Under the former United States used its agricultural surpluses as instruments of foreign policy, selling, bartering, and donating stockpiled commodities to foreign nations in an effort to win or retain their goodwill. AID, adopting a less self-serving approach, assisted less-developed nations, friendly or nonaligned, to undertake agricultural, irrigation, industrial, and transportation projects intended to improve their people's standard of living. From 1954 to 1969 donations accounted for 20 percent of the value of surplus commodities sent overseas by the Food for Peace Program. Figures varied from year to year but in the period as a whole people-to-people groups such as Catholic Relief, CARE, Church World Service, and the American Jewish Joint Distribution Committee distributed 70 percent of the donations while government-to-government programs for disaster relief and economic assistance dispersed the remainder. In addition to supplying surplus commodities, mostly food, the government paid the overseas freight costs of clothing, medicine, and other material purchased by or given to voluntary agencies by their members.

AID relied not only on the generosity and goodwill of the private sector but also on the knowledge and expertise of universities, professional organizations, and foundations. Most AID-supported projects sought to increase food production but in 1965 the agency began to accept applications for voluntary family planning programs. In the mid-1960s, although farm surpluses had ceased to be a problem, Food for Peace was retained as a means of combating world hunger. Amendments to the program in 1966 emphasized a carrot-and-stick or self-help approach: U.S. aid would be available to underdeveloped countries if they took steps to boost agricultural development and control population growth. By the early 1970s disillusionment with the results of development efforts led to another shift in official policy: The Foreign Assistance Act of 1973 changed the emphasis from promoting economic growth by "wholesale" developmental methods to a more modest "retail" program of helping the very poorest people in poor countries.

Comparatively few foundations made grants for international purposes but those that did, notably Rockefeller and Ford, complemented Food for Peace and AID-funded projects. Both foundations continued agricultural research and development programs begun before the 1960s to increase world food supplies and both gave high priority to dissemination of information on population problems and to research, training, and experimental programs in population control and family planning. In 1963 Rockefeller inaugurated an ambitious program to upgrade higher education in parts of Asia, Africa, and Latin America. Ford, which cut back some of its domestic programs in the 1970s, committed about half its budget and two-thirds of its staff in 1977 to "transnational programs" dealing with matters affecting all nations.

Both government and voluntary aid organizations had to deal not only with the "normal" transnational problems of hunger and poverty but with emergency needs caused by natural disaster and war. Famine in India and Africa, flood in Venice, drought in Africa, recurring crises in the Middle East, support for Israel, the plight of refugees in Africa and Thailand, the needs of the world's 250 million hungry, homeless, and sickly children highlighted by the United Nations Year of the Child—all taxed the resources of donors and the ingenuity of fund-raisers and relief agents. In meeting such emergencies the voluntary organizations had to deal not only with the people they sought to help but with officials of the host government, United Nations agencies, international organizations such as the International Committee of the Red Cross, voluntary organizations from other countries with their own ideas of what needed to be done and how to do it, and U.S. State Department personnel anxious to foster humanitarian relief and simultaneously promote American foreign policy. If the results, as in efforts to deal with Cambodian and Vietnamese refugees in Thailand in the late 1970s and early 1980s, left much to be desired, it was also true that the American government, voluntary organizations, and, in particular, churches, made it possible for more refugees to find homes in the United States in the decade 1975–85 than in any earlier half century of American history.

The experience of CARE, Inc., illustrates the close relationship between food aid and development. In the 1960s, having sent 100 million CARE packages to designated recipients in Europe and other parts of the world, CARE ceased individual relief efforts to concentrate on mass feeding and self-help development projects. During the 1970s CARE operated, by invitation, in thirty-seven countries, devoting about 60 percent of its resources (mainly contributed by the United States government) to feeding programs for children and pregnant women, and 40 percent to "food for work" projects employing native labor in constructing schools, or dams and irrigation systems to increase local food growth. "It's not enough to feed the kid," declared CARE's executive director Philip Johnson in 1980. "First you have to deworm him, so you also need a medical program. Otherwise you're just feeding his parasites and not the kid. And then you've got to dig wells so there's clean water instead of dirty river water to drink and he doesn't have to pick up new parasites or maybe die of the endemic intestinal diseases." An admiring *Forbes Magazine* correspondent reported that CARE had discovered the principle of leverage: "With donated U.S. government-reserve food, host country matching contributions and local labor, CARE found it could get $10 mileage out of each private donor's $1."

As CARE and other voluntary agencies approached the 1980s they found inflation curtailing support at home and high oil prices limiting the sums overseas countries could provide for matching funds. Volunteer programs were no substitute for government aid and only modestly supplemented it. The total amount furnished by all European and American voluntary agencies was about equal to Britsh government aid. It was sometimes possible, however, for voluntary organizations to enter or remain in areas where official agencies could not operate, thereby performing the mission entrusted to them: "Delivering emergency disaster aid and reconstruction assistance wherever it is needed, to whoever needs it."

I3

The Public-Private Partnership

I believe it is wrong for people who have made it
up the ladder to pull the ladder up behind them.
        THOMAS P. (TIP) O'NEILL, JR.

People are concerned about the plight in Africa,
but if there was no famine we'd have sold as many
tickets.
        LIVE AID PROMOTER, BILL GRAHAM

The public-private partnership in public service, never
dissolved but in abeyance during and for some years after
the New Deal, took on new life in the 1960s and 1970s. A
number of factors encouraged revival of the partnership:
distrust of "Washington" and "big government," dissatisfaction with "the welfare mess," belief in the inherent
superiority of private to public efforts in dealing with social
problems, and, not least, the readiness of hard-pressed
voluntary agencies to accept government's help in easing
the pinch of mounting costs and dwindling resources.

The Nixon-Ford administration supported decentralization and privatization both in theory and practice. The "New Federalism," revenue sharing, and Title XX of the Social Service Amendments of 1974 allowed states to use federal grants to fund whatever social services they deemed appropriate. The result was a great expansion in the number and dollar value of "purchase of service" agreements with private sources. Not surprisingly the emphasis shifted from preventing or reducing poverty to "enhancing human development and the general quality of life." At approximately the same time, in a fervor of "deinstitutionalization," states emptied mental hospitals, sometimes without making adequate provision for the care of released patients elsewhere, and, under the spur of the federal government, released juvenile status offenders from detention.

In some respects purchase of service agreements marked a return, although on a much larger scale, of the nineteenth-century practice of granting subsidies from public funds to private orphanages, hospitals, and relief societies. Had advocates or critics of privatization chosen to do so they might have cited examples in earlier periods of American history when towns, counties, and states delegated responsibility for the care of the poor and criminals to private contractors. Under the new dispensation, payments from government made up a larger share of many voluntary agencies' resources than did contributions from private donors. Government grants and contracts allowed existing voluntary organizations to expand their areas of usefulness and encouraged formation of new ones to provide additional and often sorely needed services. On the other hand, growing reliance on government funds raised questions about the agencies' integrity and the relative importance of service and advocacy in philanthropy. "As valuable as the direct services of voluntary agencies are, they are still decidedly secondary to the role of the voluntary sector to act as independent advocate and critic," declared Brian O'Connell, executive director of the National Association for Mental Health and first president of Independent Sector. Speaking in the same year, 1976, Leslie Dunbar of the Field Foundation said that for a foundation or voluntary organization to help the government govern "may sometimes be of a small benefit, but helping the governed to represent their needs and *enforce an accounting to them* is continuously indispensable."

The same period that saw government and voluntary service agencies working in closer cooperation also witnessed the rise of a great many advocacy organizations monitoring the performance of government and seeking to influence public policy by lobbying, demonstrations, litigation, and empowerment of beneficiaries of social programs. Sometimes in the face of official hostility, sometimes in accordance with the equal rights policies endorsed by government, groups representing blacks, Hispanics, native Americans, migrants, consumers, children, women, prisoners, homosexuals, the homeless, animals, the environment, and opponents or defenders of abortion, nuclear power, or nuclear disarmament won recognition and tax-exempt status. Nonprofit public interest law firms, some established under Ford Foundation projects, survived IRS attacks in the Nixon administration, not entirely unscathed but viable enough that conservatives emulated liberals and radicals in organizing such firms to press their positions.

Social justice and civil rights and civil liberties groups such as the NAACP Legal Defense Fund, the American Civil Liberties Union, and the Anti-Defamation League of B'nai Brith had long used litigation to defend the rights of citizens against arbitrary or discriminatory acts of government. In the 1970s voluntary organizations increasingly turned to the courts to force the release of funds appropriated by Congress but impounded by the executive branch, to monitor the expenditure of earmarked federal funds by state and local authorities, and to require executive agencies to enforce compliance with federal regulatory laws. Going beyond service, advocacy, and litigation, some voluntary agencies sought to empower the disadvantaged so that those needing services, such as the poor, the aged, the homeless, or the handicapped, might be able to obtain the necessary political and economic power to represent themselves.

Both before and after rules on lobbying by charitable organizations were clarified in 1976, national health, mental health, and social service agencies felt an obligation to represent the causes and the interests of their clients in the public arena. With professional staff in central and state headquarters and hundreds of affiliates in all sections of the country, groups like the American Lung Association and the National Association for Mental Health were able to assemble "constellations of influential people and groups" to make their views known in legislative halls and administrative agencies. In *Voluntary Agencies in the Welfare State* (1981) Ralph Kramer noted that the voluntary agencies receiving the largest government support were among the most active in advocacy. "Contrary to conventional wisdom," he concluded, "reliance on public funds is not constraining." Kramer agreed, however, with Brian O'Connell's contention that a large service-providing agency that was substantially dependent on government funds might expend much of its social action time on "legislation, appropriations, and administrative red tape which relate to the agency's own program."

Nonprofit organizations, like business firms and state and local governments, complained about the red tape involved in doing business with the federal government. Part of the red tape was the result of the equal rights laws adopted in the 1960s and 1970s. Private colleges and universities, in particular, expressed resentment at the intrusive federal presence on campuses caused by prohibitions against racial and gender discrimination in employment practices and treatment of students, and the cost of assuring "equal access" to the handicapped. The Carter administration's generally evenhanded and benign attitude toward voluntary associations, however, was illustrated in 1980 when the IRS ruled that the anti-union National Right to Work Legal Defense Foundation was entitled to exemption from federal taxation as a charitable organization, and in 1981 when the Special Counsel for the Department of Energy, on his last day in office, sent $4 million received from the Standard Oil Company (Indiana) in an overcharge settlement to four charities to help poor people pay their heating bills. (The department subsequently agreed to let the charities keep 75 percent of the $4 million.)

In the 1970s local ordinances and state laws regulating charitable solicitations posed a greater threat to philanthropy than federal legislation or administrative rulings. A number of communities, including the village of Schaumburg, Illinois, required fund-raising groups to prove that at least 75 percent of money raised in door-to-door or on-street solicitations went for "charitable purposes," defined to exclude salaries and administrative costs. Reasonable as such a requirement might seem, the effect of the limitation was to bar solicitations by advocacy organizations in which salaries of staff engaged in gathering and dispensing information about the organizations' purposes comprised a substantial amount of budgets. When Schaumburg refused permission to solicit to an environmental protection agency that could not meet the village's definition of "charitable purposes," the agency sued and won its case in the federal district and appeals courts. Recognizing the importance of the case to philanthropy and voluntary associations, the Coalition of National Voluntary Organizations, predecessor of Independent Sector, argued the case for Citizens for a Better Environment before the Supreme Court, and the National Committee for Responsive Philanthropy filed an amici curiae brief in support of the agency. In 1980, with only Justice William Rehnquist dissenting, the Supreme Court ruled (444 U.S. 620) that solicitation was so intertwined with freedom of speech that it was within the protection of the First Amendment to the Constitution, and that the 75 percent limitation violated activity protected by the First Amendment. There were other ways, the Court held, less threatening to Constitutional rights, to protect the public from fraud, crime, or undue annoyance.

The most serious blow to the public-private partnership came from avowed friends of voluntarism. The Republican Party platform in 1980 called for restoration of "the American spirit of voluntary service and cooperation, of private and community initiative." In 1981 President Ronald Reagan declared "voluntarism is an essential part of our plan to give the government back to the people." Generous with rhetorical support, the Reagan administration took few positive steps, other than appointing a task force on private sector initiatives and offering awards and citations for volunteer action, to foster the philanthropic sector. Its real interest lay elsewhere—reducing taxes, cutting federal spending on social programs, and building up national defense. Provisions of the Economic Recovery Taxation Act of 1981 permitting nonitemizers to deduct charitable contributions from income tax returns and raising the deduction corporations could take from 5 to 10 percent of taxable income were offset by the lower tax rates established in the act that, experts asserted, increased the real cost of giving and thus discouraged it.

Cuts in federal expenditures for social welfare, demanded by the Reagan administration and approved by Congress in 1981, went into effect during a period of deep recession and mounting unemployment and homelessness. In retrospect it seems unrealistic to have expected voluntary organizations, themselves heavily dependent on government funds, to take up the slack caused by sharp reductions in appropriations for child welfare, day care, nutrition for the elderly, mental health and retardation programs, and restricted eligibility for welfare, food stamps, school lunches, and energy assistance. Federal budget cuts cost nonprofit organizations an estimated $30 billion dollars in government grants and contracts in the period 1981–85. Some agencies went out of existence and others survived by putting greater emphasis on fees and charges. By 1986 increases in private giving had accounted for only about one-fourth of the lost federal revenue. In an analysis of the administration's budget plans for 1986–88 Lester M. Salamon foresaw "a federal pullout from partnership arrangements in all fields but health," and predicted that reliance on fees and charges would further reduce voluntary agencies' ability to serve the poor.

From the beginning leaders of the philanthropic community rejected the administration's assumption that private giving could replace government funding in social programs. The notion that philanthropy *should* assume the burden ran counter to the conviction that engrossing philanthropy in the task of meeting basic human needs diminished its capacity to act as advocate or innovator. According to this point of view the function of philanthropy was not to serve as a handmaid to government but to propose and promote achievement of a more just social order.

This conception of the role of philanthropy found no favor with the Reagan administration. It made its opposition clear by a dogged effort to exclude advocacy organizations from the Combined Federal Campaign (CFC), the only charitable solicitation permitted among federal government employees and military personnel. For about fifteen years after its founding in 1961 CFC raised funds by payroll deductions for traditional charities such as United Way and the American Red Cross. In the late 1970s the National Committee for Responsive Philanthropy (NCRP) began to agitate for admittance of more minority, women's, environmental, and legal defense organizations. In 1980 the Carter administration liberalized criteria for inclusion in the campaign and a federal court ruled that the National Black United Fund had been illegally excluded from it. Thereafter the number of agencies participating in the campaign increased and came to include both conservative and liberal advocacy groups. Because of the large number of prospective donors—2.4 million in 1980, 4 million in 1985—and the sum raised—$80 million in 1980, $130 million in 1985—participation in CFC was a boon agencies eagerly sought and jealously guarded.

The smoldering charity war that pitted United Way against alternative charities and national health organizations took on new intensity in 1981 when the director of the federal Office of Personnel Management drafted the first of a series of proposed executive orders intended to strengthen United Way's control of local CFC drives and to exclude agencies like the NAACP Legal Defense and Education Fund that engaged in litigation and advocacy on public policy issues from participation in CFC. The proposal, more or less modified from year to year to year, drew opposition from the American Red Cross, CARE, Inc., the American Lung Association, and the Girl Scouts of America, as well as from NCRP and Independent Sector, which warned that the measure would "deny government the combination of services and opinions it needed." President

Reagan withheld his full approval of the proposed changes in CFC until 1983.

In 1985 (*Cornelius v. NAACP-LDF*) the U.S. Supreme Court upheld the 1983 executive order on the grounds that "the President could reasonably conclude that a dollar spent on providing food or shelter to the needy is more beneficial than a dollar spent on litigation that might or might not result in aid to the needy." The Court ruled, however, that charities could not be excluded from CFC if the administration's justification was "merely a pretense for viewpoint discrimination," and remanded the case to the U.S. district court for a determination of fact on this point. In 1986, while the case was still pending, the Office of Personnel Management published revised rules for the 1986 CFC barring participation by agencies spending more than 15 percent of their total budgets on lobbying or lawsuits. Before these rules could go into effect they were blocked by an order of the district court and an amendment to the supplemental appropriations bill, leaving the situation, after five years of controversy, about as it was in 1981.

Congress designated November 15, 1986, National Philanthropy Day in recognition of America's 800,000 nonprofit philanthropic organizations. The observance came shortly after publication of a new edition of *Dimensions of the Independent Sector*, a statistical reference book portraying the size, scope, and functions of the nonprofit sector, which showed a decline since 1982 in its rate of growth in employment, earnings, and share of the national income. Social service agencies, in particular, had been hard hit by government budget cuts (42 percent in real terms, 1980–86). Virginia Hodgkinson, one of the authors of *Dimensions*, reported that although neither private contributions nor volunteer time had made up for the loss in government funding, an increase in private giving had helped some voluntary organizations compensate for declining government support.

The continuing importance and complexity of individual giving was revealed in two very different areas. According to *The Charitable Behavior of Americans* (1986), a national survey analyzed by Independent Sector, 72 percent of all individual giving went to religious institutions. In the period 1981–85 giving to religion rose at a slightly higher rate than total philanthropy. Part of the increase reflected the success of television evangelists in attracting donations from millions of viewers; some of it may have been in response to churchgoers' awareness of and desire to alleviate human needs caused by cutbacks in federal aid programs. Organized religion is both a recipient and donor of charitable contributions but, because religious organizations are not required to file reports on their activities with government, precise and comprehensive information on the services provided by churches and religion-affiliated institutions is difficult to obtain. A study conducted in the early 1980s by the Council on Foundations reported that the religious organizations responding to its survey (too few for statistical validity) were active both in overseas aid and in a variety of charitable, educational, employment, housing, social services, self-help, and advocacy programs for the needy in their own communities and in other parts of the United States.

Private givers further supported their part of the public-private partnership by contributing to mainly tax-supported institutions such as state colleges and universities, public radio and television stations, and public or endowed museums, libraries, parks, and zoos. Nearly every public educational, civic, or cultural institution cultivated "Friends" whose gifts supplemented appropriations from federal, state, or local government. In New York City in 1987 twenty public monuments in need of costly repair were put up for "adoption" by private donors; in Washington, D.C., the National Park Service, operating on a tight budget, asked private individuals to donate money to replace aging and dying cherry trees around the Tidal Basin.

In 1984 per capita giving in constant (1972) dollars reached $99, the highest figure since 1955. Many people involved in and concerned about philanthropy thought that amount could and should be higher. Independent Sector launched a campaign in 1986 to double charitable giving and increase volunteer activity by 50 percent by 1991.

Fund-raising, or development as it was increasingly called, took many forms, some traditional, some novel. Just as an increasing number of states used lotteries to raise funds for education, and some churches derived revenue from Bingo and other games of chance, so, at Christmas 1986, the National Easter Seal Society sponsored a sweepstakes offering chances at $10,000 in cash or $200 a week for a year in exchange for a "suggested contribution" of $5 for six tickets.

For almost a century and a half, charity balls had given Americans, rich and poor, an opportunity to dress up, be seen, and feel generous. Although commentators tended to deride charity galas, their durability and ubiquity indicated their continuing usefulness as a means of raising money for many causes. Some local charities and branches of national health organizations raised as much as one-third of their operating budgets by annual balls. In Columbus, Ohio, on a single weekend in December 1986, three major dances and a shopping party in a mall benefited the local ballet company, a hospice, the hearing impaired, and the district academy of osteopathic medicine.

Enlisting artists and entertainers in the service of philanthropy is a time-honored practice but the development of mass media and instantaneous communications has given the benefit concert new dimensions. In a 1971 concert for

Bangladesh, George Harrison, a former member of the Beatles, showed how rock music's appeal to young poeple could be used for charitable fund-raising. The Ethiopian famine of the 1980s—besides eliciting hundreds of millions of dollars in official international aid—roused the sympathy of musicians, record promoters, and rock music fans on both sides of the Atlantic. Bob Geldof, an Irish rock musician, raised $110 million dollars for famine relief and development aid in Ethiopia and the Sudan by a recording and two internationally broadcast Live Aid rock concerts. The latter, held in the summer of 1985, were attended by 162,000 fans in London and Philadelphia and watched by an estimated one and a half billion people around the world. Ken Kragen, a Los Angeles talent manager and promoter, organized USA for Africa (United Support of Artists for Africa) and, with Harry Belafonte, produced the recording "We Are the World," sales of which raised $52 million for African hunger relief. Both organizations discovered that raising money was easier than getting help to famine sufferers. The outpouring of funds brought vast quantities of food and medical supplies to ports and warehouses in Africa but political, economic, and logistical problems made getting relief to those in need an unexpectedly difficult and complex process.

Although Live Aid and USA for Africa had similar objectives and cooperated on some projects, the two enterprises were independent. By chance or design their 1986 fund-raisers—Geldof's Sports Aid for African relief, and Kragen's Hands Across America for the hungry and homeless in the United States—fell on the same day, May 25, 1986. Sports Aid attracted millions of runners and substantial amounts of money in Europe, Africa, and Australia; Hands Across America, however, outdrew and outgrossed Sports Aid in the United States. An estimated 5 million people including President and Mrs. Reagan, musicians, and television personalities joined hands in a living chain stretching coast-to-coast through sixteen states. The amount generated by the event, $33 million, was considerably less than the promoters had hoped for.

Corporate sponsors, including Coca-Cola and Citicorp, which contributed funds to meet Hands Across America's $16 million expenses, publicized it as a wholesome exercise in making people feel good about themselves. According to Kragen, the aim of Hands Across America was to demonstrate "a unity of purpose"; it was "a bipartisan effort, not a rap-the-government effort." Robert M. Hayes, counsel to the National Coalition for the Homeless, criticized the event as an extravaganza without content. "There seems to be no recognition," he objected, "that several million Americans are homeless as a result of deliberate public policy decision." On a more favorable note, James P. Grant, executive director of the United Nations Children's Fund, hailed Sports Aid and Hands Across America as "an incredible mass outpouring of concern and commitment—of demand—that those who hunger should be fed and those who are vulnerable should be sheltered."

Even if the most optimistic goals of Hands Across America's promoters had been reached the amount raised would have represented only a fraction of the annual cost of one government antipoverty program—food stamps. "If you really care about hunger in America," exclaimed Michael Kinsley, an unimpressed bystander, "you support government programs to feed the hungry and taxes to pay for them. Why should people have to starve for the convenience of Coca-Cola Co.?"

Coca-Cola's support for Hands Across America, like similar corporate assistance in financing the 1984 Summer Olympics and the five-year campaign for restoration of the

Statue of Liberty, involved a new and controversial approach to fund-raising—"cause-related marketing." The Statue of Liberty campaign was also a prime example of the assumption by the private sector of functions normally performed by government. In 1981 the Statue of Liberty–Ellis Island Foundation, a nonprofit corporation, undertook to relieve the federal government of the expense of and credit for restoring one of the nation's most beloved patriotic shrines. The foundation used direct-mail appeals for contributions and collected royalties from the sale of licensed novelty items, but the core of its finances came from selected corporate sponsors that each pledged sums of $3 million to $5 million to the project. In return the sponsors received exclusive rights to use the campaign symbol in advertising and promotion of their various products, including beer, wine, whiskey, soft drinks, beauty products, and aviation. The pledges were more in the nature of business expenses than gifts and were made in the expectation that sponsoring companies would be repaid in public relations benefits and by increased sales of their products.

An official of the Statue of Liberty–Ellis Island Foundation, responding to criticism that the marketing approach commercialized the Statue of Liberty, declared there was "not a single thing wrong in a free enterprise system in a marriage between proper commercialization and philanthropy." For philanthropic agencies needing funds to carry out their programs the marriage to "proper commercialization" was one of convenience. In the mid-1980s Mothers Against Drunk Driving, the Muscular Dystrophy Association, and the Arthritis Foundation entered into marketing arrangements with consumer product companies promising the organizations a donation for every money-off coupon redeemed by purchasers of the products. The arrangement differed from corporate philanthropy in that the donations were not gifts but devices to increase sales.

Experts agreed that the Tax Reform Act adopted in September 1986 would have a strong and probably unfavorable impact on philanthropy. The new law retained the income tax deduction of charitable contributions for taxpayers who itemized their gifts but ended it for the large group—approximately 75 percent of all taxpayers—who filed short forms without itemized deductions. For itemizers, the lower marginal rates established in the act increased the real price of giving by lowering the tax-reducing value of charitable contributions. Under the law's provisions contributors of large gifts of appreciated property to universities, museums, or other nonprofit organizations would also lose the advantageous tax write-offs formerly available to them. Independent Sector estimated the various provisions of the act could cost charities $11 billion a year and cause an average loss of 14 percent to the fields of education, health care, culture, social service, and religion. Even if the consequences of the Tax Reform Act were less drastic than anticipated its enactment brought to close an era in which tax policy and philanthropic giving were closely and favorably related.

The effect of tax reform was only one of a number of unresolved issues facing philanthropy toward the end of the 1980s. As on earlier occasions during the Reagan administration the advocacy function of philanthropy came under attack, this time from the Treasury Department. Ten years after passage of the law permitting public charities to spend a part of the budgets on lobbying, the Internal Revenue Service published proposed regulations to implement the act that, in the opinion of many philanthropic organizations, would make it virtually impossible for them to engage in lobbying. Nonprofit agencies in health care, physical fitness, and day care, areas formerly shunned by private enterprise, found themselves under fire from entrepreneurs crowding into the service sector of the economy in search of clients and government contracts. The newcomers charged their tax-exempt rivals with unfair competition and questioned the need for their existence. State and local officials continued efforts to regulate solicitations by secular charities and to limit fund-raising costs. In some communities conflict between public policy and religious doctrine on such matters as homosexuality, sex education, family planning, and abortion threatened the public-private partnership in child welfare and family services. Efforts by public authorities to require voluntary agencies to comply with federal wage, hour, and antidiscrimination statutes put further strains on the partnership.

Underlying all these problems were the questions of the meaning, appropriate functions, and legal status of philanthropy and voluntary nonprofit organizations in relation to government and for-profit business. These are questions on which Americans have never been and are not now in agreement. Relations between responsibilities assigned the three sectors are neither rigidly defined nor permanently fixed but shift from time to time to meet changing circumstances and needs. The central value of philanthropy, as Brian O'Connell points out in *Philanthropy in Action* (1987), lies not in performance of any particular set of tasks but in "the extra dimension it provides for seeing and doing things differently." The three sectors, despite their differences, have much in common. In a country united by love of freedom and respect for diversity, giving, like voting and buying, is part of the process by which people respond to and express their interests, preferences, and convictions.

Important Dates

1601	Statute of Charitable Uses, cornerstone of Anglo-American law of philanthropy, and Elizabethan Poor Law, basis of English and American public poor relief, enacted by Parliament
1630	John Winthrop (1588–1649) preaches "A Model of Christian Charity" to Puritans bound for New England
1638	John Harvard (1607–38) bequeaths library and half of his estate to newly founded school at Cambridge, Mass.
1646	John Eliot (1604–90) begins missionary work among Indians of Massachusetts
1649	Society for the Propagation of the Gospel in New England established by Parliament; rechartered in 1661 and continued to support Indian missions until Revolution
1657	Scots' Charitable Society, first American "friendly society," founded in Boston; reorganized 1684
1675	Massachusetts legislature provides relief for frontier settlers driven from homes by King Philip's War, thus departing from principle of exclusive local responsibility for relief
1682	William Penn (1644–1718) comes to America to launch a "holy experiment"
1702	Cotton Mather (1663–1728) publishes *Magnalia Christi*

	Americana, one of earliest celebrations of American philanthropy
1710	Cotton Mather publishes *Essays To Do Good,* a popular do-it-yourself book
1715–18	Elihu Yale (1649–1721) sends gifts to Collegiate School of Connecticut (chartered 1701); school changes name to Yale College
1727	Franklin and friends organize "Junto," a mutual and community improvement society
1729	First orphan home in present boundaries of United States established at Ursuline Convent, New Orleans
1730	St. Andrew's Society founded in Charleston, S.C., "to assist all people in distress, of whatsoever Nation or Profession"
1731	Anthony Benezet begins half century of teaching and promoting good causes in Philadelphia
	James Oglethorpe advances a number of reasons, some philanthropic, to show why a colony should be planted in Georgia
1737	Jean Louis makes gift for founding Charity Hospital, New Orleans
1739–41	George Whitefield, on second visit to America, finds religious revivals in progress and helps turn them into Great Awakening; founds orphanage in Georgia in 1740
1751–52	Dr. Thomas Bond, assisted by Benjamin Franklin and others, founds Pennsylvania Hospital, the first general hospital in the U.S.; building opened 1756
1760	New York, Virginia, Maryland, Pennsylvania, New Hampshire, and Rhode Island collect and send assistance to Boston fire sufferers
1767	Philadelphia Bettering House, sometimes called "Pauper Palace," opened
1774–75	Parliamentary act closing Boston Port creates greatest relief problem in colonial period; other towns and colonies send money, grain, and livestock to aid Boston
1776	Society for Alleviating the Miseries of Public Prisons,

earliest prison reform society, organized in Philadelphia; reactivated in 1787

1780   Pennsylvania, first state to take such action, passes Act for the Gradual Abolition of Slavery

1790   Free mulattoes of Charleston, S.C., organize Brown Fellowship Society, one of several aristocratic charitable associations of that city

Death of Benjamin Franklin; will establishes Franklin Funds in Boston and Philadelphia to lend money to "young married artificers of good character"

1793   Yellow-fever epidemic in Philadelphia; worst disaster of kind in American history

1808   Andover Theological Seminary founded; popular cause among orthodox Congregational donors

1809   Mother Elizabeth Bayley Seton establishes order of Sisters of Charity of St. Joseph at Emmitsburg, Md.

1810   American Board of Commissioners for Foreign Missions organized; sends first missionaries to India in 1812

1811   Massachusetts General Hospital, favorite beneficiary of Boston philanthropists, founded

1816   American Bible Society, oldest of national benevolent societies, established; American Tract Society (1825), American Society for Promotion of Temperance (1826), and similar organizations founded in 1820s

1817   Thomas Hopkins Gallaudet (1787–1851) establishes in Hartford, Conn., America's first free school for deaf; one son to continue active in education of deaf until 1917

1818   Postwar depression prompts establishment of New York Society for the Prevention of Pauperism; similar societies in Baltimore and Philadelphia

1819   Supreme Court decision in Dartmouth College case strengthens legal position of incorporated endowments

1821   Amherst College opens and receives liberal support from conservative Congregationalists

1824   Louis Dwight founds Boston Prison Discipline Society;

controversy over relative merits of "congregate" and
"separate" prison systems

1824–30   Samuel Gridley Howe takes part in, raises funds for, and
administers relief in Greek War for Independence

1825   Founding of New York House of Refuge, first
reformatory for juveniles; similar institutions in
Boston and Philadelphia

Robert Owen (1771–1858) opens cooperative
community in New Harmony, Ind.

1825–30   Boston Unitarians support Joseph Tuckerman's ministry
to the poor

1829   Mathew Carey (1760–1839) attempts federated fund-
raising in Philadelphia

1831   Arthur (1786–1865) and Lewis Tappan (1788–1873),
New York dry goods merchants, become active in
antislavery and manual-training college movements

Death of Stephen Girard; left largest fortune any
American had thus far accumulated to charitable
purposes

Amos Lawrence (1786–1852) retires from business to
devote full time to benevolent interests and spiritual
welfare

1832   Samuel Gridley Howe opens New England Asylum (later
Perkins Institution), leading American institution for
instruction of the blind

1835   Alexis de Tocqueville comments on American
disposition to organize and join voluntary associations
in *Democracy in America*

1836   John Lowell bequeaths $250,000 to found and support
Lowell Institute, Boston; annual lecture series begins
in 1840

1837   Samuel G. Howe begins instruction of Laura Bridgman,
blind and deaf girl

Horace Mann begins work as secretary of Massachusetts
Board of Education

Depression opens; lasts until 1840s

1841   Dorothea L. Dix (1802–87) begins crusade for better
treatment of insane; submits *Memorial* to

Massachusetts legislature in 1843; publishes *Remarks on Prisons and Prison Discipline*, 1845

1843 Robert Hartley and other charity reformers organize New York Association for Improving the Condition of the Poor

1845 Establishment of first American conference of Society of St. Vincent de Paul, charitable organization of Roman Catholic laymen

1846 After decade of debate Congress passes act creating Smithsonian Institution

1846–47 Large American contributions for Irish famine relief

1847 Abbott Lawrence makes gift of $50,000 to Harvard; gift helps support work of Louis Agassiz

1848 Girard College opens in Philadelphia; most famous orphanage in United States and classic example of the "dead hand" in philanthropy

1851 YMCA movement spreads to the United States

1853 Charles Loring Brace founds Children's Aid Society of New York, important child welfare agency

1854 Congress passes, President Pierce vetoes, Dorothea Dix's bill granting public lands to states to assist in financing care of insane

1859 Peter Cooper (1791–1883), one of best-loved American philanthropists, opens Cooper Union in New York City as center for free instruction in art and science

1861 United States Sanitary Commission, forerunner of American Red Cross, organized

1862 Freedmen's aid societies established in North to send teachers and relief supplies to former slaves

1863 Massachusetts establishes first central agency for supervising public welfare institutions

Catholic Protectory, largest institution for children in the United States, founded in New York City

1863–64 Sanitary Fairs in northern cities raise money and collect supplies for United States Sanitary Commission

1865 Freedmen's Bureau founded; active in relief and education in the South until early 1870s

1867 Peabody Fund, first of modern foundations, established

	by George Peabody (1795–1869) to assist southern education
1868	Opening of Hampton Institute in Hampton, Va.; best-endowed school for Negroes
1869	Founding of London Charity Organization Society, which served as a model for American COS movement
1871–72	Fire sufferers in Chicago and Boston relieved by contributions from other cities
1874	Organization of National Conference of Charities and Correction, now National Conference on Social Welfare
1876	Opening of Jubilee Hall, Fisk University, Nashville, Tenn.; money raised by concert tours of Fisk Jubilee Singers
1877	Buffalo Charity Organization Society established; similar organizations founded in other cities in next few years
1881	Clara Barton (1821–1912) organizes American Association of the Red Cross (name changed to American National Red Cross in 1893)
	Booker T. Washington (1858–1915) organizes Tuskegee Institute for Negroes in Tuskegee, Ala.
1882	United States ratifies Geneva Convention of 1864, which provided for neutralization of aid to wounded in time of war
	John F. Slater Fund founded to support Negro industrial schools and teacher training institutions
1884	Toynbee Hall, first social settlement, opened in London; visited by many Americans and served as model for American settlement houses
	Hebrew Sheltering and Immigrant Aid Society organized to receive and assist Jews emigrating to the U.S.
1885	Stanford University chartered (opened 1891); gifts of Leland Stanford thought to be of unprecedented size
1887	Helen Keller (1880–1968), blind and deaf, begins study with Anne Sullivan
1888	Denver experiments with federated fund-raising
1889	Andrew Carnegie publishes "Wealth"

John D. Rockefeller gives $600,000 to help found new University of Chicago

Jane Addams (1860–1935) establishes Hull House

1890   Last loan made in Massachusetts from revolving loan fund for young married tradesmen established by will of Benjamin Franklin

1892   New York *Tribune* counts 4,047 millionaires in the United States

1894   First federal income tax law exempts organizations founded and conducted solely for charitable, religious, or educational purposes

1895   Washington Gladden publishes article on "Tainted Money"

Jewish Charities in Boston adopt federated fund-raising

1898   New York School of Philanthropy inaugurates formal training courses for social work

1899   First American juvenile court established in Chicago

1900   American National Red Cross obtains charter of incorporation from Congress

1901   Rockefeller Institute for Medical Research incorporated and begins work on small scale; eventually received $60.5 million from Rockefeller

1902   General Education Board established by John D. Rockefeller; his total gifts to it were about $130 million

Carnegie endows Carnegie Institution of Washington to encourage investigation, research, and discovery

1904   National Tuberculosis Association organized

1905   Carnegie Foundation for the Advancement of Teaching established

Resumption of tainted-money controversy

1907   Russell Sage Foundation, important in development of social work, organized

1909   First White House Conference on the Care of Dependent Children recommends establishment of federal Children's Bureau and declares that poverty alone should not be grounds for removing children from families

1910   Boy Scouts of America founded (Campfire Girls, 1910; Girl Scouts, 1912)

1911   Carnegie Corporation, Carnegie's largest foundation ($125 million), established

Missouri and Illinois enact "mothers' pensions" laws permitting assistance from public funds to maintain small children in own homes

1912   Congress establishes U.S. Children's Bureau "to investigate and report upon all matters pertaining to the welfare of children and child life among all classes of our people"

1913   Rockefeller Foundation chartered by state of New York "to promote the well-being of mankind throughout the world"

American Cancer Association founded

Modern community chest movement begins in Cleveland

Revenue Act of 1913, adopted after ratification of 16th (Income Tax) Amendment, exempts organizations "organized and operated exclusively for religious, charitable, scientific, or educational purposes"; subsequent acts add "prevention of cruelty to children or animals" (1918), "literary" (1921), "community chest, fund or foundation" (1921), and "testing for public safety" (1954) to list of exempt organizations

1914   Red Cross "Mercy Ship" takes doctors, nurses, and hospital equipment to Europe at start of war

Commission for Relief in Belgium organized

American Jewish Joint Distribution Committee organized to coordinate Jewish war relief activities

Cleveland Foundation, first community trust, established

1915–16 U.S. Industrial Relations Commission investigates foundations

1917   Julius Rosenwald Fund established; active in field of Negro education

Income tax law permits individuals to deduct charitable contributions up to 15 percent of taxable income

Important Dates

Publication of Mary Richmond's *Social Diagnosis,* landmark in social work

American Friends Service Committee begins operations

Red Cross asks—and gets—$100 million, largest sum raised by voluntary organizations up to that time

1918   Harkness family establishes Commonwealth Fund "to do something for the welfare of mankind"; active mainly in health field

United War Work campaign raises $200 million for seven national war relief agencies

Bequest of John W. Sterling doubles Yale's endowment

1919   Death of Andrew Carnegie; benefactions total $350 million

Harvard uses professional fund-raising counsel in $14 million endowment fund drive

Community chest in about 40 cities; spreads to 350 in 1929

Herbert Hoover (1874–1964) director of American Relief Administration; also Director-General of Relief for Allied Governments

Twentieth Century Fund established by Edward A. Filene; specializes in economic research

1921   American Foundation for Blind founded; Helen Keller helps raise endowment

1921–22   Russian famine relief supervised by American Relief Administration, private organization headed by Herbert Hoover

1924   Total annual charitable contributions in United States reach $2 billion

1925   John Simon Guggenheim Memorial Foundation organized to aid young scholars and creative workers

1927   Restoration of Williamsburg, Va., financed by John D. Rockefeller, Jr. (1874–1960), begins

1928   Philanthropic peak of 1920s; 500 lump-sum gifts of $1 million or more

Edward S. Harkness (1874–1940) gives $11 million to Harvard for house plan

1930 Kellogg Foundation organized; interested in health and education in rural areas

Louis Bamberger and Mrs. Felix Fuld donate $8 million to found Institute for Advanced Study, Princeton, N.J.

Edward S. Harkness makes large gifts to Yale and Phillips Exeter Academy

Congress establishes National Institutes of Health, federal government's principal health research agency

1931 Red Cross refuses to consider congressional grant for drought relief

President's Organization for Unemployment Relief conducts publicity campaign for local fund appeals

As a "temporary emergency" New York State assists local communities in financing unemployment relief

1932 Dedication of Folger Shakespeare Library, Washington, D.C., gift of Henry C. Folger

Red Cross processes and distributes surplus wheat and cotton to needy

Reconstruction Finance Corporation authorized to lend money to states for unemployment relief

1933 FERA established to make emergency grants for unemployment relief

Philanthropy at depression low point

Henry Ford opens Ford Museum and Greenfield Village

Rockefeller Foundation appropriates $1.5 million to expedite discovery of remedies for the depression

1934 First President's Birthday Ball for relief of polio victims

Congress limits tax exemption to organizations "no substantial part of the activities of which is carrying on propaganda or otherwise attempting to influence legislation"

1935 Social Security Act, beginning of a permanent welfare program by national government

Heavier income and corporation taxes; corporations permitted to deduct charitable contributions up to 5 percent of taxable income

	Total contributions to philanthropy slightly exceed predepression peak
1936	Ford Foundation organized; not active nationally until about 1950
1937	Congress accepts Andrew Mellon's offer to give art collection and National Gallery building to public
	Death of John D. Rockefeller; benefactions total $530 million
1938	National Foundation for Infantile Paralysis begins concentrated program of research into the cause, prevention, and treatment of poliomyelitis
1939	Neutrality Act requires agencies engaged in relief activities in belligerent countries to register with Department of State
1941	Red Cross adopts blood-donor program
	USO organized
	Carnegie Corporation ends program begun in early 1920s to strengthen library facilities of small colleges
1942	National War Fund, Inc., organized to collect funds for both war and nonwar agencies
1943	United Nations Relief and Rehabilitation Administration (UNRRA) founded to plan and supervise postwar emergency relief on international basis
	American Council of Voluntary Agencies for Foreign Service established by approximately fifty agencies to plan and coordinate private efforts
	Frederick Douglas Patterson, president of Tuskegee Institute, organizes United Negro College Fund to raise money for twenty-seven accredited four-year colleges.
	Initiation of compulsory withholding of federal income and social security tax payment from employee pay makes possible payroll deduction for contributions to community chest
1944	Servicemen's Readjustment Act (GI Bill of Rights) provides educational and other benefits for World War II veterans

1945   Hill-Burton Hospital Construction Act makes federal
        government a major factor in health care
        CARE begins sending food parcels to Europe
1946   Voluntary agencies begin sending aid to Germany
        War Relief Control Board succeeded by Advisory
        Committee on Foreign Aid
        John D. Rockefeller, Jr., gives seventeen acres of
        downtown Manhattan land as site for United Nations
        headquarters
        Congress passes Full Employment Act, recognition of
        government's continuing responsibility to promote
        economic security
1946–48 United Jewish Appeal raises very large sums to assist
        refugees, immigrants to Israel, and government of
        Israel
1948   Senator Charles Tobey investigates use of foundations by
        business firms for nonphilanthropic purposes
        Spelman Fund of New York dissolved
1949   President Truman announces Point Four plan of
        technical assistance to underdeveloped nations
        United Fund movement begins in Detroit
1950   Revision of Internal Revenue Code subjects foundations
        engaged in certain prohibited practices to loss of tax
        exemption
        Federal government establishes National Science
        Foundation
        Lowell Institute, Boston, provides funds for WGBH
        Educational Foundation, which operates WGBH-FM
        (1951) and WGBH-TV (1953)
1951   USO reactivated
1952   Select (Cox) Committee of House of Representatives
        investigates foundations
1953   Carnegie Endowment for International Peace opens
        International Center on United Nations Plaza, New
        York
        Decision of New Jersey Supreme Court in *Barlow et al.* v.
        A. P. Smith Manufacturing Co. clarifies legal right of

corporations to make contributions to higher education

Howard Hughes makes Howard Hughes Medical Institute sole owner of Hughes Aircraft Co., leading U.S. defense contractor

1954   Special (Reece) Committee of House of Representatives widely criticized for tactics employed in investigation of foundations

1955   Ford Foundation announces largest grant in foundation history; $560 million to privately supported colleges, medical schools, and hospitals

National Merit Scholarship Corporation organized to assist talented students in attending colleges of their choice

Development of Salk Vaccine against paralytic polio climaxes seventeen years of work by National Foundation for Infantile Paralysis

1958   National Foundation for Infantile Paralysis becomes National Foundation; will combat rheumatic diseases, birth defects, and disorders of central nervous system

National Defense Education Act provides indirect subsidies to colleges and universities by underwriting student aid

1959   Disc jockey Peter Tripp stays awake longer than anyone in history; performs for 200 hours without sleep (in armed forces recruiting booth, Times Square) "in the interest of science and the March of Dimes"

1960   Estimate of Americans' total giving for philanthropic purposes is $10.92 billion

Death of John D. Rockefeller, Jr.; donations during lifetime total about $475 million

1961   Congressman Wright Patman of Texas begins investigations of private foundations

Joseph N. Mitchell, city manager of Newburgh, N.Y., denounces welfare recipients and cost of assisting them

President John F. Kennedy begins fund drive among

federal employees and military personnel later known at Combined Federal Campaign (CFC); program begins on experimental basis in 1964 and soon becomes the world's largest workplace charitable appeal

1962   Mobilization for Youth, Inc., founded in part by Ford Foundation, offers plan for prevention and control of juvenile delinquency in New York City

Benjamin Franklin's Boston Fund modified to make $1,735,549 available for loans to medical students and secondary school graduates seeking further training in technical sciences and crafts

Amendments to Social Security Act accept social work doctrine of need for service approach in public welfare

1963   Dwight Macdonald's review of Michael Harrington's *The Other America* (1962) comes to attention of President John F. Kennedy

1964   Economic Opportunity Act launches President Lyndon Johnson's War on Poverty

General Education Board dissolved

Congressman Patman charges J. M. Kaplan Fund operates as conduit for channeling CIA funds to anticommunist causes

1965   Johnson administration establishes Medicare, basic hospital insurance and supplemental insurance for doctors' bills for persons age 65 and over, and Medicaid, covering physician, hospital, and other medical expenses of low-income persons

Richard C. Cornuelle, in *Reclaiming the American Dream*, advocates reliance on voluntary organizations rather than "unlimited government" as best solution to social problems

Red Cross, USO, and forty other voluntary agencies have representatives offering services in Vietnam

1966   Robert Theobald, ed., *The Guaranteed Income*, and Gilbert Steiner, *Social Insecurity*, favor income assistance as opposed to services in fighting poverty

1967   Red Cross and Salvation Army provide food, clothing,

and shelter in all communities struck by urban riots; YMCA, Urban League, and other United Way agencies provide emergency assistance to victims of disorder

Ramparts magazine reveals connections between CIA and United States National Student Association and Foundation for Youth and Student Affairs

Amendments to Social Security Act establish WIN plan to require welfare recipients to work

1968   Ford Foundation announces it will use part of its investment portfolio for economic and social programs supported by grants; grants program totaling about $200 million a year to continue

Ferdinand Lundberg, *The Rich and Super Rich,* publicizes Patman's investigations of foundations

Joseph W. Barr, secretary of the treasury, reports that in 1967, 21 individuals with gross income over $1 million and 151 with gross income over $200,000 did not have to pay income taxes

Following federal court decisions nullifying racial restrictions in will of Stephen Girard, first black male orphans admitted to Girard College

1969   Congress approves Tax Reform Act of 1969 with punitive provisions affecting private foundations but allowing individuals to deduct 50 percent of contributions to charitable organizations other than foundations

President Nixon's executive order establishes National Center for Voluntary Action, a nonprofit, nonpartisan body to coordinate government and voluntary sectors

1970   Total contributions to philanthropy estimated to be slightly more than $21 billion

1970–73 Congress considers and eventually rejects Nixon administration Family Assistance Plan

1971   Community Service Society of New York decides to end individual and family casework services and turn instead to community organization and social reform

1972   In *The Big Foundations,* Waldemar A. Nielsen accuses major foundations of timidity and conservatism in approaching racial and social problems

1974   Carnegie Free Library in Braddock, Pa., first of 1,679 libraries Andrew Carnegie gave to 1,412 communities, closes for lack of funds

With help of Philadelphia Eagles football team and Children's Hospital of Philadelphia, McDonald's Restaurants establishes first of many Ronald McDonald houses in U.S., Canada, and Australia where parents of hospitalized children can stay near them or with children receiving outpatient treatment

1975   Airlift of 130,000 South Vietnamese civil servants, professionals, and political and military leaders to U.S.; first wave of almost 600,000 Indo-Chinese who sought refuge in U.S., 1975–85

Commission on Private Philanthropy and Public Needs issues *Giving in America;* Donee Group counters with *Private Philanthropy: Vital and Innovative or Passive and Irrelevant?*

1976   Tax Reform Act permits charitable organizations other than foundations, churches, and religion-affiliated agencies to spend limited part of budgets on lobbying

1977   Death of Eli Lilly, founder of Lilly Endowment, Inc., which, since its establishment in 1937, had donated $250 million to charity

Philadelphia Common Pleas Court rules that applicants for admission to Girard College need not be orphans; girls as well as boys admitted to institution in 1980s

1978   John D. and Catherine T. MacArthur Foundation established; one of few very large foundations created since 1960, it supports health, education, and environmental concerns

John D. Rockefeller III dies at age 72; during lifetime donated $94 million to philanthropy including organizations seeking to fight hunger and control world population

Rev. Guido John Carcich, former chief fund-raiser of

Pallotine Fathers, once one of country's largest direct-mail charity operations, pleads guilty to misappropriating $2.2 million of charitable contributions made to Pallotine order

1978–79 Yale Program on Nonprofit Organizations begins interdisciplinary research program on the role, character, organization, and impact of the American voluntary sector

1979 Coca-Cola magnates Robert and George Woodruff give $105 million to Emory University, Atlanta, the largest gift by living donors in American philanthropic history

U. S. District Court, Washington, D.C., awards damages to three U.S. Army enlisted men whose names were posted on Ft. Myer, Va., bulletin board as noncontributors to Combined Federal Campaign

Charities report increase in donations of used gas-guzzler automobiles

1980 Estimated total giving for philanthropic purposes is $48.74 billion

John D. and Catherine T. MacArthur Foundation and Atlantic Richfield Foundation purchase *Harper's Magazine* to operate as nonprofit enterprise

Forty-one accredited colleges seek to raise $20 million in United Negro College Fund drive

In *Village of Schaumburg* v. *Citizens for Better Environment,* U.S. Supreme Court rules that ordinance requiring fund-raising groups to prove that at least 75 percent of money raised goes for charitable purposes infringes freedoms protected by First Amendment

In Refugee Act federal government promises full reimbursement to states for care and medical assistance furnished 450,000 Indo-Chinese refugees entering U.S., 1979–81

1981 In *NAACP Legal Defense and Education Fund, Inc.* v. *Campbell* (504 *Fed. Supp.* 1365), Judge Gerhard Gessell of Federal District Court for District of

Columbia rules that First Amendment bars exclusion of advocacy organization from Combined Federal Campaign

President Reagan appoints Task Force on Private Initiatives chaired by William Verity

Economic Recovery Taxation Act allows nonitemizers—individuals who use standard deduction—to deduct part of contributions to charitable organizations, and raises deduction corporations are allowed to take for charitable contributions from 5 to 10 percent of taxable income

1984   In *Maryland* v. *Munson*, U.S. Supreme Court rules states cannot impose limits on amount of money charities spend on fund-raising

Death of Musketeer, last stray dog supported by estate of Eleanor Ritchey, allows Auburn University to inherit Ritchey's $12 million estate

In survey conducted by Yankelovich, Skelly and White, 89 percent of Americans reported contributing to charities in 1984; Americans gave an average of $650 (2.4 percent of household incomes) to charities in 1984

1984–85 Total gifts to American institutions of higher education reach $6.32 billion; for first time corporate gifts to higher education surpass donations from alumni

1985   "We Are the World," charity anthem by all-star rock choir, raises $52 million for African famine relief

Seven donors to American Cancer Society plead guilty to tax evasion in scheme in which fund-raisers gave them each refunds of up to 90 percent of donations made and reported to IRS as gifts to society

In *Alamo Foundation* v. *Secretary of Labor*, U.S. Supreme Court rules tax-exempt religious organization must pay federal minimum wage to employees in its business functions

As result of Howard Hughes Medical Institute's sale of Hughes Aircraft Co. to General Motors Corp. for $5 billion, institute will increase annual spending on basic research from $100 million to $200 million

1986 Danforth Foundation awards Washington University, St. Louis, $100 million, the largest amount ever given to a university by a foundation

Tax Reform Act of 1986 contains provisions expected to have adverse effect on philanthropic giving

Death of Edwin S. Lowe, 75, manufacturer and distributor of contest cards for Bingo, fund-raising game used by churches, charitable organizations, and Indian tribes

United Jewish Appeal, organized at start of World War II to rescue and resettle European Jewry, and Federation of Jewish Philanthropies of New York merge "to meet Jewish needs wherever they exist"

Independent Sector launches effort to double charitable giving and increase volunteer activity by 50 percent by 1991

Will of Beverly Hills oil heiress Liliore Green Rains leaves $40 million each to six educational and health institutions, some of which did not know who she was

New York State's highest court declares public utilities' gifts to charity from rate revenues are unconstitutional as violation of rate payers' freedom of expression; decision does not affect charitable gifts made by utilities from profits or contributions by private businesses

1987 National Center for Charitable Statistics develops system for classifying nongovernmental, nonbusiness, tax-exempt organizations in U.S. to foster accurate description of the philanthropic sector

"Agreement in principle" between Norton Simon and University of California at Los Angeles for transfer of art collections owned by the Simon Foundation to University; if consummated, estimated $750 million value of collections will make gift the largest ever made to an American university

New foundation with seven-member board of trustees, most from Marin County, Cal., to administer $435 million Buck Trust; 20 to 25 percent of trust's annual income will finance one to three projects located in Marin County but benefiting all mankind

John W. Kluge's gift of $25 million, largest donation ever received by Columbia University, will be used to recruit and support minority students

1991   Scheduled date for final distribution of capital accumulated by Boston Fund established by will of Benjamin Franklin

Suggested Reading

REFERENCE WORKS

Giving USA, published annually by the American Association of Fund Raising Counsel, is an indispensable compilation of facts and trends in philanthropy since the mid-1950s. Two publications of Independent Sector provide analytical and interpretive data on the current state of American philanthropy: Virginia Ann Hodgkinson and Murray Weitzman, eds., *Dimensions of the Independent Sector: A Statistical Profile* (1986), and *The Charitable Behavior of Americans: A National Survey* conducted by Yankelovich, Skelly and White, Inc. (1986). Walter I. Trattner and Andrew W. Achenbaum, *Social Welfare in America: An Annotated Bibliography* (1983), and Daphne N. Layton, *An Annotated Bibliography on Philanthropy, Volunteering, and Nonprofit Initiative* (1987), supplant earlier bibliographies. The Foundation Center *Foundation Directory, Edition 11* (1987) supplies current information on foundations; Harold M. Keele and Joseph C. Kiger, eds., *Foundations* (1984) contains historical information. Sam Sternberg, comp., *National Directory of Corporate Charity* (1984), and the Foundation Center, *Corporation Foundation Profiles* (1985), are informative on giving by business firms.

Peter Romanofsky, ed., *Social Service Organizations*, 2 vols.

(1977), contains excellent historical and bibliographical material on voluntary associations. The American Association of Social Workers, *Encyclopedia of Social Work, Eighteenth Edition,* 2 vols. (1987), offers a wealth of data on the history and present concerns of social work as a profession and brief biographical sketches of men and women active in organized philanthropy. Further biographical and bibliographical information is available in Walter Trattner, ed., *Biographical Dictionary of Social Welfare in America* (1986). The indexes to *National Cyclopedia of American Biography* (1893–) and to volumes 1–20 of *The Dictionary of American Biography* (1927–1937) list subjects of biographies by occupation and happily include philanthropist as an occupation. The same is true in each of the following: Frances E. Willard and Mary Livermore, *American Women* (1897–1973); Edward T. James, ed., *Notable American Women, 1607–1950,* 3 vols. (1971); and Barbara Sicherman et al., eds., *Notable American Women: The Modern Period* (1980).

GENERAL

Merle Curti's essays, "The History of American Philanthropy as a Field of Research," *American Historical Review* 62 (1957): 357–63, and "American Philanthropy and the National Character," *American Quarterly* 10 (1958): 420–37, inaugurated study of the history of American philanthropy by professional historians. While directing the history of philanthropy project at the University of Wisconsin, Curti produced *American Philanthropy Abroad* (1963) and, with Roderick Nash *American Philanthropy in the Shaping of Higher Education* (1965), both works of enduring value. Another product of the University of Wisconsin history of philanthropy project, Scott M. Cutlip's *Fundraising in the United States: Its Role in American Philanthropy* (1965), concentrates on the period 1900–1945 and includes a chapter on "The Cheats in Fundraising."

Some of the most important studies of philanthropy have been written by "philanthropoids," a word coined by Dwight Macdonald in *The Ford Foundation* (1956) to describe executives of foundations and charitable organizations. Edward C. Jenkins'

Suggested Reading

Philanthropy in America (1950) deals mainly with the organization and financing of philanthropic agencies in the twentieth century but also gives some attention to the role of philanthropy in American life. Two studies by professional fund-raisers, Arnaud C. Marts, *Philanthropy's Role in Civilization: Its Contribution to Human Freedom* (1953), and John Price Jones, *The American Giver: A Review of American Generosity* (1954), offer practical and inspirational insights into the business of giving. F. Emerson Andrews, *Philanthropic Giving* (1950), remains one of the best introductions to the complexities and technicalities of philanthropy. A collection of essays on different aspects of giving, also entitled *Philanthropic Giving*, edited by Richard Magat, is forthcoming. Brian O'Connell, president of Independent Sector, has assembled a well-chosen collection of readings, *America's Voluntary Spirit* (1983), which includes the essays "From Charity to Philanthropy" by Daniel Boorstin and "Corporate Philanthropy: Historical Background" by Stanley Katz; in *Philanthropy in Action* (1987), O'Connell provides many examples of how philanthropy has made a difference in American life.

In recent years a number of centers have been established to promote research in philanthropy. John G. Simon, in *Research in Philanthropy* (1980), reviews the experiences of the Yale University Program on Nonprofit Organizations, of which he is director. Walter Powell, ed., *The Nonprofit Sector: A Research Handbook* (1987), which brings together the results of a decade of research at the Yale program, contains, among other informative essays, "A Historical Overview of the Private Nonprofit Sector" by Peter Hall, "Partners in Public Service" by Lester M. Salamon, and "Nonprofit Organizations and Policy Advocacy" by J. Craig Jenkins.

Arthur M. Schlesinger pointed out the importance of voluntary associations in American life in "Biography of a Nation of Joiners," *American Historical Review* 50 (1944): 1–25. Oscar and Mary Handlin, in *The Dimensions of Liberty* (1961), assess voluntary associations as factors in the development of American liberty. *Voluntary Associations: Perspectives on the Literature* (1972) by

Constance Smith and Anne Freedman provides a good framework for studying the many different kinds of voluntary organizations in the United States. Ralph M. Kramer, *Voluntary Agencies in the Welfare State* (1981), compares the current role of voluntary agencies in the United States, Great Britain, Israel, and the Netherlands. James Douglas, in *Why Charity? The Case for a Third Sector* (1983), presents a spirited defense of voluntarism.

Walter I. Trattner, *From Poor Law to Welfare State: A History of Social Welfare in America* (1974); James Leiby, *History of Social Welfare and Social Work in the United States* (1978); and Michael B. Katz, *In the Shadow of the Poorhouse: A Social History of Welfare in the United States* (1986), examine both official and voluntary efforts to deal the poverty and insecurity. Robert H. Bremner et al., eds., *Children and Youth in America: A Documentary History*, 3 vols. (1970–74) records efforts on behalf of children by both public and private agencies from the colonial period to the mid-1970s. It includes material on health and education not covered in Grace Abbott, *The Child and the State*, 2 vols. (1938).

United Way of America, *People and Events, A History of the United Way* (1977), is a chronological account of the development of the community chest and federated fund-raising. H. L. Lurie, *A Heritage Affirmed* (1961), and Philip Bernstein, *To Dwell in Unity* (1983), trace the history of the Jewish federation movement before and after 1960. Marshall Sklare, ed., *Understanding American Jewry* (1982), and Marc Lee Raphael, ed., *Understanding Jewish Philanthropy* (1979), analyze and interpret recent trends in giving by Jews. Oscar Handlin's *Adventure in Freedom: Three Hundred Years of Jewish Life in America* (1954) gives a good deal of attention to charitable organizations and philanthropy. The extensive literature on Roman Catholic philanthropy includes Donald P. Gavin, *National Conference of Catholic Charities, 1910–1960* (1962), and Marguerite J. Boylan, *Catholic Church and Social Welfare* (1961). William J. Reid, "Sectarian Agencies," *Encyclopedia of Social Work, Seventeenth Issue* (1977), gives an overview of the work of religious organizations contributing to social welfare.

Daniel Boorstin's lively and informative *The Americans: The*

Suggested Reading

Colonial Experience (1958), *The Americans: The National Experience* (1965), and *The Americans: The Democratic Experience* (1973) contain interesting observations on philanthropy.

CHAPTER 1

Among the essay-biographies of "the lives of little known but remarkable human beings from the inarticulate lower strata of colonial society" included in David G. Sweet and Gary B. Nash, eds., *Struggle and Survival in Colonial America* (1981), is "Squanto: Last of the Patuxets" by Neal Salisbury.

The writings of John Winthrop, William Penn, and Cotton Mather are primary sources for philanthropic thought in the early colonial period. Winthrop's "A Model of Christian Charity" (1630) is available in the Massachusetts Historical Society's *Winthrop Papers, II* (1931), and in Darrett B. Rutman's *John Winthrop's Decision for America: 1629* (1975). Samuel Eliot Morison's *Builders of the Bay Colony* (1930) has a good chapter on Winthrop; the best recent study is by Edmund S. Morgan, *The Puritan Dilemma: The Story of John Winthrop* (1958). Richard S. Dunn, in *Puritans and Yankees: The Winthrop Dynasty of New England, 1630–1717* (1962), presents John Winthrop as a man of the Puritan Revolution, his son as a man of the Restoration. Darrett Rutman's *Winthrop's Town* (1965) considers theory and practice of charity in seventeenth-century Boston.

Frederick B. Tolles and E. Gordon Aldefer, eds., in *The Witness of William Penn* (1957), provide selections from *No Cross, No Crown* (1669, 1682, 1694), *Some Fruits of Solitude* (1693), and *More Fruits of Solitude* (1702). Edward Beatty's *William Penn as Social Philosopher* (1939) and Auguste Jorn's *The Quakers as Pioneers in Social Work* (1931) are standard interpretations of Quaker humanitarianism. Richard S. Dunn and Mary M. Dunn are general editors of *The Papers of William Penn*, 1 vol. to date (1981–). The Dunns have edited *The World of William Penn (1986),* and Mary Maples Dunn, in *William Penn: Politics and Conscience* (1967), examines two aspects of Penn's character. A recent biography is Harry Emerson Wildes, *William Penn* (1974).

Cotton Mather's *Bonafacius, or Essays To Do Good* (1710) is reprinted in O'Connell, *America's Voluntary Spirit. Magnalia*

Christi Americana (1855 ed.) 1:102, contains Mather's advice to Bostonians on the conduct of charity. Kenneth B. Murdock's introduction to his *Selections from Cotton Mather* (1926) helped revive respect for Mather; Perry Miller's *The New England Mind: From Colony to Province* (1953) offers a learned and influential analysis of Mather's thought. The following are illustrative but not exhaustive of recent scholarly interest in Mather: Robert Middlekauf, *The Mathers: Three Generations of Puritan Intellectuals, 1596–1728;* David Levin, *Cotton Mather: The Young Life of the Lord's Remembrances* (1978); Kenneth Silverman, *The Life and Times of Cotton Mather* (1984); Virginia Berhnhard, "Cotton Mather and the Doing of Good: A Puritan Gospel of Wealth," *The New England Quarterly* 49 (1976): 225–41; Richard Lovelace, *The American Pietism of Cotton Mather: Origins of American Evangelicalism* (1979); and Mitchell Robert Breitsieser, *Cotton Mather and Benjamin Franklin: The Price of Representative Personality* (1984). Elizabeth Wisner, in her article on "The Puritan Background of the New England Poor Laws," *Social Service Review* 19 (1945): 381–90, examines Mather's charitable activities from the standpoint of modern social work.

The Papers of Benjamin Franklin, ed. Leonard W. Labaree and Whitefield J. Bell, Jr., 24 vols. to date (1959–), is the definitive edition of Franklin's correspondence and writings. The most authoritative of many editions of Franklin's memoirs is *The Autobiography of Benjamin Franklin*, ed. Leonard W. Labaree et al. (1964). "Poor Richard Improved" (1758), often reprinted under the title, *The Way to Wealth*, is in *The Papers of Benjamin Franklin* 7 (1964): 326–50; for other statements by Franklin on poverty and the poor laws see *Papers* 4 (1961): 477–83; 13 (1969): 510–16; and 15 (1972): 103–107. Carl Van Doren's *Benjamin Franklin* (1938) is recognized as one of the great American biographies. The best brief biography is the sketch by Carl Becker in volume six (1931) of the *Dictionary of American Biography*. Ralph Ketcham, *Benjamin Franklin* (1965), is a study of Franklin's thought. "Benjamin Franklin and Philadelphia" in *History of Philadelphia, 1609–1884*, 3 vols., by J. Thomas Scharf and

Suggested Reading

Thomas Westcott (1884), 1:218–43, is a perceptive and entertaining essay written about a century after Franklin's death. It can be read in conjunction with Harold A. Larrabee, "Poor Richard in an Age of Plenty," *Harper's Magazine* 212 (January 1956): 64–68, an article assaying Franklin's significance on the two-hundred-and-fiftieth anniversary of his birth.

Legislation for the relief of the poor in Philadelphia during Franklin's lifetime is examined by Hannah Benner Roach, "Philadelphia's Colonial Poor Laws," *Pennsylvania Genealogical Magazine* 22 (1962): 159–85. John K. Alexander, *Render Them Submissive: Responses to Poverty in Philadelphia, 1760–1800* (1980), gives some attention to Franklin's activities. Franklin's bequests to Boston and Philadelphia are discussed in F. Emerson Andrews, *Philanthropic Foundations* (1956), 93–94, Julius Rosenwald, "Principles of Public Giving," in O'Connell, ed., *America's Voluntary Spirit*, and Howard Husock, "Ben's Bequest," *Boston Globe*, May 17, 1987.

Wallace Notestein, *The English People of the Eve of Colonization* (1954), and Louis B. Wright, *The Cultural Life of American Colonies* (1957), both volumes in the New American Nation series, are useful for orientation and social and cultural background.

Religion and education, both major concerns of philanthropy in the colonial era and later periods of American history, are thoroughly studied by Sidney Ahlstrom, *Religious History of the American People* (1973); Lawrence Cremin, *American Education: The Colonial Experience, 1607–1783* (1970); and Richard Hofstadter and Wilson Smith, *American Higher Education: A Documentary History*, 2 vols. (1961).

CHAPTER 2

A good place to begin is Richard Hofstadter's *America at 1750: A Social Portrait* (1971). James S. Henretta, *Evolution of American Society, 1700–1815* (1973), surveys change in economics, society, and culture. Bernard Bailyn's ambitious study of population movements opened with *The Peopling of British North America: An Introduction* (1986). Bailyn's *Voyages to the West: A Passage in the Peopling of America on the Even of the Revolution* (1986) considers poverty as a motive for emigration from Britain to America, 1773–76. Jackson Turner Main, *The Social Structure of Revolutionary America* (1965); James T. Lemon, *The Best Poor Man's Country* (1972); and Gary B. Nash, *Red, White and Black: The Peoples of Early America* (1974) and *The Urban Crucible: Social Change, Political Consciousness and the Origins of the American Revolution* (1979), deal with class structure and social and economic conditions.

Sidney Ahlstrom, *Religious History of the American People*, examines the general state of religion in the eighteenth century. Alan Heimert and Perry Miller, two leading scholars on the subject, have edited *The Great Awakening* (1967), a documentary history, and Edwin Gaustad, in *The Great Awakening in New England* (1957), analyzes its course and consequences. William G. McLoughlin discusses both the first and second Great Awakenings (as well as earlier and subsequent ones), and evaluates the literature concerning them in *Revivals, Awakenings, and Reform: An Essay on Religion and Social Change, 1607–1977* (1978). Stuart C. Henry, *George Whitefield, Wayfaring Wtiness* (1957); *George Whitefield's Journals* (1969, first published 1747); and John Charles Pollock, *George Whitefield and the Great Awakening* (1972) illumine Whitefield's contributions to American religion and philanthropy.

George S. Brooke's *Friend Anthony Benezet* (1937), a loving biography, includes letters to, from, and concerning Benezet and Benezet's minor writings. Anthony Benezet's *Some Observations on the Situation, Disposition, and Character of the Indian Natives of the Continent* (1784) is characteristic of the author. *A Word of Remembrance and Caution to the Rich* (1793), written about thirty years before publication and originally entitled "A Plea for the Poor," is John Woolman's best essay. Frederick B. Tolles's *Meeting House and Counting House* (1948) gives an excellent picture of the Quaker society in which Benezet and Woolman lived. Sydney V. James, *A People among Peoples: Quaker Benevolence in Eighteenth-Century America* (1963), reviews Quaker social welfare and social service activities from the 1750's to 1815. David Rothman, ed., *The Charitable Impulse in Eighteenth-Century America: Collected Papers* (1971), contains sermons and acts of incorporation of charitable societies, including the Brown Fellowship Society of Charleston, South Carolina.

Carl and Jessica Bridenbaugh, in *Rebels and Gentlemen: Philadelphia in the Age of Franklin* (1942), discuss the Pennsylvania Hospital and other benevolent institutions. Richard H. Shryock's *The Development of Modern Medicine* (1936) related medical developments to humanitarian movements and shows the relationship between European and American activity. This relationship is the subject of Michael Kraus's "Eighteenth Century Humanitarianism: Collaboration between Europe and America," *Pennsylvania Magazine of History and Biography* 60 (1936): 270–86. Merrill Jensen's *The New Nation* (1950) has a chapter surveying humanitarian progress during the Confederation period. Benjamin Rush's *Essays, Literary, and Philosophical* (1806) is a fascinating miscellany by one of America's greatest humanitarian reformers. George W. Corner's edition of *The Autobiography of Benjamin Rush* (1948) is valuable as is L. H. Butterfield's *Letters of Benjamin Rush* (1951). David Freeman, *Benjamin Rush, Revolutionary Gadfly* (1971), follows Rush's career to 1790; Abraham Blinderman deals with Rush's interest in education in *Three Early Champions of Education: Benjamin Franklin, Benjamin Rush, and Noah Webster* (1976). John Harvey Powell, in *Bring Out Your Dead* (1949), deals with Philadelphia's reaction to the yellow-fever epidemic of 1793 in a manner both vivid and scholarly. John Bach McMaster, in *The Life and Times of Stephen Girard* (1918), makes Girard's career dull; Harry Emerson Wildes's *Lonely Midas: The Story of Stephen Girard* (1943) overcompensates for McMaster's defects but is more satisfactory. Neva R. Deardorff's "The New Pied Pipers," *Survey* 52 (1924): 31–47, 56–61, comments on Girard's legacy and its influence on other donors.

Alexander, *Render Them Submissive*, cited in Chapter I, and Raymond A. Mohl, *Poverty in New York, 1783–1825* (1971), deal with responses to urban poverty before and after the Revolution. Voluntary efforts at moral and social reform in late eighteenth- and early nineteenth-century New York are examined by M. J. Heale in "Humanitarianism in the Early Republic," *Journal of American Studies* 2 (1968):161–75, and "The New York Society for the Prevention of Pauperism," *New York Historical Society Quarterly* 55 (1971):52–72. John Resch, "Federal Welfare for Revolutionary War Veterans," *Social Service Review* 56 (1982):171–95, studies implementation of the 1818 Revolutionary War Pension Act. Hyman B. Grinstein, *The Rise of the Jewish Community of New York, 1654–1860* (1945), deals with both philanthropy and mutual aid.

CHAPTERS 3 AND 4

Russell B. Nye, *The Cultural Life of the New Nation, 1776–1830* (1960) and *Society and Culture in America, 1830–1860* (1974), provide the social and intellectual background for philanthropic developments in the first half of the nineteenth century. A contemporary source, Emerson Davis, *The Half Century* (1851), is well worth consulting; and *Niles' Register* (1811–49), which is indexed, contains information on charity and relief.

Nearly all European travelers' accounts, including those of Tocqueville and Dickens, devote space to American philanthropic institutions. One of the lesser known but valuable accounts is George Combe's *Notes on the United States of North America* (1841). George Wilson Pierson's *Tocqueville and Beaumont in America* (1938) presents a panorama of the United States in 1831–32. Frederika Bremer, in *The Homes of the New World* (1853), comments on the American prospensity for associated action. "This People," she wrote, "associate as easily as they breathe."

Edith Abbott's *Some American Pioneers in Social Welfare* (1937) contains biographical sketches and selections from the writings of Thomas Eddy, Stephen Girard, Samuel Gridley Howe, Dorothea L. Dix, and Charles Loring Brace. Joseph Tuckerman, *On the Elevation of the Poor* (1874), reprints selections from Tuckerman's reports on his ministry to the poor in Boston. Mathew Carey's proposal for federated financing in Philadelphia in 1829 is reprinted in the *Social Service Review* 29 (1955): 302–5. *The Works of William E. Channing, D.D.* (1887)

includes "Remarks on Associations" and other relevant essays and addresses. William R. Lawrence's *Extracts from the Diary and Correspondence of the Late Amos Lawrence* (1855) is illuminating; and Lewis Tappan's *Is It Right to be Rich?* (1869) follows in the pattern of Mather's *Essays To Do Good.* Both Emerson and Thoreau made pointed observations on philanthropy in their journals and essays. "Self-Reliance" (1836–39), "Man the Reformer" (1841), and "New England Reformers" (1844) give Emerson's views. *Walden* (1854) contains Thoreau's comments.

Helen E. Marshall's *Dorothea Dix, Forgotten Samaritan* (1937) and Harold Schwartz's *Samuel Gridley Howe, Social Reformer* (1956) are two good studies of important reformers. Biographies of other philanthropists and reformers include Daniel T. McColgan, *Joseph Tuckerman* (1940); Benjamin P. Thomas, *Theodore Weld* (1950); R. V. Harlow, *Gerrit Smith, Philanthropist and Reformer* (1939); and Edward Clarence Mack, *Peter Cooper, Citizen of New York* (1949). Cooper and his son-in-law are the subjects of Allan Nevins, *Abram S. Hewitt with Some Account of Peter Cooper* (1935). Gerda Lerner's *The Grimké Sisters from Carolina: Rebels against Slavery* (1967) throws light on both abolitionism and the women's rights movement. Franklin Parker, *George Peabody: A Biography* (1971), deals mainly with the philanthropic aspects of Peabody's career. *The Lowells and Their Institute* (1966) by Edward Weeks is a family and institutional study extending through the nineteenth and much of the twentieth centuries.

Alice Felt Tyler, *Freedom's Ferment: Phases of American Social History to 1860* (1944), is a pioneer study of the pre–Civil War "thrust for reform." Henry Steele Commager, in *Era of Reform* (1960), and David B. Davis, in *Anti-Bellum Reform* (1967), offer, respectively, source readings and a selection of articles and essays on the reform movements. Bremner et al., eds., *Children and Youth in America,* vol. 1 (1970), deals with philanthropically inspired efforts on behalf of children and young people in the fields of health, education, dependency, child labor, deliquency, and services for black and native American children. Homer Folks, *Care of Destitute, Neglected and Deliquent Children* (1902), and Henry W. Thurston, *The Dependent Child: The Story of Changing Aims and Methods in the Care of Dependent Children*

(1930), are works of continuing interest. Charles Loring Brace, *The Dangerous Classes of New York and Twenty Years' Work among Them* (1872) is a fascinating account of "child saving."

Two important studies of women's roles are Nancy F. Cott's *The Bonds of Womanhood: "Women's Sphere" in New England, 1780–1835* (1977), and Barbara J. Berg's *The Remembered Gate, Origins of American Feminism: The Woman and the City* (1978). Mary Bosworth Treudley, "The 'Benevolent Fair': A Study of Charitable Organizations among American Women in the First Third of the Nineteenth Century," *Social Service Review* 14 (1940): 509–22, deals with the early history of female charitable organizations.

Among older but still useful studies of humanitarian reform are Albert Deutsch, *The Mentally Ill in America* (1949); Merle Curti, *The Social Ideas of American Educators* (1935) and *Peace or War* (1936); Ishbel Ross, *Journey into Light: The Story of the Education of the Blind* (1951); and Harry Best, *Blindness and the Blind in the United States* (1934) and *Deafness and the Deaf in the United States* (1943). More recent studies, representing different emphases and different points of view, include David J. Rothman, *The Discovery of the Asylum: Social Order and Disorder in the New Republic* (1971); Gerald Grob, *Mental Institutions in America: Social Policy to 1875* (1973); Robert M. Mennel, *Thorns and Thistles: Juvenile Delinquents in the United States, 1825–1940* (1973); Frances A. Koestler, *The Unseen Minority: A Social History of the Blind* (1976); and Steven Schlossman, *Love and the American Delinquent: The Theory and Practice of "Progressive" Juvenile Justice, 1825–1920* (1977).

Religious and moral reform have attracted the interest of numerous scholars. John R. Bodo, *The Protestant Clergy and Public Issues, 1812–1848* (1954); Timothy L. Smith, *Revivalism and Social Reform: American Protestantism on the Eve of the Civil War* (1957); Charles I. Foster, *An Errand of Mercy: The Evangelical United Front, 1790–1837* (1960); Clifford Griffin, *Their Brothers' Keepers: Moral Stewardship in the United States, 1800–1865* (1960); Charles C. Cole, *The Social Ideas of Northern Evangelists* (1954); and Carroll Smith Rosenberg, *Religion and the Rise of the American City: The New York City Mission Movement,*

1812–1870 (1971), are prominent among, but do not exhaust, the list of valuable monographs.

There is a vast literature on abolitionism, much of it produced since 1960. Bibliographic expansion and changes in interpretation can be followed from Gilbert H. Barnes, *The Antislavery Impulse* (1934), through Louis Filler, *The Crusade against Slavery 1830– 1860* (1960), to such representative works as James Brewer Steward, *Holy Warriors: The Abolitionists and American Slavery* (1976), and Lawrence J. Friedman, *Gregarious Saints: Self and Community in American Abolitionism* (1982).

Lawrence Cremin's *American Education: The National Experience, 1783–1876* (1980) is the best guide to developments in education. Neil Harris's *The Artist in American Society: The Formative Years* (1966) and Lillian B. Miller's *Patrons and Patriotism: The Encouragement of Fine Arts in the United States, 1790–1860* (1966) are complementary studies. Harris's *Humbug: The Art of P. T. Barnum* (1973) notes Barnum's use of philanthropy for promotional purposes. Irwin G. Wyllie, "The Search for an American Law of Charity," *Mississippi Valley Historical Review* 46 (1959): 203–21, and Howard S. Miller, *The Legal Foundations of Philanthropy, 1776–1844* (1961), examine court decisions allowing development of a permissive rather than restrictive law of charity in the United States.

CHAPTER 5

Two general surveys help put philanthropic efforts in perspective: David Herbert Donald, *Liberty and Union* (1978), and James M. McPherson, *Ordeal by Fire: The Civil War and Reconstruction* (1981). Clement Eaton's *A History of the Southern Confederacy* (1954) and Emory M. Thomas's *The Confederate Nation* (1979) give overviews of the Confederacy from different points of view. Attitudes of intellectuals and writers, some of whom were involved in relief activities, are surveyed in George M. Frederickson, *The Inner Civil War: Northern Intellectuals and the Crisis of the Union* (1965), and Daniel Aaron, *The Unwritten War: American Writers and the Civil War* (1973).

Linus P. Brockett's and Mary C. Vaughn's *Women's Work in the Civil War* (1867); the chapter on charity in Emerson David Fite's

Social and Industrial Conditions in the North during the Civil War (1910); and Holland Thompson's "Private Agencies of Relief," in Francis Trevelyan Miller, ed., The Photographic History of the Civil War, 10 vols. (1911), 7:321–44, are still useful. Mary Elizabeth Massey's Bonnet Brigades (1966) is a study of women's contributions to the war effort on both sides of the conflict. Her book, Refugee Life in the Confederacy (1964), and Paul D. Escott's article, " 'The Cry of the Sufferers': The Problem of Welfare in the Confederacy," Civil War History 23 (1977): 228–40, shed light on home front problems in the South and efforts to deal with them. Robert H. Bremner, The Public Good: Philanthropy and Welfare in the Civil War Era (1980), deals with philanthropic rivalries involving aid to soldiers and freedman. Robert Lester Reynolds examines the struggle between supporters of the United States Sanitary Commission and the Christian Commission in Benevolence on the Home Front in Massachusetts during the Civil War (1970).

William Quentin Maxwell's Lincoln's Fifth Wheel: The Political History of the United States Sanitary Commission (1956) traces the fortunes of an important philanthropic agency engaged in both service and advocacy for Union servicemen. Additional information on the Sanitary Commission can be found in George Worthington Adams's Doctor in Blue: The Medical History of the Union Army in the Civil War (1952) and in Laura Wood Roper, FLO: A Biography of Frederick Law Olmsted (1973).

George R. Bentley's A History of the Freedman's Bureau (1955), John A. Carpenter's Sword and Olive Branch: Oliver Otis Howard (1964), and William S. McFeeley's Yankee Step Father: O. O. Howard and the Freedman (1968) contain information on efforts of voluntary agencies to assist the freedmen. Henry Lee Swint's The Northern Teacher in the South, 1862–1870 (1941) is an early and still useful treatment of the freedman's aid societies. Willie Lee Rose's Rehearsal for Reconstruction: The Port Royal Experiment (1964) discusses the beginning of philanthropic work with former slaves. In Been in the Storm So Long: The Aftermath of Slavery (1978) Leon Litwack records former slaves' attitudes toward freedmen's aid and missionary societies. J. L. M. Curry

Suggested Reading

gives an informative account of the origin and work of the Peabody Education Fund in *A Brief Sketch of George Peabody, and a History of the Peabody Education Fund through Thirty Years* (1898, 1969). Franklin Parker reviews Peabody's contributions to philanthropy in *George Peabody, A Biography* (1971).

CHAPTER 6

John A. Garraty, *The New Commonwealth, 1877–1890* (1968), and Harold B. Faulkner, *Politics, Reform and Expansion* (1959), supply political and social background for philanthropic developments in the late nineteenth century. Samuel Rezneck reviews the impact of two economic depressions in "Distress, Relief, and Discontent in the United States during the Depression of 1873–78," *Journal of Political Economy* 58 (1950): 494–512, and "Patterns of Thought and Action in an American Depression, 1882–1886," *American Historical Review* 61 (1955–56): 284–307. Leah H. Feder's *Unemployment Relief in Periods of Depression* (1936) covers the years 1857–1922; Alexander Keyssar's *Out of Work: The First Century of Unemployment in Massachusetts* (1986) deals with agencies aiding the unemployed, 1870–1920.

Verl S. Lewis's "Charity Organization Society," *Encyclopedia of Social Work, Seventeenth Issue* (1977), 1:96–100, condenses much information into brief space. The entire issue of *Social Casework* (February 1968) is devoted to "Who Spoke for the Poor, 1880–1914." Amos G. Warner's *American Charities* (1894) is indispensable for an understanding of the point of view of charity reformers in the late nineteenth century. Robert H. Bremner, in "'Scientific Philanthropy,' 1873–93," *Social Service Review* 30 (1956): 168–73, gives citations to the voluminous contemporary literature on the subject. Jane Addams et al., *Philanthropy and Social Progress* (1893), presents the attitude of more advanced social workers in the 1890s. William Rhinelander Stewart's *The Philanthropic Work of Josephine Shaw Lowell* (1911) is still the only full-length study of one of the most important women of the late nineteenth century. Frances A. Goodale's anthology, *The Literature of Philanthropy* (1893), describes in winning fashion the work of women volunteers in many undertakings. Sheila M.

Rothman, *Women's Proper Place: A History of Changing Ideals and Practices, 1870 to the Present* (1978), traces shifts in movements supported by women since the late nineteenth century. Roy Lubove's *The Professional Altruist: The Emergence of Social Work as a Career, 1880–1930* (1965) is the standard work on the subject. Emma O. Lundberg's *Unto the Least of These* (1947) is a history of social services for children, and Margaret E. Rich's *A Belief in People: A History of Family Social Work* (1980) outlines the origins and development of the family service movement. Recent articles dealing with different aspects of late nineteenth-century philanthropy include F. Emerson Andrews, "A Note on Nineteenth Century Foundations," *Foundation News* 15 (March–April 1974): 39–41, and Edward N. Saveth, "Patrician Philanthropy in America," *Social Service Review* 54 (1980): 76–91.

The religious response to problems of city life is dealt with in Aaron I. Abell, *The Urban Impact on American Protestantism, 1865–1900* (1944), and *American Catholicism and Social Action, 1865–1950* (1961); Robert D. Cross, ed., *The Church and the City, 1865–1910* (1967); Nathan Huggins, *Protestants against Poverty: Boston's Charities, 1870–1900* (1971); Alan S. Horlick, *Country Boys and Merchant Princes: The Social Control of Young Men in New York* (1975); and Paul Boyer, *Urban Masses and Moral Order in New York, 1820–1920* (1978). Two helpful sources of information on Jewish charities are Herman D. Stein's "Jewish Social Work in the United States (1654–1954)," *American Jewish Yearbook* 57 (1956): 3–98, and *Trends and Issues in Jewish Social Welfare in the United States, 1899–1952* (1966), ed. Robert Morris and Micahel Freund. Timoth L. Smith reviews the Judeo-Christian ethic in "Biblical Ideals in American Christian and Jewish Philanthropy, 1880–1920," *American Jewish History* 74 (1984–85): 3–26.

The most acceptable biography of Clara Barton is *Angel of the Battlefield* (1956) by Ishbel Ross. Foster Rhea Dulles's *The American Red Cross* (1950) deals with all aspects of Red Cross history. Clyde E. Buckingham's *Red Cross Disaster Relief* examines the origin and development of an important aspect of

Red Cross work. Charles Hopkins's *History of the Y.M.C.A. in North America* (1951) is readable and objective. Daniel L. Macleod's *Building Character in the American Boy: The Boy Scouts, YMCA, and Their Forerunners, 1870–1920* (1983) contrasts and compares two leading agencies involved in work with boys.

CHAPTER 7

Andrew Carnegie's "Wealth," *North American Review* 148 (1889): 653–64, and "Best Fields for Philanthropy," *North American Review* 149 (1889): 682–98, are reprinted in his *The Gospel of Wealth* (1901). Burton J. Hendrick, in *The Life of Andrew Carnegie* (1932), sketches the background and reception of the gospel of wealth and gives some information on Carnegie's major gifts. Joseph Frazier Wall's *Andrew Carnegie* (1970) is a superior biography. Carnegie's benefactions are summarized by Robert M. Lester in *Forty Years of Carnegie Giving* (1941). Florence Anderson's *Carnegie Corporation Library Program, 1911–1961* (1963) notes contributions to library services as well as library buildings. Ellen Condliffe Lageman, *Private Power for the Public Good* (1963), is an excellent history of the Carnegie Foundation for the Advancement of Teaching. Barry D. Karl and Stanley N. Katz, in "The American Private Foundation and the Public Sphere, 1890–1930," *Minerva* 19 (1981): 236–70, examine the origins and significance of foundations.

John D. Rockefeller, in *Random Reminiscences of Men and Events* (1909), states his philosophy and program for giving. Allan Nevins's *Study in Power: John D. Rockefeller, Industrialist and Philanthropist* (1953) describes the difficulties Rockefeller encountered in carrying out his stewardship. *American Heritage* 6 (April 1955): 65–86, contains the memoirs of Frederick T. Gates, Rockefeller's adviser on philanthropy, with an introduction and postscript by Allan Nevins. Raymond B. Fosdick's *John D. Rockefeller, Jr.* (1956) shows the broadening influence exerted on the younger Rockefeller by Gates and others with whom he was associated in managing the family benefactions. John Ettling, *The Germ of Laziness: Rockefeller Philanthropy and Public Health in the South* (1981), is an account of the eradication of hookworm disease.

Albert Shaw, in "American Millionaires, and Their Public Gifts," *Review of Reviews* 7 (1893): 48–60, surveys the extent to which the gospel of wealth was being practiced by millionaires in the 1890s. Sarah K. Bolton's *Famous Givers and Their Gifts* (1896) deals with several almost forgotten donors as well as with many well-known ones. Edward C. Kirkland's *Dream and Thought in the Business Community, 1860–1900* (1956) and Irvin G. Wyllie's *The Self-Made Man in America* (1954) are useful on businessmen's attitudes toward philanthropy. Washington Gladden, with his article "Tainted Money," *Outlook* 52 (1895): 886–87, opened a celebrated controversy.

Gunnar Myrdal et al., in *An American Dilemma* (1944), 2:887–93, offers a quick survey of philanthropic activity in the field of southern education. E. Franklin Frazier's *Black Bourgeoisie* (1957) and Louis R. Harlan's *Separate and Unequal: Public School Campaigns and Racism in the Southern Seaboard States, 1901–1915* (1958) are critical of the influence of northern philanthropists on Negro education; Horace Mann Bond, *The Education of the Negro in the American Social Order* (1934) and Joseph C. Kiger, "The Large Foundation in Southern Education," *Journal of Higher Education* 27 (1956): 125–32, are informative and balanced accounts.

In *When Social Work Was Young* (1939) Edward T. Devine records the variety of causes in which social workers were active around and after the turn of the century. The antituberculosis crusade, which touched on many other issues, is treated in Richard H. Shryock's *National Tuberculosis Association, 1904–1954* (1957). Robert H. Bremner, in *From the Depths: The Discovery of Poverty in the United States* (1956), and Allen F. Davis, in *Spearheads for Reform: The Social Settlements and the Progressive Movement, 1890–1914* (1967), discuss the role of social workers in reform movements of the Progressive Era. James B. Lane, "Jacob A. Riis and Scientific Philanthropy during the Progressive Era," *Social Service Review* 47 (1973): 32–48; Edward S. Shapiro, "Robert A. Woods and the Settlement House

Impulse," *Social Service Review* 52 (1978): 215–25; and James A. Hijiya, "Four Ways of Looking at a Philanthropist: A Study of Robert Weeks de Forest," *Proceedings of the American Philosophical Society* 124 (1980): 404–18, provide further insights on philanthropy and reform. Jane Addams, *Democracy and Social Ethics* (1902, 1964) and *Twenty Years at Hull-House* (1910) illumine the practical idealism of the settlement movement. Allen F. Davis and Mary Lynn McCree, eds., in *Eighty Years at Hull House* (1969), assemble photographs and excerpts from the writings of the founders, residents, supporters, and critics of Hull House. Another settlement house and settlement leader are memorialized in R. L. Duffus's *Lillian Wald* (1938). Florence Kelley's "Labor Legislation and Philanthropy in Illinois," *Charities Review* 10 (1900–1901): 287–88, is a characteristic article by a formidable reformer. Her biographer is Josephine Goldmark, *Impatient Crusader: Florence Kelley's Life Story* (1953). Herbert A. Wisbey, Jr., *Soldiers Without Swords: A History of the Salvation Army in the United States* (1955), and Beatrice Plumb, *Edgar James Helms, the Goodwill Man* (1965), deal with two still-flourishing organizations. Daniel M. Fox, *Engines of Culture: Philanthropy and Art Museums* (1963); Helen Lefkowitz Horowitz, *Culture and the City: Cultural Philanthropy in Chicago from 1880 to 1917* (1976); and Kathleen McCarthy, *Noblesse Oblique: Charity and Culture in Chicago, 1849–1929* (1982), examine philanthropic support of the arts.

CHAPTER 8

Dulles, *American Red Cross*, and Hopkins, *Y.M.C.A.*, are essential for war relief activities in World War I. Portia B. Kernodle's *The Red Cross Nurse in Action, 1882–1948* (1949) is thorough and unsentimental. Raymond B. Fosdick, in *Chronicle of a Generation: An Autobiography* (1958), describes the confusion resulting from the desire of numerous private agencies to serve the soldier. Frank M. Surface and Raymond L. Bland's *American Food in the World War and Reconstruction Period* (1931) is a methodical account of relief operations directed by Herbert Hoover in the decade after 1914. Two studies deal with special phases of Hoover's work: Suda L. Bane and Ralph H. Lutz, *Organization of American Relief in Europe, 1918–1919* (1943), and H. H. Fisher, *The Famine in Soviet Russia, 1919–1923: The Operations of the American Relief Administration* (1927). Frank Alfred Golder and Lincoln Hutchinson, in *On the Trail of the Russian Famine* (1927), report the observations of two ARA investigators. Hoover's *An American Epic*, 4 vols. (1959–63), a "history of American enterprises of compassion," begins with a volume on the CRB.

John R. Seeley et al., in *Community Chest: A Case Study in Philanthropy* (1958), focuses on Indianapolis but presents the historical background and development of the community chest movement. Willford Isbell King's *Trends in Philanthropy* (1928) studies patterns in giving in New Haven, 1900–1925. Henry S. Pritchett's "A Science of Giving," in Carnegie Corporation of New York, *Report of the Acting President* (1922), 13–20, is a foundation executive's presentation of the difficulties of giving. A foundation founder discusses the same problem in Julius Rosenwald, "The Burden of Wealth," *Saturday Evening Post*, January 5, 1929, pp. 12–13. Cornelia Cannon's "Philanthropic Doubts," *Atlantic Monthly*, 128 (1921): 289–300, critical of the philanthropic approach to social problems, received wide attention in the 1920's. "Giving—the Great American Game," *Saturday Evening Post*, December 28, 1928, p. 28, and "The New Gospel of Wealth," *Literary Digest*, November 30, 1929, pp. 22–23, are examples of the celebration of American philanthropy in the late 1920's.

In *Graham Taylor, Pioneer in Social Justice* (1964) and *Seedtime of Reform: American Social Service and Social Action, 1918–33* (1963), Louise C. Wade and Clarke Chambers, respectively, examine the activities of a settlement house leader and activist social workers in the 1920s. Harold C. Coffman, *American Foundations: A Study of Their Role in the Child Welfare Movement* (1936); Steven Schlossman, "Philanthropy and the Gospel of Child Development," *History of Education Quarterly* 21 (1981): 275–99; and Neil A. Radford, *The Carnegie Corporation and the Development of American College Libraries*

(1984), consider different aspects of foundation work in the 1920's. Morell Heald's *The Social Responsibilities of Business: Company and Community, 1900–1960* (1970) gives considerable attention to business and the community chest movement.

John H. Mariano's *The Second Generation of Italians in New York City* (1921) contains information on benevolent organizations and other voluntary associations. In *Steel City: Urban and Ethnic Patterns in Gary, Indiana, 1906–1950* (1986) Raymond A. Mohl and Neil Betten contrast programs of settlement houses and the International Institute in dealing with immigrants. Caroline W. Ware's *Greenwich Village, 1920–1930* (1935) examines social services available to residents of an urban community in the 1920s.

CHAPTER 9

The Crisis of the Old Order, 1919–1933 (1957) by Arthur M. Schlesinger, Jr., is a good guide to the thought and literature of the early depression years. Jonathan Leonard's *Three Years Down* (1939) preserves some of the flavor of the period. U.S. Senate Committee on Manufactures, 72 Congress, 1 session, *Unemployment Relief: Hearings on S. 174 . . . and S. 262* (1932), contains a mine of information. R. M. MacIver's *The Contributions of Sociology to Social Work* (1931); Reinhold Niebuhr's *The Contributions of Religion to Social Work* (1932); and Philip Klein's "Social Work," *Encyclopedia of the Social Sciences* 14 (1935): 165–73, are all important sources for the orientation of social workers' thought in the early 1930s. Rich, *A Belief in People*, is particularly good on the impact of the depression on family welfare agencies. Abraham Epstein, in "Do the Rich Give to Charity?" *American Mercury* 23 (May 1931): 22–30, discusses the inadequacy of philanthropy as a means of meeting social needs.

Harris G. Warren, in *Herbert Hoover and the Great Depression* (1959), attempts to do justice to the Hoover administration. The former president presents his own case in *The Memoirs of Herbert Hoover: The Great Depression, 1929–41* (1952). William Starr Myers's *The State Papers and Other Public Writings of Herbert Hoover* (1934) is the standard source for

Hoover's statements on charity and other subjects. Bernard Bellush, in *Franklin D. Roosevelt as Governor of New York* (1955), and Frank Freidel, in *Franklin D. Roosevelt: The Triumph* (1956), trace the development of Roosevelt's policy on unemployment relief. Dorothy Kahn's *This Business of Relief* (1936) is good on the situation in the mid-thirties. Josephine C. Brown's *Public Relief, 1929–1939* (1940) remains a useful study of a complicated problem. Mabel Newcomer, in "Fifty Years of Public Support of Welfare Functions in the United States," *Social Service Review* 15 (1941): 651–60, records and comments on the changes in the financing of public welfare, 1890–1940. Marguerite T. Boylan's *Social Welfare in the Catholic Church* (1941) shows the impact of the depression and New Deal on organized Catholic charities. Judith Trolander, in *The Settlement Houses and the Great Depression* (1975), considers the effect of community chest affiliation on settlement house programs.

The best one-volume history of the New Deal is William E. Leuchtenburg's *Franklin D. Roosevelt and the New Deal, 1932–1940* (1963). John A. Garraty's *Unemployment in History, Economic Thought and Public Policy* (1978) compares the New Deal attack on unemployment with policies and programs followed in other countries, including Nazi Germany. Roy Lubove, in *The Struggles for Social Security, 1900–1935* (1968), considers the background of the Social Security Act, and Edwin C. Witte, in *The Development of the Social Security Act* (1963), traces the steps toward its enactment. James T. Patterson's *America's Struggle against Poverty, 1900–1980* (1981) contrasts New Deal relief and work projects with the War on Poverty programs of the 1960s. Robert H. Bremner, in "The New Deal and Social Welfare," in Harvard Sitkoff, ed., *Fifty Years Later: The New Deal Evaluated* (1985), puts New Deal programs for relief and welfare in historical perspective and lists suggested readings on the topic.

CHAPTER 10

F. Emerson Andrews's *Philanthropic Foundations* (1956) and Warren Weaver's *U.S. Philanthropic Foundations: Their History,*

Suggested Reading

Structure, Management, and Record (1967) deal impressively with the aims and achievements of American foundations. Frederick P. Keppel's *The Foundation: Its Place in American Life* (1930) reflects the thoughtful and humane outlook of the author, who was president of the Carnegie Corporation. *Funds and Foundations* (1952), by Abraham Flexner, a foundation pioneer, is critical of foundation policies since the mid-1920s. There are histories of a number of the major foundations. Among the best are Raymond B. Fosdick's *The Story of the Rockefeller Foundation* (1952) and *Adventures in Giving: The Story of the General Education Board* (1962); the least reverent is Dwight Macdonald's *The Ford Foundation* (1956). Eduard C. Lindeman, in *Wealth and Culture* (1936), and Horace Coon, in *Money to Burn* (1938), emphasize the conservatism of the foundations. Joseph C. Kiger's *Operating Principles of the Larger Foundations* (1954) is a judicious study by the director of research for the Cox investigating committee. *Hearings before the Select (Cox) Committee to Investigate Tax-Exempt Foundations* (1953) is well worth consulting. Edwin R. Embree's "Timid Billions: Are the Foundations Doing Their Job?" *Harper's Magazine* 198 (March 1949): 28–37, is the most challenging of the many articles criticizing the foundations in the late 1940s and early 1950s. Business contributions to philanthropy are the subject of F. Emerson Andrews's *Corporation Giving* (1952) and Richard Eels's *Corporation Giving in a Free Society* (1956). The origin of several influential service and advocacy organizations is dealt with in Alfred H. Katz's *Parents of the Handicapped: Self-Organized Parents and Relatives Groups for Treatment of Ill and Handicapped Children* (1961). Edwin Corbin Jenkins's *Philanthropy in America* (1950) surveys the quarter-million churches, social agencies, colleges, museums, and hospitals supported by private gifts and endowments in the years 1924 to 1948.

Joseph C. Hyman's *Twenty-five Years of American Aid to Jews Overseas* (1939) is a modest and moving record of the work of the Joint Distribution Committee. David Hinshaw's *Rufus Jones, Master Quaker* (1951) contains material on the American Friends Service Committee in the 1920s and 1930s. *Voluntary War Relief during World War II* (1946), a report by the U.S. President's War Relief Control Board, is a useful summary. A history of the National War Fund, *Design for Giving* (1947) by Harold J. Seymour, is particularly good on fund-raising. George Woodbridge's *UNRRA: The History of the United Nations Relief and Rehabilitation Administration* (1950) is a distinguished official history. Edward McSweeney's *American Voluntary Aid to Germany, 1945–50* (1950) is a short summary. The Congressional (House) Special Subcommittee of the Committee on Foreign Affairs, in its *Final Report on Foreign Aid* (1948), concluded that Americans could afford to send private assistance overseas and could not afford to discontinue it. Walter R. Sharp, in *International Technical Assistance* (1952), attempts to inventory and evaluate United States government, United Nations, and regional assistance programs. William Adams Brown, Jr., and Redvers Opie, in *American Foreign Assistance* (1953), appraise twelve years (1941–52) of overseas aid. Volume four (1964) of Hoover's *An American Epic* covers the years 1939–63.

The private agencies' tasks are explored by the American Council of Voluntary Agencies for Foreign Service in *The Role of Voluntary Agencies in Technical Assistance* (1953). Alvah Myrdal, Arthur J. Altmeyer, and Dean Rusk describe the challenge of *America's Role in International Social Welfare* (1955). Max F. Millikan and W. W. Rostow, in *A Proposal: Key to an Effective Foreign Policy* (1957), argue for expanded, long-term American participation in economic development of undeveloped areas. Grant S. McClellan's *United States Foreign Aid* (1957) presents arguments pro and con; and *Current History* 33 (1957): 129–67, devotes an entire issue to an objective review of foreign-aid problems.

J. Frederic Dewhurst and Associates, in *America's Needs and Resources: A New Survey* (1955), 430–68, describe the domestic welfare scene in the 1950s. Ida C. Meriam's "Social Welfare in the United States, 1934–54," *Social Security Bulletin* 18 (October 1955): 3–14, presents developments since the New Deal. There are many helpful insights in Max Lerner's *America as a Civilization* (1957); the section entitled "The Sinews of Welfare," pp. 123–39, is particularly rewarding. Marion K. Sanders' "Mutiny of the Bountiful," *Harper's Magazine* 226 (December 1958): 23–31, deals with financing of voluntary health organizations. Wayne McMillen, in "Financing Social Welfare Service," *Social Work Yearbook* (1957), 260–67, discusses the United Fund movement, and in "Charitable Fraud: An Obstacle in Community Organization," *Social Service Review* 29 (1955): 153–71, he describes the more common charity rackets and examines their direct and indirect costs.

CHAPTER 11

Giving USA, published annually by the American Association of Fund-Raising Council, provides information on the estimated total, sources, and objectives of American giving each year since 1960. The Commission on Private Philanthropy and Public Needs, in *Giving in America* (1975), describes the situation in the mid-1970s, and Virginia Hodgkinson and Murray S. Weitzman, *Dimensions of the Independent Sector* (1984, 1986), provide current statistical data on the nonprofit sector. In "25 Years and Change," and "25 Years' Worth," *Foundation News* 25 (November–December 1984): 14–16, 22–25, Kathleen D. McCarthy and Kathleen Halloran and James Gorman, respectively, review foundation developments since 1960 and highlights in the history of *Foundation News* during its first twenty-five years.

Marion Fremont-Smith deals with supervision of foundations by federal and state governments in *Foundations and Government* (1965) and with legal aspects of corporate philanthropy in *Philanthropy and the Business Corporation* (1972). Books and articles dealing with the Patman investigations of foundations and the background of the Tax Reform Act of 1969 include Morton M. Caplin, "Foundations and Government," *Foundation News* 4 (May–June 1963): 1–3; Philip M. Stern, *The Great Treasury Raid* (1964); Julian Levi, "Foundation in the Public Eye," *Foundation News* 5 (January–February 1964): 5–8; F. Emerson Andrews, *Patman and Foundations* (1968); and Thomas C. Reeves, ed.,

Foundations under Fire (1970). Useful studies of the provisions of the Tax Reform Act of 1969 include Stanley S. Weithorn, "Summary of the Tax Reform Act as It Affects Foundations," *Foundation News* 11 (May–June 1970): 85–89; U.S. Congress, Joint Committee on Internal Revenue Taxation, *General Explanation of the Tax Reform Act of 1969* (1970); and William H. Smith and Carolyn P. Chiechi, *Private Foundations Before and After the Tax Reform Law of 1969* (1974).

CHAPTER 12

Fred Schnaue's observation on giving and taxation is taken from *Giving USA, 1980,* which surveys philanthropic ups and downs in the 1970s. *The Foundation Directory, Edition 5* (1975) contains data on foundation problems in the early 1970s. Other studies of foundations include Fritz F. Heinemann, ed., *The Future of Foundations* (1973); Waldemar A. Nielsen, *The Big Foundations* (1972); and Alan Pifer, *Philanthropy in an Age of Transition* (1984). *The Research Papers of the Committee on Private Philanthropy and Public Needs,* 5 vols. (1977) contain a mine of information on nearly all aspects of philanthropy; there is a summary description of the papers at the start of volume 1. Both the commission's report and recommendations and the Donee Group's report and recommendations are in volume 1, part 1.

On the trends in voluntary agencies in the 1970s see Jane Dunstan, "Marking 75 Years: Foundation for Child Development Looks Ahead," *Foundation News* 16 (January–February 1975): 30–35; Gertrude S. Goldberg, "New Directions for Community Service Society of New York," *Social Service Review* 54 (1980): 184–219; and Steven Martin Cohen, "Trends in Jewish Philanthropy," *American Jewish Yearbook* 80 (1980): 29–51. Carl Bakal, *Charity USA* (1979), is a journalist's survey of "the hidden world of the multi-billion-dollar charity industry" in the 1970s.

A new edition of Merle Curti's *American Philanthropy Abroad* with an introduction surveying American overseas aid since 1960 is forthcoming. *Private Foreign Aid: U.S. Philanthropy for Relief and Development* (1982) by Landrum R. Bolling with Craig Smith is a comprehensive history. Theresa Hayton and Catherine

Watson, in *Aid: Rhetoric and Reality* (1985), are critical of international assistance furnished by governments and minimize the quantitative importance of aid provided by voluntary agencies. William Shawcross's *Quality of Mercy: Cambodia, Holocaust, and the Modern Conscience* (1984) calls attention to the ambiguities and complexities of foreign aid. In "Who Cares?" *Forbes* (August 18, 1980), pp. 86–88, Harold Seneker presents a favorable account of CARE, Inc. "Starting Over," *Foundation News* 27 (May–June 1986): 16–22, by Jim Gorman, deals with self-help groups and voluntary and government agencies assisting Indo-Chinese refugees to adjust to life in the United States. Dan Jacobs's *The Brutality of Nations* (1987) is a distressing account of political factors that prevented aid to famine victims in Biafra in the Nigerian civil war, 1968–70.

CHAPTER 13

O'Neill's statement is in "When Government was a Friend in Need," *The New York Times* (May 16, 1986); Graham is quoted in Samuel G. Freedman, "In Live Aid, Echoes of the Woodstock Generation," *The New York Times* (July 18, 1985).

Michael B. Katz, *In the Shadow of the Poorhouse* (1986), and Neil Gilbert, "The Transformation of Social Services," *Social Service Review* 51 (1977): 624–41, discuss the growth in the use of public funds to purchase service from voluntary agencies. Observations by Brian O'Connell and Leslie Dunbar on the importance of the advocacy function of philanthropy can be found, respectively, in O'Connell, "Voluntary Agencies Must Ask: What Price Independence?" *Foundation News* 17 (July–August 1976): 16–20, and Patrick Kennedy, "Surveillance, Civil Liberties, Amensty, National Policy," *Foundation News* 17 (July–August 1976): 40–43. Additional sources on advocacy include Ralph Kramer, *Voluntary Agencies in the Welfare State* (1981), and J. Craig Jenkins, "Nonprofit Organizations and Policy Advocacy," in Walter Powell, ed., *The Nonprofit Sector* (1987).

Dimensions of the Independent Sector and *The Charitable Behavior of Americans*, both cited in the General Works section of this essay, picture the state of philanthropy in the 1980s. Virginia

Hodgkinson comments on the situation in "Slowdown in the Sector," *Foundation News* 21 (September–October 1986): 56–58. Lester M. Salamon analyzes the effects of Reagan administration cuts in social spending in "Nonprofit Organizations: The Lost Opportunity," in John L. Palmer and Isabell V. Sawhill, eds., *The Reagan Record: An Assessment of America's Changing Domestic Priorities* (1984). The Salamon quotation is from "Federal Budget: Deeper Cuts Ahead," *Foundation News* 26 (March–April 1985): 48–54. Alan Green, "No End in Sight," *Foundation News* 27 (May–June 1986): 23–28, reviews the controversy over the Combined Federal Campaign; Donald J. Devine presents the Reagan administration's side of the story in *Politicizing Charity: A Case Study* (1986).

In *The Golden Donors* (1985) Waldemar A. Nielsen assesses the recent performance of major foundations. A. McGehee Harvey, M.D., and Susan L. Abrams recount the work of an important foundation in *"For the Welfare of Mankind": The Commonwealth Fund and American Medicine* (1986). Robert Arnove, ed., *Philanthropy and Cultural Imperialism* (1980), and Edward H. Berman, *The Influence of Carnegie, Ford, and Rockefeller Foundations on Foreign Policy* (1983), are, for the most part, critical of foundations.

Recent studies of corporate giving include Council on Foundations, *Corporate Philanthropy: Philosophy, Management, Trends, Future, and Background* (1982); Arthur White and John Bartholomew, *Corporate Giving; The Views of Chief Executive Officers of Major American Corporations* (1982); and Alex J. Plinio and Joanne B. Scanlan, *Resource Raising: The Role of Non-Cash Assistance in Corporate Philanthropy* (1986).

Paul Desruisseaux, in "Organized Religion: Major Donor to Charity," *Chronicle of Higher Education* (February 20, 1985), 26, discusses the findings of the Council on Foundations' survey of religious giving. The study is entitled *The Philanthropy of Organized Religion* (1985).

Articles on Live Aid appeared in *The New York Times* on October 1, 1985, and May 26, 1985. Roger M. Williams discusses Bob Geldof's contributions to fund-raising in "What Hath Geldof

Suggested Reading

Wrought," *Foundation News* 28 (January–February 1987): 31–37. Robert Payton's *Famine and Philanthropy* (forthcoming) considers problems encountered in bringing relief to famine areas of Africa in the 1980s.

Robert M. Hayes's and James P. Grant's comments on Hands Across America appear in *The New York Times,* May 26 and June 6, 1986. The quotation by Michael Kinsley is in *The Wall Street Journal,* October 31, 1985. Financing of the Statue of Liberty restoration is reviewed by Stanley Penn in "Taking Liberties," *The Wall Street Journal,* February 14, 1986, and criticized by Maurice G. Gurin in "Marketing of Statue Affects Philanthropy," *The New York Times,* August 4, 1986. Jon Pratt draws a distinction between cause-related marketing and corporate charity in "When Corporate Philanthropy Is Not Charity," *Foundation News* 27 (September–October 1986): 62–64. In *Fund Raising Management* 19 (January 1987): 72–76, a professional fund-raiser, Maurice G. Gurin, asks, "Is Marketing Dangerous for Fund Raising?" and answers that it is.

America's Wealthy and the Future of Foundations (1987) by Teresa Odendahl et al. is an impressive study that brings together current and historical data on the motives and instincts of wealthy donors, especially in regard to formation of foundations. It is summarized in *Foundation News* 27 (March–April 1986): 22–29. In *Federal Tax Policy and Charitable Giving* (1985), Charles T. Clotfelter reviews evidence on the effect of the charitable deduction on contributions to philanthropy. Two useful sources of information about current issues and problems in philanthropy are *IS Update,* a newsletter on giving and volunteering published by Independent Sector; and *Responsive Philanthropy,* the newsletter of the Committee for Responsive Philanthropy.

Acknowledgments

It is a pleasure to recall and acknowledge the help offered by Merle Curti at the start of my work on the history of philanthropy. Richard Magat's kind words encouraged me to update *American Philanthropy*. Institutions and publications such as the Foundation Center, *Foundation News,* and *Giving USA* have facilitated the task of bringing the book up to date. All students of philanthropy in recent years are indebted to the endeavors made by Brian O'Connell, Virginia Hodgkinson, and Robert Payton of Independent Sector to promote research in giving, volunteering, and nonprofit enterprise.

I am particularly grateful to Catherine Marting Bremner who assisted me in countless ways, to Maria Mazon who prepared the manuscript for publication with competence and unfailing good humor, and to James Rohrer for help when it was most needed. I am happy to acknowledge financial assistance provided by a publication grant from the Graduate School and the College of Humanities of The Ohio State University.

Index

Index

Astor, John Jacob, 42, 44, 52
Astor Library, 52
Atlanta University, 83
Atlantic Richfield Foundation, 233
Auburn, N.Y., 61
Auburn University, 234
Augustus, John, 62
Australia, 161

Bahama Islands, 5
Baker, Newton D., 126
Baldwin Locomotive Co., 75
Baltimore, Md., 48, 52, 103, 104, 110, 219
Bamberger, Louis, 226
Barlow et al. v. A.P. Smith Manufacturing Co., 228
Barr, Joseph W., 231
Barton, Clara, 119, 222; characterized, 88; in Civil War, 74; as Red Cross leader, 89–90; and Red Cross movement, 87–89
Bates, Joshua, 52
Beekman, James, 46
Belafonte, Harry, 212
Belgium, relief of, in World War I, 120–22
Bellamy, Edward, quoted, 177–78
Bellows, Henry W., 73, 76, 79, 87–88
Benevolent associations, 45, 83, 84
"Benevolent Empire," 45–46, 91
Benezet, Anthony, 64, 218; antiwar tracts of, 27; charitable activities of, 25–26; defends Indian rights, 28; and struggle for Negro rights, 28–30
Bennett, James Gordon, 93
Bible, 13, 31, 45, 75
Bible Society of the Confederacy, 75

Bickerdyke, "Mother" Mary Ann, 74
Bicknell, Ernest, 122
Big Foundations (Nielson), 187, 231
Bingo, 235
Blind, the, 43, 92, 146; Foundation for, 148; Howe and, 63; "talking books" for, 148
Blithedale Romance, The (Hawthorne), 62
Boardman, Mabel, 119
Bolling, Landrum, 196
Bond, Dr. Thomas, 24, 218
Bonifacius (Mather), 12. See also *Essays to Do Good*
Boston, Mass., 14, 18, 23, 42, 51, 52, 54, 57, 59, 61, 62, 219; Associated Charities, 99; fires in, 25, 89, 218, 222; freedmen's aid societies, 80–81; Jewish Charities, 118, 223; Mather on charity in, 1, 14; philanthropy, 43, 104; relief crisis of 1774–75, 218
Boston House of Reformation, 59
Boston Prison Discipline Society, 61, 219
Boston Public Library, 52
Boston Tea Party, 25
Boudinot, Elias, 44, 45
Boy Scouts of America, 117, 224
Boys Town, 189
Brace, Charles Loring, 60–61, 221
Bradford, William, 6
Bridgman, Laura, 63, 220
British Sanitary Commission, 76
British War Relief, 160
Brooks, Peter Chardon, 43
Broun, Heywood, 153
Brown, John, 70–71
Brussels, Belgium, 120

Index

Index

Index